NEUROPSYCHOLOGICAL

ASSESSMENT OF

dementia
and
depression

IN OLDER ADULTS:

A CLINICIAN'S GUIDE

NEUROPSYCHOLOGICAL

ASSESSMENT OF

dementia

and

depression

IN OLDER ADULTS:

A CLINICIAN'S GUIDE

Edited by Martha Storandt
and Gary R. VandenBos

American Psychological Association, Washington, DC

Sixth printing January 2005

Published by
American Psychological Association
750 First Street, NE
Washington, DC 20002

Copies may be ordered from
APA Order Department
P.O. Box 92984
Washington, DC 20090-2984

In the UK and Europe, copies may be ordered from
American Psychological Association
3 Henrietta Street
Covent Garden, London
WC2E 8LU England

Typeset in Goudy by Techna Type, Inc., York, PA

Printer: Data Reproductions Corporation, Rochester Hills, MI
Cover Designer: Grafik Communications, Ltd., Alexandria, VA
Technical/Production Editor: Mark A. Meschter

Library of Congress Cataloging-in-Publication Data
Neuropsychological assessment of dementia and depression in older
    adults : a clinician's guide / edited by Martha Storandt and Gary R. VandenBos.
        p.   cm.
    Includes bibliographical references and index.
    ISBN 1-55798-437-9 (acid-free paper)
    I. Storandt, Martha.   II. VandenBos, Gary R.
    [DNLM: 1. Dementia—in old age.   2. Dementia—diagnosis.
3. Depressive Disorder—in old age.   4. Depressive Disorder—
diagnosis.   5. Neuropsychological Tests.   WM220 N4943 1994]
RC524.N49   1994
618.97'683—dc20
DNLM/DLC
for Library of Congress   94-4735
                                                                                              CIP

British Library Cataloguing-in-Publication Data
A CIP record is available from the British Library

Printed in the United States of America

CONTENTS

CONTRIBUTORS

F. Marcus Brown III, Department of Psychology, Connecticut Valley Hospital, Middletown, CT

Meryl A. Butters, Department of Psychiatry, University of Pittsburgh Medical Center, Pittsburgh, PA

Nelson Butters, San Diego Veterans Affairs Medical Center, San Diego, CA, and Department of Psychiatry, University of California at San Diego, La Jolla, CA

Gina DiTraglia Christenson, Department of Psychology, University of Arizona, Tucson, AZ

Perry Eimon, Brockton Veterans Affairs Medical Center, Brockton, MA

Richard C. Erickson, Seattle Veterans Affairs Medical Center, Seattle, WA

Thomas Grisso, Department of Psychiatry, University of Massachusetts Medical Center, Worcester, MA

Margaret Gatz, Department of Psychology, University of Southern California, Los Angeles, CA

Nancy Hebben, McLean Hospital, Belmont, MA

Alfred W. Kaszniak, Department of Psychology, University of Arizona, Tucson, AZ

Bob G. Knight, Leonard Davis School of Gerontology, University of Southern California, Los Angeles, CA

David P. Salmon, Department of Neurosciences, University of California at San Diego, La Jolla, CA

Forrest R. Scogin, Department of Psychology, University of Alabama, Tuscaloosa, AL

Martha Storandt, Department of Psychology, Washington University, St. Louis, MO

Gary R. VandenBos, Office of Communications, American Psychological Association, Washington, DC

Jack G. Wiggins, Jr., Psychological Development Center, Inc., Cleveland, OH

PREFACE

By virtue of their expertise in assessment, psychologists are uniquely capable of contributing to the differential diagnosis of two of the most common psychological disorders of later life: dementia and depression. The purpose of this book is to provide psychological practitioners with the latest information about the assessment of dementia and depression in older adults. Because of an intense national research effort focusing on Alzheimer's disease, there has been an explosion of new knowledge on aging in the last decade, particularly about dementia compared with normal aging. Also in recent years, there has been increased attention to the detection of depression in later life. In this book, nationally recognized experts in neuropsychology and aging provide up-to-date reviews of the current knowledge about the diagnosis of dementia and depression. These experts also make recommendations to practitioners concerning the unique aspects of evaluating older individuals.

In chapter 1, Jack G. Wiggins, Jr., provides a historical context by describing national policy concerning the provision of mental health services to older individuals. He describes the constraints on psychologists' practice with older adults, as well as the opportunities. In chapter 2, Martha Storandt reviews the psychological changes that accompany normal aging and that may influence the assessment process. She also describes cultural values about aging that may influence psychologists who work with older clients.

Chapters 3 and 4 focus on the assessment of dementia and the assessment of depression, respectively. In chapter 3, Meryl A. Butters, David P. Salmon, and Nelson Butters describe the neuropsychological evaluation of individuals with dementia. They illustrate the effects of Alzheimer's disease, a cortical dementia, on cognitive abilities in contrast with Huntington's disease, a subcortical dementia. In chapter 4, Forrest R. Scogin reviews depression in later life, as well as the tests that are commonly used to assess it. He pays special attention to instruments that are useful in routine practice. Alfred W. Kaszniak and Gina DiTraglia Christenson, in chapter 5, provide an integration of the elements of differential diagnosis of dementia and depression. These authors carefully describe differences in specific assessment responses and behavior that provide evidence for one diagnosis or the other. They also point out that the two disorders can coexist.

Thomas Grisso focuses on functional ability and competence in chapter 6. He provides an outline of the issues that psychologists may be asked to address in the legal contexts of guardianship, conservatorship, and consent to treatment. In chapter 7, Bob G. Knight describes the all-important matter of providing clinical interpretations to clients and family. His focus is from a family-systems perspective. Finally, in chapter 8, Margaret Gatz describes treatment strategies for depression and dementia and discusses the application of information gained in the assessment process to decisions concerning interventions as well as to monitoring outcomes.

This book ends with two appendixes. The first, by F. Marcus Brown III and Jack G. Wiggins, Jr., contains the results of a postconference mail survey of the participants in a conference titled "Neuropsychological Assessment of Older Adults: Dementia and Depression." This conference was held in St. Louis, Missouri, in May 1993 and served as the impetus for this book. The survey results provide information about the participants' practices with older individuals. The second appendix is a bibliography of references to norms for older adults on cognitive tests that psychologists may find useful in their practices with older adults. The availability of an earlier version of this bibliography was announced in *The Clinical Neuropsychologist* (1992, Vol. 6, pp. 98–102). Richard C. Erickson, Perry Eimon, and Nancy Hebben updated this bibliography for inclusion in this book.

We wish to acknowledge additional special contributors to this book. Jack G. Wiggins, Jr., recognized the need to communicate the information that is contained herein to psychological practitioners and called for this effort during his presidency of the American Psychological Association (APA). Alfred W. Kaszniak prepared the initial proposal. The APA's Practice Directorate and Office of Communication, as well as the Psychological Corporation, provided partial funding for the just-mentioned conference, which brought the book's contributors together. Emily Barge and Julia Haines of the Washington University Alzheimer's Disease Research Center ably managed the conference arrangements. Finally, we thank the many researchers who have devoted themselves to research on aging; without their efforts, we would have little to communicate to practitioners.

MARTHA STORANDT
GARY R. VANDENBOS

1

INTRODUCTION

JACK G. WIGGINS, JR.

The need to distinguish reversible from irreversible conditions is a fundamental goal of good health care. To be able to identify individuals with treatable conditions, compared with those whose conditions can only be managed, is an essential skill of health practitioners. Depression can be treated, whereas most of the various dementias must be managed, at least at the present time.

Depression can be precipitated by a variety of circumstances and responds to many interventions. Because depression has many manifestations, physicians in office-based primary care practices often fail to identify it. Simon (1993) suggested that the recognition rate is about 62%. Even when recognized, physicians often treat depression as if it were a symptom of a physical disorder rather than a comorbid condition. "Testing" for depression is often done by trial-and-error drug challenges to find a medication that relieves the patient's symptoms.

Although depression is underdiagnosed and undertreated in the general population, it poses a special diagnostic problem in older adults who seek medical assistance—often for more than one physical disorder. Even if the depression is recognized by the attending physician, it is often discounted. It may be attributed to life circumstances such as the recent loss of a spouse, to one of the physical conditions, or simply to old age. Contrary to popular opinion, the frequency and intensity of depression does not necessarily increase with age (Myers et al., 1984).

The consequence of ignoring or failing to treat depression puts the older adult at further risk. Herbert and Cohen (1993) found a linear relation between intensity of affect and immune system function as measured by lymphocyte functioning. Older adults who are already experiencing the ravages of one or more health problems may be even more vulnerable to others if they are depressed. On the positive side, active psychological interventions can allay the effects not only of depression (e.g., Thompson, Gallagher, & Breckenridge, 1987) but also of other behaviors that may complicate the clinical picture of a patient. Therefore, depression must be evaluated carefully by practitioners who have a thorough knowledge of the psychological aspects of depression.

Failure to identify and treat depression compounds the problems in the diagnosis of Alzheimer's disease and other dementias, as described later in this book. Current estimates of the prevalence of Alzheimer's disease, the most common of the dementias of later life, vary with age, ranging from 3% between the ages of 65 and 74 years to 47% in those who are over 85 years old (Evans, 1989). Too often, however, cognitive deficits are attributed to dementia when they may result from a treatable condition—depression. It is imperative that psychologists develop assessment guidelines for these conditions that are based on psychological tests and then apply their skills to the assessment of older adults.

One wonders why this has not already been done. A brief historical review may be helpful. At the beginning of this century, the average life expectancy was 49 years (National Center for Health Statistics, 1992); therefore, there were not large numbers of older people. Until the enactment of the Social Security Act in 1935, families were expected to support their relatives. (It should be pointed out that they still do to a large extent. Spouses and adult children provide the bulk of care for frail or ill older adults.) If there were no surviving family members, then there were county homes for the aged, county infirmaries, and state asylums for the mentally ill. These were feared last resorts.

By the middle of the century, the average life expectancy had increased to 68 years (National Center for Health Statistics, 1992). After World War II, the American Psychological Association (APA) experienced a rapid period of expansion. Twenty new divisions were formed. One of these was Division 20, now called Adult Development and Aging. This brought together a small but growing cadre of psychologists who were interested in the aging process—mainly from a research perspective. Meager federal funding of programs for the psychological needs of the older populace resulted in little progress in the development of techniques or training of personnel for the assessment and treatment of older adults.

When Medicare (Title XVIII of the Social Security Act) was adopted in 1965, older adults received badly needed government assistance for their health care needs. The focus, however, was on acute hospitalization for physical ailments. Outpatient treatment benefits for mental health conditions were limited to $250 per year, with a 50% copayment; the amount of these benefits did not change until 1987. Furthermore, psychologists were not included as independent providers of services. Medicare authorized psychological testing only on referral from a physician. The primary site for psychological testing became hospitals rather than offices because the referring physician had to be present in order for reimbursement to occur. Psychological services for older adults in acute medical/surgical hospitals were very restricted because psychologists were not members of the hospital staffs. These restrictions proved to be almost insurmountable barriers to the psychological assessment of older people. Because psychologists were not actively involved as providers of services to older adults, there was little impetus to train psychologists to work with them or to develop the tools needed to address the special needs of older clients.

These impediments to the access to psychological expertise by older adults remained for nearly a quarter of a century. Then, the Budget Reconciliation Act of 1989 authorized psychologists to be independent providers for Medicare beneficiaries in community mental health clinics and in rural health centers, and the $250 annual cap on outpatient benefits was raised on a phased-in basis to $1,375. Psychological assessment and treatment of older adults became a reality, even though "proposed regulations" have yet to be written.

Another impediment to the provision of services to older adults centered on Medicaid (Title XIX of the Social Security Act), which provides health services to the poor of all ages. Medicaid also pays for long-term care in nursing homes. Almost immediately, states began to shift elderly patients from mental health facilities to nursing homes to take advantage of the federal financial support for these individuals. This shift, however, placed older people in facilities in which the staff had little training in mental health.

As a result of the lack of standards for treatment of individuals with mental illness in skilled nursing facilities, a new law regulating Preadmission Screening and Annual Resident Review (PASARR) was enacted in 1987. Although the implementation of the final regulations surrounding PASARR issued in 1992 resulted in significant delays in service and payments for the needed evaluations, this was a legislative breakthrough. It paved the way for psychologists to be included in the PASARR program for older adults in nursing homes.

Psychological assessment of emotional disorders and cognitive function has great potential for the early recognition and effective treatment or management of depression and dementia, as well as other emotional and health problems. Psychological evaluations can result in significant cost savings in national health care reform initiatives. For example, if depression in older adults is identified and treated early in the course of the episode, then costly inpatient treatment may be avoided. Effective screening and evaluation of functional ability in individuals with dementia—along with provision of outpatient services to them and their caregivers—may delay costly nursing home placement.

To meet this challenge, psychologists must increase their skills in working with the older population. Two national conferences on training psychologists to work with older people have been sponsored by the APA: one in 1981 and one in 1992. Both called for expanded continuing education opportunities for practitioners. These recommendations, combined with the legislative breakthroughs in the late 1980s concerning Medicare and Medicaid, prompted me to request the APA Practice Directorate to sponsor a conference titled "Neuropsychological Assessment in Older Adults: Dementia and Depression," which served as the impetus for this book. The enthusiastic reception of the attendees at this heavily oversubscribed conference attests to the interest of psychologists in working with older people, the significance of the differential diagnostic questions involved, and the quality of the program, which was ably organized and directed by Martha Storandt, PhD, of the Department of Psychology, Washington University, St. Louis, Missouri. This conference has also laid the groundwork for additional continuing education workshops designed to provide psychologists with information about the most recent research findings related to the assessment and treatment of older adults. The goal of these efforts and of this book is to promote access to psychological expertise for older people.

REFERENCES

Budget Reconciliation Act of 1989 (PL 101-239, December 19, 1989). *Code of federal regulations.* (1987, October). 42 C.F.R. 415.10(a)(b). St. Paul, MN: West.

Evans, D. A. (1989). Prevalence of Alzheimer's disease in a community population of older persons. *Journal of the American Medical Association, 226,* 2551–2556.

Herbert, T. B., & Cohen, S. (1993). Depression and immunology: A meta-analytic review. *Psychology Bulletin, 113,* 472–486.

Myers, J. K., Weissman, M. M., Tischler, G. L., Holzer, C. E., Leaf, P. J., Orvaschel, H., Anthony, J. C., Boyd, J. H., Burke, J. D., Kramer, M., & Stoltzman, R. (1984). Six-month prevalence of psychiatric disorders in three communities: 1980–1982. *Archives of General Psychiatry, 41,* 959–967.

National Center for Health Statistics. (1992). *Vital statistics of the United States, 1989: Life tables. Vol. 2, Sect. 6.* Hyattsville, MD: Author.

Simon, G. E. (1993, May). *Depression and primary care: Treatment and outcome.* Paper presented at the 146th annual meeting of the American Psychiatric Association, San Francisco, CA.

Thompson, L. W., Gallagher, D., & Breckenridge, J. S. (1987). Comparative effectiveness of psychotherapies for depressed elders. *Journal of Consulting and Clinical Psychology, 55,* 385–390.

2

GENERAL PRINCIPLES OF ASSESSMENT OF OLDER ADULTS

MARTHA STORANDT

Why might the assessment of older adults be different from the assessment of people in the earlier years of adulthood? What is unique about assessing an older person?

In this chapter, I review some of the special characteristics and concerns that may influence the assessment techniques and procedures a psychologist uses to assess depression and dementia in older clients in light of unique aspects of this population. For example, there are cohort differences even within the older population. Psychologists may automatically recognize that a generation separates a 22-year-old and a 43-year-old client but may fail to make this distinction between a 63-year-old and an 84-year-old client. Both of the latter may be viewed simply as old. Thus, the variability within and among older adults is explored first.

Sensory and psychomotor changes that accompany the aging process are explored next because these can influence test performance. Only rarely

Preparation of this chapter was supported, in part, by National Institute on Aging training grant AG 00030.

must these variables be considered in the assessment of younger adults; they are extraneous in the sense that the vast majority of younger people can hear and see, for example, at levels that do not interfere with psychological testing. This may not be the case with an older client.

The last section of this chapter deals not with older clients themselves, but with attributes of psychologists that may affect their interactions with an older client. These include cultural stereotypes of older adults as well as special issues of transference and countertransference. Clinical assessment requires two actors—a performer (i.e., the older person) and an observer (i.e., the clinical psychologist). Although the focus of the evaluation should be on the performer, as a responsible professional, the clinical psychologist must also reflect on how he or she consciously or unconsciously shapes the outcome.

VARIABILITY

Clinical psychologists are accustomed to measuring individual differences. It is one of the unique contributions that they make to the mental health enterprise. At the same time, clinical psychologists who are inexperienced in working with older adults may fail to recognize the extent of individual variability in older adults. Neugarten (1977) pointed out that old age spans many years and suggested that psychologists differentiate the "young-old" from the "old-old." For example, those who are young-old may still be in the work force, now that mandatory retirement has been eliminated, whereas a larger proportion of the old-old may be frail and in poor health. Thus, the range of abilities that the clinical psychologist may observe in older clients may be quite wide.

Just as older people may be quite variable in their abilities, they are also highly variable in their life experiences. Table 1 shows the age of different cohorts at the time of major events in this century, as well as their age today. For example, a man who is 95 years old today may have served in the armed forces during World War I, he was probably trying to support

TABLE 1
Age of Individuals Born at Different Times (Cohorts) During Major Events in This Century

Cohort	World War I	Great Depression	World War II	1993
1898	20	35	45	95
1908	10	25	35	85
1918		15	25	75
1928		5	15	65
1938			5	55

a growing family during the Great Depression, and one or more of his children may have died during World War II. In contrast consider a man who is 75 years old today. He was a teenager during the Depression and probably served in the armed forces during World War II. In other words, he is of a different generation.

In addition to generational differences among older people, there are substantial sex differences. According to the U.S. Bureau of the Census (1986), women outnumber men in the older population because they have longer life expectancies than do men (approximately 79 years compared with 72 years). For example, among those over age 85, there are more than twice as many women as men (U.S. Bureau of the Census, 1986). Furthermore, older people come from a variety of ethnic backgrounds. There are elderly African Americans, Asian Americans, Hispanic Americans, and Native Americans in addition to White Americans. Some elderly people were born in other countries and immigrated to the United States as children, young adults, or even more recently as older adults.

The different and variable life experiences of older people shape the values, attitudes, and concerns that older clients bring to the assessment setting. Few may have had prior experience with the mental health system or with psychological assessment. The effective clinician must be sensitive to these individual differences when explaining the purpose of the assessment and introducing the testing procedures.

PHYSICAL HEALTH

Chronic Illness

Increased physical health problems may contribute to the increased variability among older people. One cannot expect people to do their best on psychological tests if they are sick. Older people have more chronic health problems than do younger age groups. This is illustrated in Figure 1, which shows the average total number of diagnoses per individual in the Baltimore Longitudinal Study (Fozard, Metter, & Brant, 1990). Prevalence of disease increases with age, even in this sample of relatively healthy and well-educated men. The 10 most common chronic conditions experienced by older people are shown in Table 2. More than 80% of people over age 65 have at least one chronic illness, and many have multiple conditions.

Some of these chronic health problems may have an obvious, direct effect on psychological test performance. For example, 50% of women and 35% of men in a national probability sample over the age of 55 reported that they had arthritis (Verbrugge, Kepkowski, & Konkol, 1991). Arthritis can interfere with grasping (Verbrugge et al., 1991). Thus, an older woman with severe arthritis in her hands may find it painful to hold a pencil, and her drawings of Benton's (1963) Revised Visual Retention Test figures may

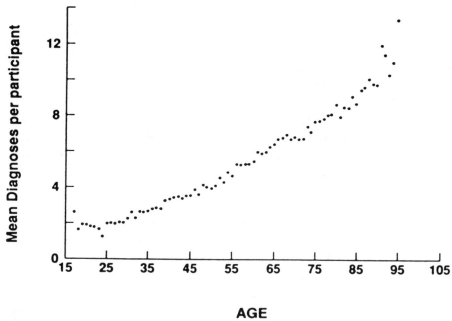

AGE

Figure 1. Average total number of diagnoses per individual (prevalence) in male participants in the Baltimore Longitudinal Study of Aging. From "Next Steps in Describing Aging and Disease in Longitudinal Studies" by J. L. Fozard, E. J. Metter, and L. J. Brant, 1990, *Journal of Gerontology: Psychological Sciences, 45,* p. P124. In the public domain.

suffer. Indeed, she might refuse to attempt the drawings at all or might discontinue after a few items, not because of problems with memory, but because of performance difficulty.

Other age-associated health problems may influence test performance in less obvious ways. Consider, for example, hypertension. Elias, Robbins,

TABLE 2
The 10 Most Common Chronic Health Conditions of People Age 65 Years and Older

Chronic condition	Percentage
Arthritis	48
Hypertension	37
Hearing impairment	32
Heart condition	30
Orthopedic impairment	18
Cataracts	17
Sinusitis	14
Diabetes	10
Tinnitus	8
Varicose veins	8

Note. From *Current Estimates From the National Health Interview Survey, 1991* by P. F. Adams and V. Benson, 1992, Hyattsville, MD: National Center for Health Statistics. In the public domain.

Schultz, and Pierce (1990) studied the relation of blood pressure to performance on tests from the Halstead–Reitan battery (Reitan & Davison, 1974). They found that higher diastolic blood pressure was associated with poorer test performance after adjusting for age, sex, and education. Because blood pressure increases with age in many people, older adults are therefore at greater risk of declines in cognitive performance that may be related to hypertension, even though the mechanism by which this occurs is not yet understood.

Because of the chronic health problems that they experience, many older people take many medications. As shown in Figure 2, the number of prescription medications taken in a week increases with age, even though in this sample older people did not rate their health as poorer than younger adults rated theirs (Salthouse, Kausler, & Saults, 1990). Health was rated on a 5-point scale ranging from excellent (1) to poor (5). Medical treatments in this figure refer to treatment of heart or blood pressure problems in the last 5 years.

Some medications, such as the anticholinergic drugs, produce side effects that impair psychological functions such as memory and cognition.

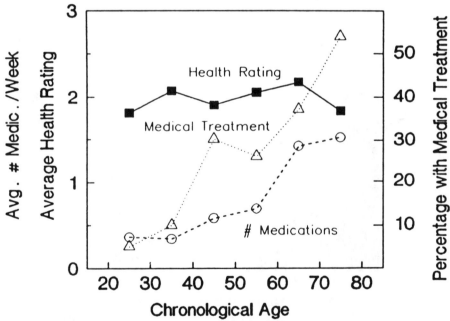

Figure 2. Means at each decade for self-rated health (filled squares), average number of prescription medications per week (open circles), and percentage of people reporting treatment in last 5 years for blood pressure or heart problems (open triangles). From "Age, Self-Assessed Health Status, and Cognition" by T. A. Salthouse, D. H. Kausler, and J. S. Saults, 1990, Journal of Gerontology: Psychological Sciences, 45, p. P157. Copyright 1990 by The Gerontological Society of America. Reprinted by permission.

These drugs include antipsychotics, antidepressants, antiparkinsonism medications, over-the-counter sedatives, and antihistamines. A disturbing study conducted by Blazer, Federspiel, Ray, and Schaffner (1983) revealed that many older people take multiple anticholinergic drugs, setting the stage for drug toxicity. They examined the prescription records of 5,902 nursing home residents and an equal number of ambulatory Medicaid recipients in Tennessee. As shown in Figure 3, they found that many people were taking more than one anticholinergic drug at the same time. The filled bars are based on conservative calculations of prescription overlap; the hatched bars indicate the increase in the estimates if liberal criteria were used. The actual values are probably somewhere in between. Although it is clear that nursing home residents are at greatest risk for anticholinergic toxicity, a substantial number of community-dwelling individuals take more than one of these

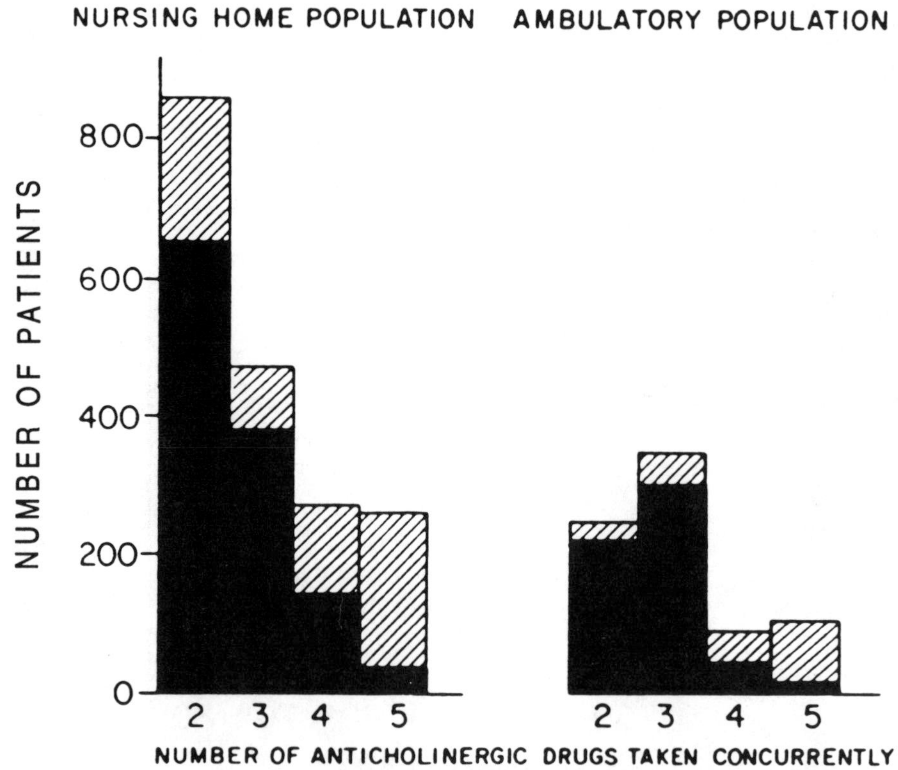

NURSING HOME POPULATION   AMBULATORY POPULATION

NUMBER OF ANTICHOLINERGIC DRUGS TAKEN CONCURRENTLY

Figure 3. Potentially concurrent use of more than one anticholinergic drug in 5,902 continuous nursing home residents and a like number of ambulatory Medicaid recipients, Tennessee, July 1975 through June 1976. The filled bars represent the maximum dosage calculation; the hatched bars indicate the minimum dosage calculation. From "The Risk of Anticholinergic Toxicity in the Elderly: A Study of Prescribing Practices in Two Populations" by D. G. Blazer II, C. F. Federspiel, W. A. Ray, and W. Schaffner, 1983, Journal of Gerontology, 38, p. 33. Copyright 1983 by The Gerontological Society of America. Reprinted by permission.

medications. Older people are at risk for drug toxicity not only when they take multiple drugs but also if dosages are not modified to accommodate the lower clearance rates in older adults.

Drugs may also interact with each other or with foods to produce negative effects on mood or cognition. If the older person sees a number of medical specialists for the treatment of various health problems, then the potential for such drug interactions is increased. Even careful monitoring of prescription drugs may not be sufficient. Older people also use many over-the-counter preparations, and sometimes they try a friend's prescription.

Given the potential negative influences of medications on test performance, the clinical psychologist may wish to include a drug inventory as part of the assessment. This information might be provided by a collateral source, or the client could be asked to bring the medications to the assessment session. If the psychologist has reason to be concerned about the influence of the medications on the older person's behavior, then the client should be referred to a geriatric physician for a comprehensive evaluation of the drug regimen.

Sensory Impairment

Vision

Visual acuity—the ability to see at a distance—declines with age. Perhaps more important to satisfactory performance on psychological tests are some of the other visual changes that occur with age. For example, many older people suffer from cataracts, or clouding of the lens of the eye. Figure 4 shows the decline in the percentage of light that is transmitted through the lens with increasing age (Lerman, 1983). Cataract removal is a common medical procedure that corrects this problem for large numbers of older adults. If the cataracts have not been surgically corrected, then the person may have difficulty seeing stimuli such as some of those used in the Wechsler Adult Intelligence Scale–Revised (WAIS-R; Wechsler, 1981) performance tests.

Clouding of the lens of the eye also causes problems with glare. Light passing through the lens is refracted at varying angles, rather than passing through in a straight line. It is important to make sure that test materials are presented so as to minimize glare. Materials printed on glossy surfaces are particularly troublesome.

During assessment, the psychologist will need to balance the older adult's need for reduced glare with the need for sufficient illumination, because this need increases with age. This problem becomes noticeable in the midyears but progresses in later life. Figure 5 shows data from a survey of 302 people between the ages of 20 and 100 who were asked to rate the difficulty they experienced in performing a variety of tasks (Kosnik, Wins-

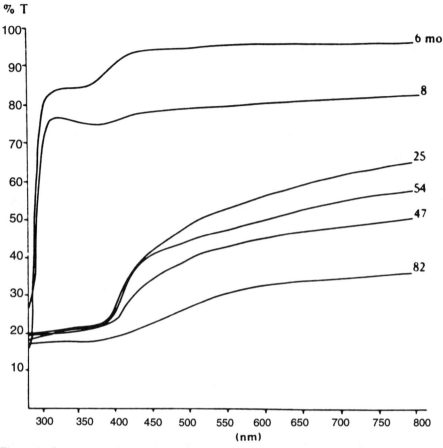

Figure 4. Percentage transmission (T) of different wavelengths of light (ultraviolet and visible) by the normal human lens at different ages ranging from 6 months to 82 years. From "An Experimental and Clinical Evaluation of Lens Transparency and Aging" by S. Lerman, 1983, *Journal of Gerontology, 38,* p. 295. Copyright 1983 by The Gerontological Society of America. Reprinted by permission.

low, Kline, Rasinski, & Sekuler, 1988). The older people reported more difficulty in adjusting to dim lights, seeing in dim lights, and seeing at dusk.

This same survey found an age-related increase in the difficulty of reading small print (Figure 6) (Kosnik et al., 1988). Stimuli might be made larger for older people; however, few standard instruments have such alternate forms. The clinical psychologist might consider having written instructions or self-report instruments produced in larger print for use with older clients. For example, J. M. Vanderplas and J. H. Vanderplas (1980) and J. H. Vanderplas and J. M. Vanderplas (1981) reported better performance by older people on a test of verbal ability when the test was printed in 14-point type rather than the standard 9-point type that is generally used for many tests. They cautioned, however, that increases beyond 14-

Dim Illumination

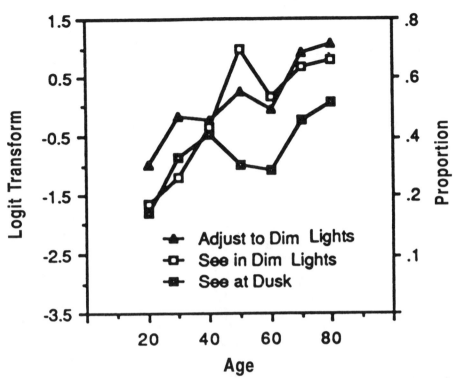

Figure 5. Proportion of survey respondents reporting difficulty under conditions of dim illumination is shown on the right vertical axis. Values on the left vertical axis represent transformed values used in statistical analysis. From "Visual Changes in Daily Life Throughout Adulthood" by W. Kosnik, L. Winslow, D. Kline, K. Rasinski, and R. Sekuler, 1988, *Journal of Gerontology: Psychological Sciences, 43,* p. P68. Copyright 1988 by The Gerontological Society of America. Reprinted by permission.

point type could interfere with normal reading processes and thereby impair legibility.

With increased age, the lens of the eye becomes more rigid and is less able to change shape to achieve focus on close objects. Most people first experience this in their 40s when they begin to use reading glasses or bifocals. Older people may have to wear trifocals to achieve good focus of near, far, and middle-distance objects. The clinical psychologist should be aware that the older person may need to shift between these three components of their eye glasses to achieve good focus on test materials at different distances.

Other visual changes with age include some loss of peripheral vision (Cerella, 1985). Loss of peripheral vision is probably more important to such everyday tasks as driving than it is to taking standard psychological

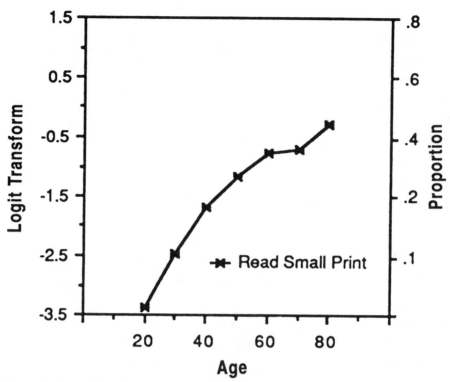

Near Vision

Figure 6. Proportion of survey respondents reporting difficulty with reading small print is shown on the right vertical axis. Values on left vertical axis represent transformed values used in statistical analysis. From "Visual Changes in Daily Life Throughout Adulthood" by W. Kosnik, L. Winslow, D. Kline, K. Rasinski, and R. Sekuler, 1988, *Journal of Gerontology: Psychological Sciences, 43*, p. P68. Copyright 1988 by The Gerontological Society of America. Reprinted by permission.

tests. The yellowing of the lens of the eye also makes it more difficult for older people to distinguish shades of blue and green (Cooper, Ward, Gowland, & McIntosh, 1991). Few standard psychological tests, however, require such distinctions.

Hearing

Hearing loss with increased age is especially apparent for high-frequency tones and is more severe in men than in women (Figure 7) (Ordy, Brizzee, Beavers, & Medart, 1979). Ordy et al. speculated that this sex difference may be related to past occupational differences that resulted in exposure of more men to damage to the cochlea from loud noises in factories or from using rifles to hunt. Equal opportunity in exposure to stereos and

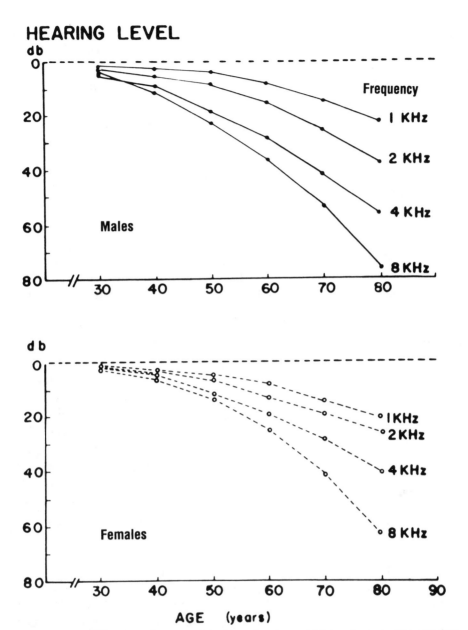

Figure 7. Age differences in age-related hearing loss at higher frequencies ranging from 1 to 8 kHz for men (top) and women (bottom). The data from eight published hearing surveys were compiled by Spoor (1967) and converted to ANSI-1969 standards by Lebo and Reddell (1972). From *Aging: Vol. 10. Sensory Systems and Communication in the Elderly* (p. 156) edited by J. M. Ordy and K. R. Brizzee, 1979, New York: Raven Press. Copyright 1979 by Raven Press. Reprinted by permission.

headsets may nullify this difference in future cohorts. Older adults' high-frequency hearing may present special communication problems to women psychologists with relatively high-pitched voices. They may wish to use a lower pitched voice than usual when speaking to older clients.

Older people are especially susceptible to masking. That is, they may have great difficulty hearing normal speech when there is substantial background noise (the classic cocktail party problem). Thus, the usual requirement of a quiet examination room is very important when testing older people.

The examiner does not necessarily need to speak more loudly to an older person, but he or she does need to speak more slowly. The rate of information processing slows with age (e.g., Lima, Hale, & Myerson, 1991). In addition to speaking relatively slowly (without overdoing it), it is also a good idea to maintain eye contact to facilitate lip reading. Many older people learn to depend on these visual cues as their hearing deteriorates. Frequent eye contact may have the added benefit of developing and maintaining rapport.

Frailty

As mentioned earlier, some of the old-old may also be quite frail. Of those over age 85, it is estimated that 29% suffer from severe disability (Kunkel & Applebaum, 1992). In some cases it may be difficult for the client to come to the psychologist's office for assessment. Therefore, many geropsychologists perform in-home assessments. This has the added benefit of allowing the psychologist to assess the environment as well as the individual. Frequently, the evaluations that a psychologist will be asked to provide for an older client will focus not only on the person's personality and behavior but also on the ability of the individual to function in his or her own setting. To provide useful recommendations, the psychologist will need to evaluate that environment.

When the psychologist conducts an in-home assessment, it is important to make arrangements for appropriate work space. Often a kitchen or dining room table serves best. If the elderly person is confined to a wheelchair, then the examiner needs to make certain that the chair can be positioned such that the work surface is comfortably within reach. The psychologist must make sure that the illumination is satisfactory and that the room is quiet. In most instances, it will be important to assure privacy; sometimes it may be necessary to ask a family member to leave. On the other hand, some psychologists have found it useful to allow a family member to be present during the assessment, especially if the diagnostic question is one of cognitive dysfunction. Observation by the family member can demonstrate not only the older person's weaknesses but also his or her remaining strengths. These arrangements should be made in advance, when the appointment is scheduled.

In some cases, the elderly person may be bedridden. Just as is the case with hospital patients, it is usually possible to administer most of the psychological battery even under these circumstances.

SLOWING OF RESPONSES

One of the best known "facts" of aging is that older people are slower than younger people. Francis Galton (1899, as cited in Wilkinson & Allison, 1989) provided the first empirical data on simple reaction times. He tested almost 10,000 people at the International Health Exhibition and at the South Kensington Museum in London in the 1890s. More recently, Wilkinson and Allison (1989) replicated Galton's findings, testing over 5,000 people at the Science Museum in London (Figure 8). Simple reaction times are slowest in childhood, fastest in the 20s, and increasingly slowed with adult age thereafter. Slowing in choice reaction time for both verbal and nonverbal tasks has also been well documented (e.g., Lima et al., 1991). Although these results are based on cross-sectional comparisons, data from Schaie's (1989) longitudinal study of intelligence illustrate similar longitudinal age changes in perceptual speed adjusted for attrition and practice.

Slowing with age is apparent in the everyday world as well as in the laboratory. For example, in the survey of visual changes in daily life conducted by Kosnik et al. (1988), older people reported slower reading speed and more time spent on visual tasks (Figure 9).

In summary, the psychologist can expect an older client to take longer to complete all aspects of the test battery—both verbal and nonverbal. In my experience, this time will be extended even more if the client is demented. Not only will the demented person perform more slowly, but he or she will probably need more time for reinstruction because the demented individual may not understand what is required at first. On the other hand, the time taken to assess severely demented people may, in fact, be relatively brief because of their inability to do many of the psychologist's standard tests.

Psychologists sometimes "test the limits" by allowing continued effort past standard cut-off times on tests such as the WAIS. In an examination of standard termination procedures in healthy older adults, Storandt (1977) found slight underestimations when using standard cutoffs on the Arithmetic and Block Design subtests but concluded that, generally, the standard time limits are appropriate for older people. The age differences in speed of responding are reflected primarily in terms of bonus points.

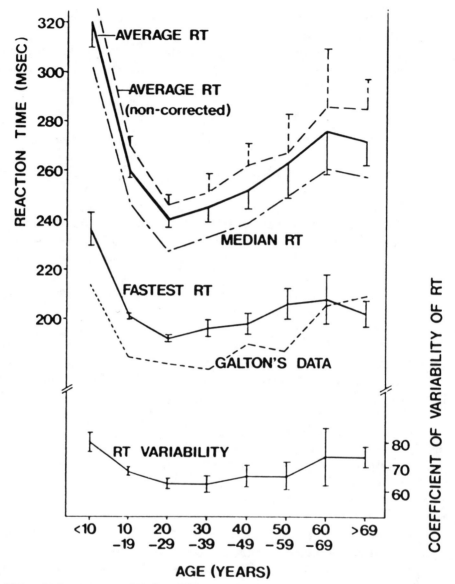

Figure 8. Average reaction time (RT; in milliseconds), fastest RT, RT variability, and median RT as a function of age in eight groups. Confidence limits (95%) are shown for the first three scores. The variable breadth of these limits in each group is a function of the widely varying numbers in each age group as well as the intrinsic variability of subjects within each group. The broken-line curve gives average RT data derived as for the full curve for that score but without removing unduly long RTs more than twice the duration of the average for the test concerned. The dotted-line curve shows, for comparison, Galton's (1899) data plotted on the same scale and for approximately the same age groups. From "Age and Simple Reaction Time: Decade Differences for 5,325 Subjects" by R. T. Wilkinson and S. Allison, 1989, *Journal of Gerontology: Psychological Sciences,* *44,* p. P31. Copyright 1989 by The Gerontological Society of America. Reprinted by permission.

Visual Processing Speed

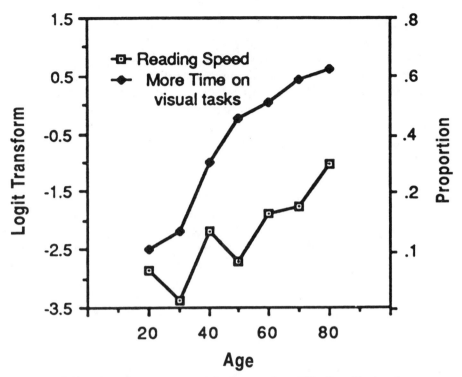

Figure 9. Proportion of survey respondents reporting difficulty with visual processing speed is shown on the right vertical axis. Values on the left vertical axis represent transformed values used in statistical analysis. From "Visual Changes in Daily Life Throughout Adulthood" by W. Kosnik, L. Winslow, D. Kline, K. Rasinski, and R. Sekuler, 1988, *Journal of Gerontology: Psychological Sciences, 43*, p. P68. Copyright 1988 by The Gerontological Society of America. Reprinted by permission.

Older adults receive fewer bonus points for very rapid responses than do younger adults.

Because older people may take longer to complete the psychologist's battery of tests, it is often suggested that frequent rest periods be provided to avoid fatigue. This may be especially desirable if the client is frail and in poor health. It may be preferable to schedule several sessions, rather than one. At the same time, not all older people are fragile. Cunningham, Sepkoski, and Opel (1978) compared the performances of healthy, community-dwelling older people on a battery of cognitive tests administered under varying conditions, including rest periods and fatigue-producing pretests. They found little evidence of fatigue in test batteries up to 2.5 hr in length. Few psychologists would expect younger people to work longer than that without a break. Perhaps the best practice is to make it clear to the client that rest periods are available as needed.

MOTOR IMPAIRMENT

Older people may have health-related motor impairments that could affect their ability to perform on psychological tests. One example would be paralysis of the writing hand resulting from stroke. Others might include tremor associated with Parkinson's disease or difficulty holding a pencil because of severe arthritis. People with Parkinson's disease may be especially slow in their verbal responses. In these cases, the psychologist will have to rely on tests that are not influenced by these impairments. Sometimes it may be possible to devise alternate forms. For example, if the psychologist typically uses Benton's (1963) Revised Visual Form Retention Test to assess nonverbal memory, then he or she could instead use the Visual Form Discrimination Test (Benton, Hamsher, Varney, & Spreen, 1983). The latter test is not designed to be used as a memory task; it has a recognition format in which the person is required to pick one of four alternatives that matches the stimulus card while the stimulus is in view. To make it a memory test, the stimulus card could be removed before the response choices are presented.

OTHER CLIENT CHARACTERISTICS

Verbosity

Just as the psychologist will need to consider the physical health status of the client, there are several other characteristics of older clients that may influence the assessment procedure. One common observation of many novice testers of older people relates to loquaciousness. The older client may be quite verbose compared with younger clients. For example, Botwinick and Storandt (1974) found that older people gave good explanations on the Vocabulary subtest of the WAIS, rather than the one-word synonyms supplied by younger people.

Not only may the older client's responses to the psychologist's questions be longer, the client may stray from the topic at hand. Such off-target verbosity was studied by Gold, Andres, Arbuckle, and Schwartzman (1988) in a sample of 340 elderly, community-dwelling Canadian veterans. They found that loquacious individuals were under greater stress in their lives and were more extraverted. Verbosity, however, was not related to loneliness; in fact, the more socially active the person, the more talkative he was.

Gold et al. (1988) also had access to a measure of nonverbal intelligence that was used to classify recruits in the Canadian Army 40 years earlier. They found that greater declines in nonverbal intelligence were related to increased loquaciousness. Thus, they offered two possible explanations of increased off-target verbosity with age—one relatively benign and the other more malignant. In the first, a life-long extraverted individual may engage in excessive talkativeness as he or she experiences the stresses of aging. In the second, "poorer cognitive functioning associated with verbosity could be indicative of central nervous system impairment" (Gold et al., 1988, p. P32).

People who have less experience with testing situations may think that they are expected to respond as they would in other social settings. Gold et al. (1988), however, found that off-target verbosity was more common in men who were less concerned about presenting themselves in a socially desirable way. Therefore, the examiner may wish to allow some extra time for interaction at the end of the assessment, pointing out that during the testing period itself there's much to be covered. A pleasant but businesslike attitude on the part of the examiner during the assessment period is generally a sufficient reminder to the client.

Personality

In some cases, formal personality assessment will be one of the psychologist's goals. In others, the focus will be on cognitive function. In the latter instance, it is important to recognize that the personality of the client may influence the evaluation. The extraverted, socially responsive client may be able to mask cognitive deficits in superficial situations. It is important for the psychologist to recognize this and not be led astray from the objective test performance.

Personality is generally very stable with age. Costa et al. (1986) reported only minimal correlations (<.20) between age and neuroticism, extraversion, or openness to experience (Figure 10). These data were from a representative sample of more than 9,000 individuals, 35–84 years old, who were interviewed as part of the National Health and Nutrition Examination Survey Epidemiologic Follow-up Study (Cernoni-Huntley et al., 1983).

Similarly, there is little evidence that some types of psychopathology increase with age. Butcher et al. (1991) reported data from the Boston Normative Aging Study for the MMPI-2 (revised Minnesota Multiphasic Personality Inventory). As can be seen in Figure 11, there were few differences among men of different ages on either the validity or clinical scales. The same was true of the content scales (Figure 12). It should be noted that these data are from relatively well-educated men who were participating in a longitudinal study and therefore are not representative of the population at large. There is little evidence in the literature, however, of differences in psychopathology between older men and women. After pointing out the

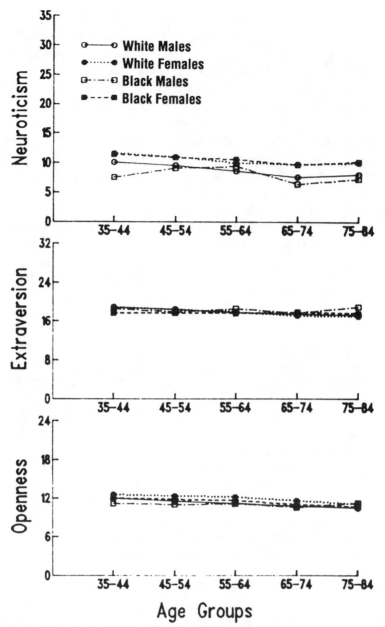

Figure 10. Mean levels of neuroticism, extraversion, and openness to experience for 10-year age groups of white men (open circles), black men (filled circles), white women (open squares), and black women (filled squares), from 35 to 84 years old. From "Cross-Sectional Studies of Personality in a National Sample: 2. Stability in Neuroticism, Extraversion, and Openness" by P. T. Costa, Jr., R. R. McCrae, A. B. Zonderman, H. E. Barbano, B. Lebowitz, and D. M. Larson, 1986, *Psychology and Aging, 1*, p. 147. In the public domain.

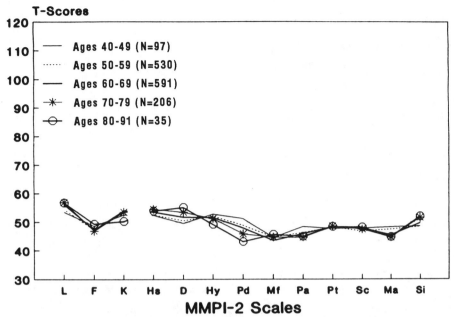

Figure 11. Boston Normative Aging Study age groups, validity, and clinical scales. L = Lie; F = Fake Bad; K = Subtle Defensiveness; Hs = Hypochondriasis; D = Depression; Hy = Hysteria; Pd = Psychopathic Deviate; Mf = Masculinity–Femininity; Pa = Paranoia; Pt = Psychasthenia; Sc = Schizophrenia; Ma = Hypomania; and Si = Social Introversion; MMPI-2 = revised Minnesota Multiphasic Personality Inventory. From "Personality and Aging: A Study of the MMPI-2 Among Older Men" by J. N. Butcher, C. M. Aldwin, M. R. Levenson, Y. S. Ben-Porath, A. Spiro III, and R. Bosse, 1991, *Psychology and Aging, 6,* p. 368. Copyright 1991 by the American Psychological Association.

lack of normative changes in psychopathology with increased age in their study, Butcher et al. concluded that there was no need for separate MMPI-2 norms for older people.

Although, in general, the older adult will come to assessment with the same personality and psychopathology (or lack thereof) that would have been exhibited at an earlier age, there are instances in which recent personality changes may be reported by either the client or family members. For example, Rubin, Morris, Storandt, and Berg (1987) described three types of behavioral changes that were often reported by collateral sources in individuals suffering from mild senile dementia of the Alzheimer's type. These were increased self-centeredness, passivity, and agitation. These symptoms were even more common in more severely demented individuals (Rubin, Morris, & Berg, 1987). With respect to depression, of course, current feelings of unhappiness and emotional distress are central to the diagnosis. This is discussed in detail in Chapter 4.

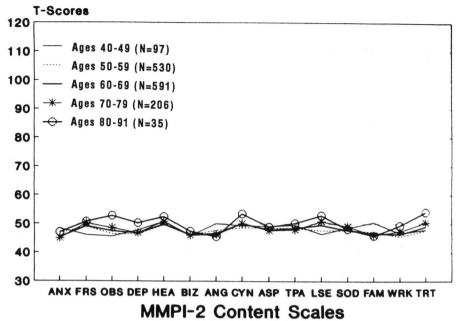

MMPI-2 Content Scales

Figure 12. Boston Normative Aging Study age groups and content scales.
ANX = Anxiety; FRS = Fears; OBS = Obsessiveness; DEP = Depression;
HEA = Health Concerns; BIZ = Bizarre Mentation; ANG = Anger; CYN =
Cynicism; ASP = Antisocial Practices; TPA = Type A; LSE = Low Self-Esteem;
SOD = Social Discomfort; FAM = Family Problems; WRK = Work Interferences;
and TRT = Treatment Indicators; MMPI-2 = revised Minnesota Multiphasic
Personality Inventory. From "Personality and Aging: A Study of the MMPI-2 Among
Older Men" by J. N. Butcher, C. M. Aldwin, M. R. Levenson, Y. S. Ben-Porath, A.
Spiro III, and R. Bosse, 1991, *Psychology and Aging, 6*, p. 369. Copyright 1991 by
the American Psychological Association.

EXAMINER CHARACTERISTICS

Cultural Stereotypes

Psychologists are members of their culture and, therefore, psychologists
practicing in the U.S. may harbor many of the same attitudes and stereotypes about older people that are generally prevalent in U.S. society. I
would expect that some psychologists are hesitant to work with older clients
because of these stereotypes. What is surprising to many psychologists,
however, is the multiplicity of stereotypes that exist about older people.
Schmidt and Boland (1986) found that, in addition to a cluster of physical
features such as gray hair and wrinkled skin, college students had many,
often conflicting, stereotypes about older adults. Using a sorting technique
for a wide range of traits, followed by a cluster analysis that grouped the
traits according to those the students thought usually appeared together,

Schmidt and Boland identified four positive and eight negative stereotypes of older adults. These are shown in Figures 13 and 14.

The stereotype of the severely impaired older person is most applicable to the psychologist's concerns about dementia. The traits associated with this stereotype are shown in Figure 14. They include "senile," which is probably a synonym for dementia. The psychologist may also be concerned about the stereotype of the despondent older adult, also shown in Figure 14. But there is also the stereotype of the sage, as well as that of the perfect grandparent (Figure 13).

Stereotypes are overly simplified generalizations. Psychologists need to remember that their clients are complex individuals with multiple facets to their personalities. For example, the severely impaired older woman may have been until very recently the perfect grandparent. Alternatively, she may have been a shrew. These traits may very well influence assessments; they most certainly will influence treatment plans.

Transference and Countertransference

Although concerns about transference and countertransference are usually more germane to the therapeutic process, some aspects may be pertinent to assessment as well. Classically, transference places the therapist in the role of parent. This may occur less readily when the client is an older adult. Robiner (1987) found that elderly pseudoclients viewed older counselors as peers and younger counselors as more similar to their own children. As he pointed out, such reverse transference on the part of an elderly client may elicit an unusual countertransference on the part of the psychologist. That is, the psychologist may need to recognize a tendency to view the elderly client as a parent. This can present a very unsettling situation. On the other hand, the psychologist will need to resist the tendency to treat elderly people—especially those who are frail and vulnerable—as children. Also, the psychologist should recognize that personal attitudes and fears about the aging process may influence his or her responses to an elderly client. Perhaps more so than with clients of other ages, it is important for the psychologist who works with older adults to follow the admonishment to "know thyself."

SUMMARY

The geropsychologist must be sensitive to the wide range of individual differences in older adults. In addition to varied life experiences, health conditions and sensory impairment (especially in vision and hearing) may influence test performances. Frailty in the very old may require in-home assessment. Older people are generally slower than younger adults; thus,

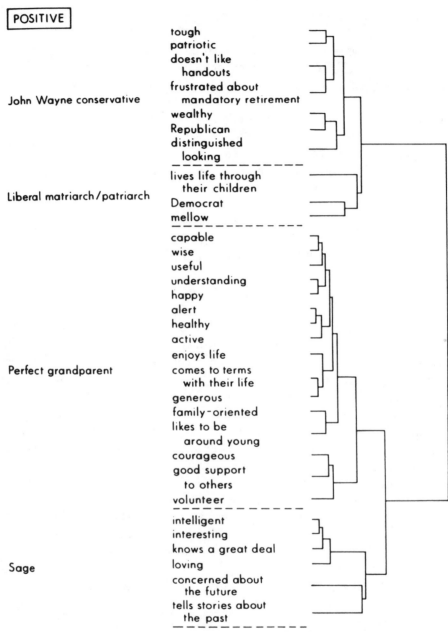

POSITIVE

John Wayne conservative
- tough
- patriotic
- doesn't like handouts
- frustrated about mandatory retirement
- wealthy
- Republican
- distinguished looking

Liberal matriarch/patriarch
- lives life through their children
- Democrat
- mellow

Perfect grandparent
- capable
- wise
- useful
- understanding
- happy
- alert
- healthy
- active
- enjoys life
- comes to terms with their life
- generous
- family-oriented
- likes to be around young
- courageous
- good support to others
- volunteer

Sage
- intelligent
- interesting
- knows a great deal
- loving
- concerned about the future
- tells stories about the past

Figure 13. Tree diagram showing positive trait clusters. Stereotypic traits are between broken lines, and stereotype labels are in the margin. From "Structure of Perceptions of Older Adults: Evidence for Multiple Stereotypes" by D. F. Schmidt and S. M. Boland, 1986, *Psychology and Aging, 1*, p. 258. Copyright 1986 by the American Psychological Association.

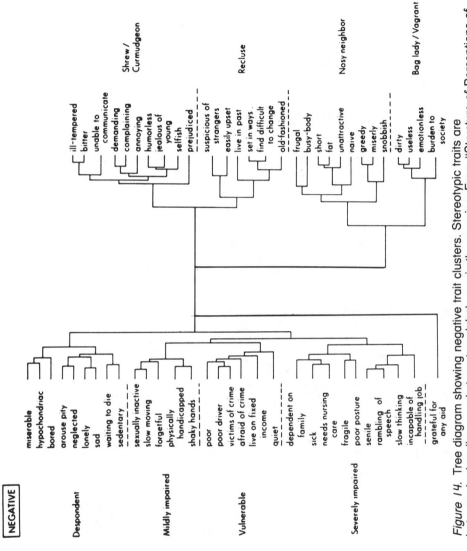

Figure 14. Tree diagram showing negative trait clusters. Stereotypic traits are between broken lines, and stereotype labels are in the margins. From "Structure of Perceptions of Older Adults: Evidence for Multiple Stereotypes" by D. F. Schmidt and S. M. Boland, 1986, *Psychology and Aging, 1,* p. 257. Copyright 1986 by the American Psychological Association.

test sessions may be longer. Some older adults may also tend to be verbose. Psychologists should be aware of their stereotypes about older people; common cultural generalizations can influence the way psychologists interpret assessment information. Unusual transferences and countertransferences can also be unsettling to psychologists who may be accustomed to working with younger adults.

REFERENCES

Adams, P. F., & Benson, V. (1992). *Current estimates from the National Health Interview Survey, 1991* (Vital and Health Statistics, Series 10, No. 184). Hyattsville, MD: National Center for Health Statistics.

Benton, A. L. (1963). *The Revised Visual Retention Test: Clinical and experimental applications.* New York: Psychological Corporation.

Benton, A. L., Hamsher, K. deS., Varney, N. R., & Spreen, D. (1983). *Contributions to neuropsychological assessment: A clinical manual.* New York: Oxford University Press.

Blazer, D. G. II, Federspiel, C. F., Ray, W. A., & Schaffner, W. (1983). The risk of anticholinergic toxicity in the elderly: A study of prescribing practices in two populations. *Journal of Gerontology, 38,* 31–35.

Botwinick, J., & Storandt, M. (1974). Vocabulary ability in later life. *Journal of Genetic Psychology, 125,* 303–308.

Butcher, J. N., Aldwin, C. M., Levenson, M. R., Ben-Porath, Y. S., Spiro, A. III, & Bosse, R. (1991). Personality and aging: A study of MMPI-2 among older men. *Psychology and Aging, 6,* 361–370.

Cerella, J. (1985). Age-related decline in extrafoveal letter perception. *Journal of Gerontology, 40,* 727–736.

Cernoni-Huntley, J., Barbano, H. E., Brody, J. A., Cohen, B., Feldman, J. J., Kleinman, J. C., & Madans, J. (1983). National Health and Nutrition Examination Survey Epidemiologic Follow-up Study. *Public Health Reports, 98,* 245–251.

Cooper, B. A., Ward, M., Gowland, C. A., & McIntosh, J. M. (1991). The use of the Lanthony New Color Test in determining the effects of aging on color vision. *Journal of Gerontology: Psychological Sciences, 46,* P320–P324.

Costa, P. T., Jr., McCrae, R. R., Zonderman, A. B., Barbano, H. E., Lebowitz, B., & Larson, D. M. (1986). Cross-sectional studies of personality in a national sample: 2. Stability in neuroticism, extraversion, and openness. *Psychology and Aging, 1,* 144–149.

Cunningham, W. R., Sepkowski, C. M., & Opel, M. P. (1978). Fatigue effects on intelligence test performance in the elderly. *Journal of Gerontology, 28,* 96–100.

Elias, M. F., Robbins, M. A., Schultz, N. R., Jr., & Pierce, T. W. (1990). Is blood pressure an important variable in research on aging and neuropsychological test performance? *Journal of Gerontology: Psychological Sciences, 45*, P128–P135.

Fozard, J. L., Metter, E. F., & Brant, L. J. (1990). Next steps in describing aging and disease in longitudinal studies. *Journal of Gerontology: Psychological Sciences, 45*, P116–P127.

Galton, F. (1899). Exhibition of instruments (1) for testing perception of differences of tint and (2) for determining reaction time. *Journal of the Anthropological Institute, 19*, 27–29.

Gold, D., Andres, D., Arbuckle, T., & Schwartzman, A. (1988). Measurement and correlates of verbosity in elderly people. *Journal of Gerontology: Psychological Sciences, 43*, P27–P33.

Kosnik, W., Winslow, L., Kline, D., Rasinski, K., & Sekuler, R. (1988). Visual changes in daily life throughout adulthood. *Journal of Gerontology: Psychological Sciences, 43*, P63–P70.

Kunkel, S. R., & Applebaum, R. A. (1992). Estimating the prevalence of long-term disability for an aging society. *Journal of Gerontology: Social Sciences, 47*, S253–S260.

Lebo, C. P., & Reddell, R. C. (1972). The presbycusis component in occupational hearing loss. *Laryngoscope, 82*, 1399–1409.

Lerman, S. (1983). An experimental and clinical evaluation of lens transparency and aging. *Journal of Gerontology, 38*, 293–301.

Lima, S. D., Hale, S., & Myerson, J. (1991). How general is general slowing? Evidence from the lexical domain. *Psychology and Aging, 6*, 416–425.

Neugarten, B. L. (1977). Personality and aging. In J. E. Birren & K. W. Schaie (Eds.), *Handbook of the psychology of aging.* New York: Van Nostrand Reinhold.

Ordy, J. M., Brizzee, K. R., Beavers, T., & Medart, P. (1979). Age differences in the functional and structural organization of the auditory system in man. In J. M. Ordy & K. R. Brizzee (Eds.), *Aging: Vol. 10. Sensory systems and communication in the elderly* (pp. 153–166). New York: Raven Press.

Reitan, R. M., & Davison, L. A. (1974). *Clinical neuropsychology: Current status and applications.* New York: Wiley.

Robiner, W. N. (1987). An experimental inquiry into transference roles and age. *Psychology and Aging, 2*, 306–311.

Rubin, E. H., Morris, J. C., & Berg, L. (1987). The progression of personality changes in senile dementia of the Alzheimer type. *Journal of the American Geriatrics Society, 35*, 721–725.

Rubin, E. H., Morris, J. C., Storandt, M., & Berg, L. (1987). Behavioral changes in patients with mild senile dementia of the Alzheimer's type. *Psychiatry Research, 21*, 55–62.

Salthouse, T. A., Kausler, D. H., & Saults, J. S. (1990). Age, self-assessed health status, and cognition. *Journal of Gerontology: Psychological Sciences, 45*, P156–P160.

Schaie, K. W. (1989). Perceptual speed in adulthood: Cross-sectional and longitudinal studies. *Psychology and Aging, 4,* 443–453.

Schmidt, D. F., & Boland, S. M. (1986). Structure of perceptions of older adults: Evidence for multiple stereotypes. *Psychology and Aging, 1,* 255–260.

Spoor, A. (1967). Presbycusis values in relation to noise-induced hearing loss. *International Audiology, 6,* 48–57.

Storandt, M. (1977). Age, ability level, and method of administering and scoring the WAIS. *Journal of Gerontology, 32,* 175–178.

U.S. Bureau of the Census. (1986). *Estimates of the population of the United States by age, sex and race* (Current Population Reports Series P-25, No. 985). Washington, DC: Government Printing Office.

Vanderplas, J. H., & Vanderplas, J. M. (1981). Effects of legibility on verbal test performance of older adults. *Perceptual and Motor Skills, 53,* 183–186.

Vanderplas, J. M., & Vanderplas, J. H. (1980). Some factors affecting legibility of printed materials for older adults. *Perceptual and Motor Skills, 50,* 923–932.

Verbrugge, L. M., Kepkowski, J. M., & Konkol, L. L. (1991). Levels of disability among U.S. adults with arthritis. *Journal of Gerontology: Social Sciences, 46,* S71–S83.

Wechsler, D. (1981). *Manual for the Wechsler Adult Intelligence Scale–Revised.* New York: Psychological Corporation.

Wilkinson, R. T., & Allison, S. (1989). Age and simple reaction time: Decade differences for 5,325 subjects. *Journal of Gerontology: Psychological Sciences, 44,* P29–P35.

3

NEUROPSYCHOLOGICAL ASSESSMENT OF DEMENTIA

MERYL A. BUTTERS, DAVID P. SALMON, and NELSON BUTTERS

The neuropsychological assessment of dementia has become a major concern of clinical neuropsychology over the past several decades as the prevalence of dementing disorders has increased with the aging of the United States' population. This increased interest has led to extensive neuropsychological research that has helped to identify the subtle cognitive changes that are an indication of the onset of a dementing process and the unique patterns of cognitive deficits that are associated with particular dementing disorders. As a result, it is now frequently possible to detect the presence and determine the etiology of dementia in its earliest stages.

Dementia is a clinical syndrome characterized by deterioration in intellectual ability of sufficient severity to interfere with usual social or occupational functioning. According to the clinical criteria established in the revised third edition of the *Diagnostic and Statistical Manual of Mental Dis-*

The preparation of this chapter was supported, in part, by National Institute on Aging grant AG-05131 and National Institute of Mental Health grant MH-48819 to the University of California, San Diego (La Jolla), and by funds from the Medical Research Service of the Department of Veterans Affairs. Portions of this chapter are based on Bondi, Salmon, and Butters (1994).

33

orders (*DSM-III-R*; American Psychiatric Association, 1987), the cognitive manifestations of dementia must include impairment in short- and long-term memory in association with impairment in abstract thinking, impaired judgement, other disturbances of higher cortical function, or personality change. The diagnostic criteria for dementia also require that a specific organic factor (or factors) can be either demonstrated or presumed (through the exclusion of all "functional" mental disorders) to be related etiologically to the cognitive and behavioral disturbance.

Dementia may be caused by more than 50 disorders (Katzman, 1986), but the most common causes are neurodegenerative diseases such as Alzheimer's disease, Huntington's disease, and Parkinson's disease. Although it has been known for some time that dementia can arise from these etiologically and neuropathologically distinct disorders, the diversity in the cognitive manifestations of various dementing disorders has been recognized only recently. In the past, dementia was considered a ubiquitous condition of global intellectual impairment. In the last 15–20 years, however, investigators have demonstrated that distinct patterns of relatively preserved and impaired cognitive abilities are associated with different dementing diseases.

This diversity has been captured in the distinction that has been drawn between the dementia syndromes associated with neurodegenerative diseases that primarily involve regions of the cerebral cortex (e.g., Alzheimer's disease) and those that have their primary locus in subcortical brain structures (e.g., Huntington's disease, progressive supranuclear palsy; Albert, Feldman, & Willis, 1974; Cummings, 1990; McHugh & Folstein, 1975). Dementia of the Alzheimer type (DAT)—a prototypical "cortical" dementia—is characterized by prominent anterograde and retrograde amnesia, with additional deficits in language and semantic knowledge, abstract reasoning, other "executive" functions, and constructional and visuospatial abilities. The scope of the cognitive deficiencies that are associated with Alzheimer's disease is consistent with the widespread neuropathological changes that occur in the disorder. Although the numerous well-known pathological changes (e.g., neurofibrillary tangles, neuritic plaques, loss of neurons, presence of amyloid) that are associated with Alzheimer's disease appear to usually begin in the hippocampus and surrounding temporal lobe structures (Hyman, Van Hoesen, Damasio, & Barnes, 1984), they eventually involve all anterior and posterior association cortices in both hemispheres (Terry & Katzman, 1983; Terry, Peck, DeTeresa, Schechter, & Horoupian, 1981).

In contrast with DAT, the "subcortical" dementia of Huntington's disease (Folstein, 1989; Hayden, 1981)—a genetically transmitted disorder that results in progressive neuronal loss in the neostriatum (primarily the caudate nucleus; Bruyn, Bots, & Dom, 1979)—is characterized by memory disturbances, attentional dysfunction, problem-solving deficits, visuoperceptual and constructional deficits, and a deficiency in performing arithmetic (Brandt & Butters, 1986; Butters, Sax, Montgomery, & Tarlow, 1978). Unlike Alzheimer's disease, Huntington's disease results in little or no aphasia, although patients may be dysarthric due to the inherent motor dysfunction of the disease. A summary comparison of the neuropsychological deficits that are associated with Alzheimer's disease (i.e., cortical dementia) and Huntington's disease (i.e., subcortical dementia) is presented in Table 1. Because Huntington's disease most commonly occurs in the 3rd or 4th decade of life, and because Alzheimer's disease is a disease of the elderly, the patterns of neuropsychological deficits presented in Table 1 are relative to the performance of healthy middle-aged and older adults, respectively.

With this background in mind, we discuss in this chapter the neuropsychological evaluation of dementia both in terms of differentiating the cognitive deficits that are associated with the early stages of dementia from the mild changes that are a normal consequence of aging and in terms of identifying patterns of neuropsychological deficits that may be useful for the differential diagnosis of various dementing disorders. We focus our discussion primarily on Alzheimer's disease because of the prevalence of this disorder and its importance as a major public health issue (Terry & Katzman, 1992). The dementia syndrome that is associated with Alzheimer's disease is compared with that of Huntington's disease to illustrate the important role that a thorough neuropsychological evaluation can play in the differential diagnosis of dementing disorders.

NEUROPSYCHOLOGICAL EVALUATION OF DEMENTIA

As we just discussed, dementia is a global disorder of intellectual functioning that may affect a wide variety of cognitive processes. The

TABLE 1
Neuropsychological Features Associated With Cortical and
Subcortical Dementia

Cortical dementia: Alzheimer's disease
1. Severe memory deficits: Anterograde and retrograde amnesia
2. Problem-solving deficits
3. Anomic aphasia
4. Visuoperceptual and constructional deficits

Subcortical dementia: Huntington's disease
1. Forgetfulness: Retrieval deficits
2. Attentional dysfunction
3. Problem-solving deficits
4. Visuoperceptual and constructional deficits
5. Arithmetic deficiencies
6. Little or no aphasia

---

particular cognitive processes that are affected and the severity of a particular cognitive dysfunction, especially early in the course of a progressive neurological disease, can vary both within and between dementing disorders. Therefore, the neuropsychological evaluation of dementia must include the thorough assessment of a wide range of cognitive abilities. In general, the selected battery of tests should contain measures of verbal and nonverbal memory, executive functions such as problem solving and abstraction, language, visuospatial and visuoperceptual abilities, and attention.

The prevalence and significance of memory dysfunction in dementia require that its assessment be a major focus of the neuropsychological evaluation of the potentially demented elderly patient. Memory impairment is a cardinal feature of dementia and, in the usual case, the most prominent patient complaint in the initial stage of the disorder (Corkin, Davis, Growdon, Usdin, & Wurtman, 1982; Moss & Albert, 1988). The prominence of memory dysfunction in all forms of dementia is acknowledged by its inclusion as a necessary component in the criteria for dementia of most standardized diagnostic schemes (e.g., *DSM-III-R*). Although memory impairment is ubiquitous in dementia, recent studies have shown that various aspects of memory may be affected differently in different dementing disorders and that these differences have important diagnostic implications (see the Assessment of Memory in Dementia section).

Deficiencies in abstract thinking, problem solving, and the ability to shift and maintain cognitive set are also prominent features of most forms of dementia and should be thoroughly assessed in the dementia evaluation (Albert & Moss, 1988; Bondi, Monsch, Butters, Salmon, & Paulsen, 1993; Cummings & Benson, 1992; Hart, Kwentus, Wade, & Taylor, 1988). Although these deficits may not occur in the early stages of all dementing disorders, they invariably arise during the course of the dementing process.

The assessment of language in the potentially demented patient should minimally include measures of confrontation naming, fluency (i.e., generative naming), and comprehension. Although syntactic and grammatical abilities appear to remain relatively intact in patients with DAT (Bayles & Kaszniak, 1987; Kemper et al., 1993; Kempler, Curtiss, & Jackson, 1987), confrontation naming deficits are evident in these patients in the early to middle stages of the disease (Bayles & Tomoeda, 1983; Hart, 1988; Hodges, Salmon, & Butters, 1991; Nebes, 1989). In contrast, confrontation-naming deficits are not readily apparent in subcortical dementing disorders, such as Huntington's disease, until the very late stages (Butters et al., 1978). Fluency deficits, on the other hand, occur relatively early in almost all dementing disorders (Butters, Granholm, Salmon, Grant, & Wolfe, 1987). As we discuss later, the different patterns of impairment on naming and fluency tasks in the various dementing disorders are likely to be indicative of different underlying linguistic and semantic memory deficits.

Impairment of constructional and visuospatial abilities occurs in varying degrees in most forms of dementia (Cummings & Benson, 1992). Although often not prominent in the early stages of DAT, constructional deficits are usually present by the middle stages of the disease. It is also noteworthy that a small number of patients with neuropathologically proven Alzheimer's disease initially presented with visuospatial impairment (Crystal, Horoupian, Katzman, & Jotkowitz, 1982; Martin, 1987).

Although attention deficits are not a pronounced problem in the early stages of DAT, they are often an important characteristic of the dementia associated with other disorders (Cummings & Benson, 1992) and should be assessed. This is particularly important because impaired attention can detrimentally affect performance on other neuropsychological tests that require effortful cognitive processing. Because verbal and nonverbal attention mechanisms can be impaired selectively, they should be evaluated independently.

A number of neuropsychological tests are available to assess each of the cognitive domains just described, and test batteries composed of these tests have been created for the assessment of dementia in older adults (e.g., Albert & Moss, 1988; Salmon & Butters, 1992; Storandt, Botwinick, Danziger, Berg, & Hughes, 1984). For example, the neuropsychological test battery used for the assessment of dementia at the University of California, San Diego (La Jolla), Alzheimer's Disease Research Center (Salmon & Butters, 1992) is presented in Table 2. This test battery evaluates each of the major cognitive domains that may be affected in DAT and other dementing disorders and provides measures that have proven to be particularly sensitive to dementia in its earliest stages. This test battery has also been useful for elucidating patterns of cognitive deficits that differentiate various dementing disorders.

In addition to neuropsychological tests that fully assess a specific cognitive function, a number of standardized mental status examinations that briefly evaluate each cognitive domain have been used as dementia screening instruments. Three widely used mental status examinations are the Mini-Mental State Examination (Folstein, Folstein, & McHugh, 1975), the Fuld (1978) adaptation of the Information–Memory–Concentration Test (Blessed, Tomlinson, & Roth, 1968), and the Mattis (1976) Dementia Rating Scale. Each of these tests briefly assesses a number of the different cognitive domains described in the first part of this section, and each has been shown to have reasonable sensitivity and specificity for the detection of DAT in the relatively early stages of the disease (Folstein et al., 1975; Fuld, 1978; Salmon, Kwo-on-Yuen, Heindel, Butters, & Thal, 1989). These brief procedures may also be useful in tracking the progression of DAT over several years (Becker, Huff, Nebes, Holland, & Boller, 1988; Brandt, Folstein, & Folstein, 1988; Katzman et al., 1988; Ortof & Crystal,

TABLE 2
Neuropsychological Test Battery Used at the University of California, San Diego (La Jolla), Alzheimer's Disease Research Center

Mental status
  1. Blessed Information–Memory–Concentration Test
  2. Mini-Mental State Examination
  3. Dementia Rating Scale
Attention
  1. Digit Span Test (WAIS-R)
  2. Visual Span Test (WMS-R)
Memory
  1. Visual Reproduction Test (WMS)
  2. California Verbal Learning Test
  3. Selective Reminding Test
  4. Logical Memory Subtest (WMS-R)
  5. Number Information Test
Abstraction/problem solving
  1. Modified Wisconsin Card Sorting Test
  2. Trail Making Test: Parts A and B
  3. Arithmetic Subtest (WAIS-R)
  4. Similarities Subtest (WAIS-R)
Language
  1. Vocabulary Subtest (WAIS-R)
  2. Boston Naming Test
  3. Letter and Category Fluency Tests
  4. American National Adult Reading Test
Constructional/visuospatial
  1. Block Design Subtest (WISC-R)
  2. Digit Symbol Substitution Test (WAIS-R)
  3. Clock Drawing Test
  4. Clock Setting Test
  5. Copy-a-Cube Test
Motor
  1. Grooved Pegboard Test
  2. Grip Strength Test

Note. WAIS-R = Wechsler Adult Intelligence Scale–Revised; WISC-R = Wechsler Intelligence Scale for Children–Revised; WMS = Wechsler Memory Scale; WMS-R = Wechsler Memory Scale–Revised.

1989; Salmon, Thal, Butters, & Heindel, 1990; Thal, Grundman, & Golden, 1986; Vitaliano et al., 1984). The Mattis Dementia Rating Scale is particularly effective in tracking progression in the more advanced stages of the disease (Salmon et al., 1990) because it assesses a wide range of cognitive abilities with both difficult and very simple test items.

ASSESSMENT OF MEMORY IN DEMENTIA

Although many cognitive abilities are affected in dementia, assessment of the specific deficits that are associated with memory dysfunction has proven to be most useful in detecting and differentiating various forms of dementia in their early stages. Consistent differences between the performances of early-stage DAT patients and normal older adults are observed on most memory tests that require the learning and retention of new information (i.e., anterograde amnesia) or the recollection of information from the past (i.e., retrograde amnesia). In addition, studies of age-related changes in normal elderly individuals indicate that a decrement in the availability of processing resources at the time of encoding and retrieval may underlie their subtle memory deficits (Craik & Rabinowitz, 1984; Kaszniak, Poon, & Riege, 1986), rather than the consolidation deficit that is apparent in patients with DAT (see the Consolidation Deficit subsection). Thus, although normal elderly individuals may accurately note a subtle decline in episodic memory abilities with advancing age, the memory deficits that are associated with DAT are clearly of greater magnitude and involve aspects of memory that are relatively spared by aging (see Butters, Heindel, & Salmon, 1990; Nebes, 1989).

Patients with DAT evidence a severe impairment of episodic memory (i.e., memory for information that depends on temporal and/or spatial contextual cues for its retrieval), which is thought to be mediated by damage to the hippocampus and entorhinal cortex (Hyman et al., 1984; Tomlinson, Blessed, & Roth, 1970) as well as to the cholinergic neurotransmitter system (Drachman, 1977; Weingartner, Sitaram, & Gillin, 1979; Whitehouse et al., 1982). The deficit is characterized by ineffective consolidation or storage of new information, a rapid rate of forgetting, and an increased susceptibility to proactive interference. Patients with DAT also exhibit severe and temporally graded retrograde amnesia, as well as a breakdown in the structure and organization of semantic memory (i.e., the general fund of knowledge that consists of overlearned facts and concepts that are not dependent on contextual cues for retrieval).

In contrast with the storage deficiency of DAT patients, the moderate memory impairment of patients with Huntington's disease is thought to result from difficulty in initiating systematic retrieval strategies when attempting to recall information from either episodic or semantic memory. The retrieval deficit of Huntington's disease patients results in a memory disorder that is characterized by performance that is less impaired on recognition tasks than on free-recall tasks, relatively intact rates of forgetting on tests of episodic memory, a moderate remote memory loss that is equally severe across all decades of the patients' lives, and—despite deficits on some language tasks—intact structure and organization of semantic memory. The empirical evidence demonstrating these divergent patterns of memory performance and the clinical significance of these characteristics are discussed in the remainder of this chapter.

Consolidation Deficit

The severe episodic memory deficit that is apparent in even the earliest stages of DAT (Butters, Salmon, & Heindel, 1990; Carlesimo & Oscar-

Berman, 1992; Nebes, 1992) appears to result primarily from a failure to adequately consolidate or store new information. A deficiency in transferring information from short- to long-term storage is supported by the observations that DAT patients exhibit little improvement in acquiring information over repeated learning trials (Buschke & Fuld, 1974; Delis et al., 1991; Masur et al., 1989; Moss, Albert, Butters, & Payne, 1986; Wilson, Bacon, Fox, & Kaszniak, 1983) and that they tend to recall only the most recently presented information (i.e., demonstrate a heightened recency effect) in free-recall tasks (Delis et al., 1991; Miller, 1971; Wilson et al., 1983). In addition, DAT patients are likely to recall items from short-term storage rather than from long-term storage in tasks using the selective reminding procedure of Buschke and Fuld (Buschke & Fuld, 1974; Masur et al., 1989; Nebes, 1992; Ober, Koss, Friedland, & Delis, 1985).

Further evidence that a consolidation deficit underlies the impaired episodic memory performance of DAT patients is their inability to benefit normally from effortful or elaborative encoding at the time of acquisition (Knopman & Ryberg, 1989). When forced to engage in elaborative or semantic processing of information during the study phase of a free-recall task, the performance of normal elderly adults, but not that of DAT patients, is enhanced (Craik & Rabinowitz, 1984; Schacter, 1987).

The inability of DAT patients to adequately consolidate new information is also evident in their failure to demonstrate a normal improvement in performance when memory is tested in a recognition rather than recall format. Delis et al. (1991) compared the performance of DAT patients, Huntington's disease patients, and alcoholics with Korsakoff's syndrome on the California Verbal Learning Test (Delis, Kramer, Kaplan, & Ober, 1987). This standardized memory test assesses rate of learning, retention after short- and long-delay intervals, semantic encoding ability, recognition (i.e., discriminability), intrusion and perseverative errors, and response biases. Subjects are verbally presented five presentation/free-recall trials of a list of 16 shopping items (4 items in each of four categories) and are then administered a single trial using a second, different list of 16 items. Immediately after this final trial, subjects are administered first a free-recall test and then a cued-recall (using the names of the four categories) test for the items on the first shopping list. Twenty minutes later, the free-recall and cued-recall tests are repeated, followed by a *yes–no* recognition test consisting of the 16 items on the first shopping list and 28 distractor items.

Delis et al. (1991) found that despite comparable free- and cued-recall deficits in all three patient groups, Huntington's disease patients, but not DAT or Korsakoff's syndrome patients, benefitted substantially when memory was tested with a recognition format. This finding suggests that the severe episodic memory impairment of DAT patients is not primarily due to difficulties in retrieving information but rather reflects a deficit in consolidation or storage (Butters, 1984; Delis et al., 1991; Martin, Browers,

Cox, & Fedio, 1985). If DAT patients had stored the items but were simply unable to retrieve them, then their performance would have improved on the recognition test as it did for patients with Huntington's disease (also see Butters, Wolfe, Martone, Granholm, & Cermak, 1985).

Rapid Forgetting

An important characteristic of the memory impairment that is associated with DAT is rapid forgetting of information over time (Hart, Kwentus, Harkins, & Taylor, 1988; Knopman & Ryberg, 1989; Welsh, Butters, Hughes, Mohs, & Heyman, 1992). The rate of forgetting that is exhibited by DAT patients has been shown to be greater than that of normal elderly adults, patients with other dementing disorders, and patients with circumscribed amnesia (Butters et al., 1988; Moss et al., 1986; Troster et al., 1993). Accordingly, rapid forgetting, as measured by delayed-recall (e.g., number of words recalled after several minutes delay) and savings scores (e.g., percentage retained over a period of time), has been proposed as an important neuropsychological marker for the early and differential diagnosis of DAT.

The utility of measures of forgetting for distinguishing mildly demented patients with DAT from normal elderly individuals was demonstrated by Welsh, Butters, Hughes, Mohs, and Heyman (1991). These investigators compared the performances of DAT patients and those of normal elderly adults on several verbal memory measures (i.e., immediate-recall scores for each of three learning trials, delayed free recall, savings scores, recognition memory, and the number of intrusion errors) derived from a list-learning task of the Consortium to Establish a Registry for Alzheimer's Disease (CERAD). Of all the memory measures examined, the highest accuracy (90%) in differentiating mildly demented DAT patients from normal elderly adults was achieved with the delayed free-recall measure (10-min delay). The percentage-of-savings measure also provided relatively good differentiation, but other memory measures (i.e., immediate recall, intrusion errors, and recognition memory) had poor overall discriminability.

The severity of the rapid forgetting that was exhibited by DAT patients in the Welsh et al. (1991) study was evident in the floor effects that occurred on the delayed-recall measure in even the mildly demented patients. Because of these floor effects, delayed recall (i.e., forgetting) was not particularly useful for discriminating between moderately and severely demented DAT patients. Indeed, in a subsequent study, Welsh et al. (1992) demonstrated that measures of naming ability, fluency, and constructional ability from the CERAD neuropsychological test battery were more useful than indices of forgetting in differentiating among mildly, moderately, and severely demented DAT patients.

The effectiveness of a delayed-recall measure for distinguishing mildly demented DAT patients from normal elderly people was also examined by

Knopman and Ryberg (1989). This study differed from that of Welsh et al. (1991) in that test conditions were established to maximize discriminability between DAT and normal elderly individuals. Thus, the verbal memory test that was used by Knopman and Ryberg required subjects to engage in elaborative encoding procedures (i.e., a sentence-generation task) at the time of stimulus presentation and to freely recall the information after a 5-min delay. The results of this study demonstrated that DAT patients were severely impaired in delayed free recall and that this measure discriminated DAT patients from elderly normal control subjects with better than 95% accuracy.

It is important to note that the just-described clinical demonstrations of the utility of delayed recall (or savings scores) for distinguishing mildly demented DAT patients from normal elderly adults are not an artifact of comparing groups of individuals who differ in their ability to initially learn new material. To circumvent this potentially confounding factor, Hart, Kwentus, Harkins, and Taylor (1988) compared the rates of forgetting exhibited by normal elderly adults and mild DAT patients who were equated for level of initial learning. These investigators equated initial learning by allowing DAT patients additional initial exposure to the to-be-remembered stimulus material. Despite the advantage of multiple repetitions of the material at the time of presentation (i.e., learning to criterion), DAT patients exhibited faster forgetting than did the healthy elderly adults.

A clinically useful attribute of savings scores that is not shared by delayed-recall or other memory measures is the relative insensitivity to subject demographic characteristics such as age and level of education. Studies have demonstrated that savings scores that are derived from the Logical Memory and Visual Reproduction subtests of the original Wechsler Memory Scale (Wechsler, 1945) (Haaland, Linn, Hunt, & Goodwin, 1983; Ivnik et al., 1990), the Wechsler Memory Scale–Revised (Wechsler, 1987) (Cullum, Butters, Troster, & Salmon, 1990), or the Auditory Verbal Learning Test (Ivnik et al., 1990) are not correlated significantly with age or years of education. Thus, savings scores (and perhaps other indices of rate of forgetting) appear to be of special clinical and diagnostic significance because they are very sensitive for detecting early DAT and have the added benefit of being relatively unaffected by educational factors and normal age-related memory decline.

Indices of rapid forgetting are not only useful for detecting DAT in its early stages, but they have also proven to be effective for differentiating DAT from other dementing illnesses (e.g., basal ganglia dementias such as Huntington's disease and Parkinson's disease). For example, Butters et al. (1988), using delayed-memory indices and savings scores calculated for the Logical Memory and Visual Reproduction subtests of the Wechsler Memory Scale–Revised, showed that DAT patients forgot verbal and figural materials more quickly than did equally demented Huntington's disease patients.

Troster et al. (1993) obtained similar results and found that discriminant function analyses based on Logical Memory and Visual Reproduction savings scores provided satisfactory to excellent overall classification accuracy in differentiating DAT and Huntington's disease patients from control groups (DAT vs. elderly controls: 94%; Huntington's disease vs. middle-aged controls: 81%), as well as in differentiating DAT from Huntington's disease patients in the early stages of the diseases (82%).

The clinical utility of forgetting rates for differentiating various forms of dementia was also shown in the Delis et al. (1991) study with the California Verbal Learning Test. In this study, patients with DAT and Korsakoff's syndrome produced significantly lower savings scores (i.e., Long-Delay Free Recall divided by Trial 5–List A Free Recall) than did Huntington's disease patients. Furthermore, when the difference between Recognition Discriminability Index and Trial 5 Free Recall was analyzed, patients with Huntington's disease tended to perform better on the discriminability index than on Trial 5 Free Recall, whereas DAT patients exhibited the opposite relationship. As noted previously, some of this difference is due to the DAT patients' inability to store new information; however, rapid forgetting also likely contributes to the DAT patients' unusually poor discriminability scores, because the recognition test of the California Verbal Learning Test is administered 20 min after Trial 5 Free Recall.

Intrusion Errors

A third prominent feature of DAT patients' episodic memory deficit is the tendency of previously learned information to intrude into the attempted recall of new materials. Such intrusion errors have been noted when DAT patients are asked to sequentially recall a series of short stories or passages (Butters et al., 1987) or a series of geometric designs (Jacobs, Troster, Butters, Salmon, & Cermak, 1990). DAT patients will often intrude facts from the first story into their attempts to recall an ensuing story and will incorporate components of one design into their drawings of subsequent ones.

Although increases in intrusion errors have been noted in a number of neurological patient groups (Kramer, Levin, Brandt, & Delis, 1988; Shindler, Caplan, & Heir, 1984), their ubiquity in patients with DAT suggests that they may have diagnostic significance in the early stages of the disorder (Butters et al., 1987; Delis et al., 1991; Fuld, 1983; Fuld, Katzman, Davies, & Terry, 1982; Kramer et al., 1988). For example, Fuld and her colleagues (Fuld, 1983; Fuld et al., 1982) found that nearly 90% of the mildly demented DAT patients that they examined made intrusion errors on episodic memory tests, mental status examinations, and several verbal subtests of the WAIS, whereas only 35% of non-DAT dementia patients made such errors. Fuld et al. (1982) also suggested that DAT patients' tendency to produce intrusion errors has important neurological significance, because the number of intrusion errors that was measured during the last year of life was significantly correlated with the number of neuritic plaques and amount of acetylcholine depletion in postmortem brains of DAT patients.

Because of the potential diagnostic usefulness of the qualitative features of errors on memory tests, the California Verbal Learning Test provides scoring guidelines and normative data for intrusion and perseverative errors. Delis and his colleagues (Delis et al., 1991; Kramer et al., 1988) compared DAT, Huntington's disease, and alcoholic Korsakoff's syndrome patients in terms of the number of intrusion errors produced on the California Verbal Learning Test. The results of this comparison revealed that DAT and amnesic Korsakoff's syndrome patients produced significantly more intrusion errors than did Huntington's disease patients. Notably, nearly 70% of the total responses of the DAT and amnesic patients on the cued-recall portion of this test were intrusions, whereas only 20% were intrusions in the Huntington's disease group.

Criteria for scoring intrusion errors on the Visual Reproduction subtest of the original Wechsler Memory Scale and the Wechsler Memory Scale–Revised were developed by Jacobs and her colleagues (Jacobs, Salmon, Troster, & Butters, 1990; Jacobs, Troster, Butters, Salmon, & Cermak, 1990). When these criteria were applied to the performances of DAT and Huntington's disease patients and normal elderly individuals, it was shown that patients with DAT produced significantly more intrusion errors than did either of the other two groups. Despite being as severely demented as the DAT patients, patients with Huntington's disease produced intrusion errors only occasionally, and normal elderly individuals typically did not produce such errors.

Although DAT patients are consistently more likely to make intrusion errors on the Visual Reproduction subtest than are equally demented Huntington's disease patients, the number of intrusion errors produced by both patient groups is lower on the Wechsler Memory Scale–Revised than on the original Wechsler Memory Scale (Jacobs, Salmon, Troster, & Butters, 1990). Jacobs and her colleagues hypothesized that the original version of the test is more likely to evoke figural intrusion errors in both patient groups, because the greater dissimilarity between items on the revised test (i.e., linear and circular figures) may create less interference in the recall of subsequent items than does the use of all linear figures in the original (for further discussion see Jacobs, Salmon, Troster, & Butters, 1990; Troster, Jacobs, Butters, Cullum, & Salmon, 1989).

Although intrusion errors on tests of memory for verbal and figural information appear to be a consistent behavioral marker in DAT, some caution should be exercised when using such errors as a diagnostic aid in a clinical setting. Intrusion errors occur in patients with forms of dementia other than DAT (e.g., Huntington's disease) and in some patients with circumscribed amnesia (e.g., Korsakoff's syndrome). Thus, they are not by themselves a pathognomonic sign of DAT (Jacobs, Salmon, Troster, & Butters, 1990). Furthermore, several studies have shown that measures of intrusion errors by themselves have very limited predictive value in differentiating DAT patients from healthy elderly controls (Christensen, Hadzi-Pavlovic, & Jacomb, 1991; Welsh et al., 1991, 1992). Thus, the occurrence of intrusion errors on episodic memory tests should be considered only a single indicator of a significant memory disturbance.

Despite these caveats, intrusion errors in conjunction with other memory measures (e.g., total recall, recognition memory, rate of forgetting) can be used to create powerful clinical algorithms for differentiating DAT from other types of dementia (Delis et al., 1991; Massman, Delis, Butters, Dupont, & Gillin, 1992). For example, Delis et al. (1991) developed a discriminant function equation using the scores of DAT and Huntington's disease patients on two measures from the California Verbal Learning Test: (a) the percentage of cued recall intrusions and (b) the difference between recognition discriminability and recall on Trial 5 of List A. (Because recognition testing occurs after a delay period, this latter measure assesses both retention over time and any potential benefit of a recognition format over free recall.) With this equation, these investigators were able to correctly classify 17 of 20 DAT patients and 16 of 19 patients with Huntington's disease. Interestingly, 100% of alcoholic Korsakoff's syndrome patients were classified as DAT-like with the discriminant equation.

In a related study, Massman et al. (1992) were able to discriminate between patients with DAT and depressed patients using a similar discriminant function. When the scores of 49 depressed patients were subjected to discriminant equations based on California Verbal Learning Test measures of total recall over the five learning trials, the percentage of cued recall intrusions, and the difference between recognition discriminability and recall on Trial 5 of List A, 49% were classified as *normal*, 22.4% were classified as *not well*, 28.6% were classified as *Huntington's disease*, and none were classified as *DAT*. It appears that when affective disorders produce deficits in cognitive abilities, the pattern of deficits is similar to that of patients with basal ganglia disorders.

Retrograde Amnesia

In addition to their deficits in learning and retaining new information, patients with DAT are severely impaired in recollecting autobiographical information and public events that they had successfully learned and remembered before the onset of their disease (Beatty & Salmon, 1991; Beatty, Salmon, Butters, Heindel, & Granholm, 1988; Hodges, Salmon, & Butters,

1993; Kopelman, 1989; Sagar, Cohen, Sullivan, Corkin, & Growdon, 1988; Wilson, Kaszniak, & Fox, 1981). In general, a number of studies have shown that DAT patients are severely impaired in relation to normal elderly adults in remembering events across all decades of their lives. In the early stages of the disease, their remote memory loss is temporally graded with memories from the distant past (i.e., childhood and early adulthood) that are relatively better remembered than memories from the more recent past (i.e., middle and late adulthood). The remote memory loss of DAT patients does not appear to be limited to one type of information, as it has been demonstrated with tests requiring the identification of famous people or scenes from the past (Beatty et al., 1988; Hodges et al., 1993; Kopelman, 1989; Sagar et al., 1988; Wilson et al., 1981), past public events (Beatty et al., 1988; Sagar et al., 1988), geographical information from past areas of residence (Beatty & Salmon, 1991), and remote autobiographical information (Kopelman, 1989).

The temporal gradient that is observed in the remote memory deficit of patients with DAT suggests that their remote memory loss is not simply due to a retrieval deficit, but rather to a defect in storing or consolidating information over time. If a general retrieval deficit was responsible for their remote memory loss, then memories from all decades of their lives would be expected to be equally affected. On the other hand, the better preservation of more distant than more recent remote memories suggests that the older memories have become better consolidated through repeated processing, rehearsal, or reexposure and thus are less susceptible to the deleterious effects of brain damage. (For a discussion of the role of consolidation in temporally graded retrograde amnesia see Zola-Morgan & Squire, 1990.)

In contrast with patients with DAT, patients with subcortical dementia arising from Huntington's disease (Albert, Butters, & Brandt, 1981; Beatty et al., 1988) or Parkinson's disease (Freedman, Rivoira, Butters, Sax, & Feldman, 1982) have only a mild remote memory deficit that is equally severe across all decades of the patients' lives. This pattern of remote memory impairment is consistent with these patients' postulated general retrieval deficit.

Semantic Memory Deficits

In addition to their severe episodic memory impairment, patients with DAT often exhibit language deficits, such as word-finding difficulties in spontaneous speech and mild anomia, during the course of the disease. These language deficits are accompanied by decrements in DAT patients' general fund of knowledge concerning common facts of history, geography, arithmetic, and science. Investigators have only recently begun to examine the language and knowledge deficits that are associated with DAT within the framework of current cognitive psychological models of semantic memory (e.g., Collins & Loftus, 1975), which propose that human representations of knowledge are organized as a network of interrelated categories, concepts, and attributes.

Studies examining the ability of DAT patients to verbally generate words that are members of restricted phonemic (e.g., words beginning with a particular letter) or semantic (e.g., animals, fruits, vegetables) categories were among the first to demonstrate semantic memory deficits in these patients. In one of these studies, Butters et al. (1987) examined the verbal fluency of mildly demented DAT patients, Huntington's disease patients, and patients with alcoholic Korsakoff's syndrome using both letter and category tasks. In these tasks, subjects verbally generated for 1 min words beginning with the letters F, A, and S or exemplars from the semantic category "animals." The results of this study showed that Huntington's disease and Korsakoff's syndrome patients demonstrated, respectively, severe and moderate deficits on both fluency tasks, presumably because of a general retrieval deficit that is related to the inherent frontal lobe dysfunction of these neurological disorders. In contrast, DAT patients, who were matched with the other patient groups for overall severity of dementia, were impaired only on the category-fluency task.

In view of the results reported by Butters et al. (1987), Monsch et al. (1992) compared the efficacy of the category- and letter-fluency tasks for differentiating between DAT patients and normal elderly individuals. Consistent with the findings of Butters et al. (1987), these investigators found that the category-fluency task was superior to the letter-fluency task in differentiating between not only moderately demented DAT patients and normal elderly individuals, but also between normal elderly individuals and patients in the earliest stages of DAT (see Table 3).

The Butters et al. (1987) results were recently replicated in a study that compared the performances of 44 patients with DAT, 42 Huntington's disease patients, and their respective age- and education-matched control subjects on the letter-fluency (F, A, and S) and category-fluency (animals, fruits, and vegetables) tasks (Monsch et al., 1994). When the performances of the two patient groups were expressed as fluency scores standardized to their respective control groups, Huntington's disease patients were severely and equally impaired on both letter- and category-fluency tasks (see Figure 1). Patients with DAT were also clearly impaired on both tasks but demonstrated a much greater impairment on the semantically based category-fluency task than on the letter-fluency task.

The disproportionately severe fluency impairment that was exhibited by DAT patients when generating exemplars from a specific semantic category, compared with generating words that begin with a particular letter, is indicative of a loss of semantic knowledge or, at least, a breakdown in the organization of semantic memory. Although normal older adults are able to use the organization within a well-defined and restricted semantic

TABLE 3
TABLE 3
Sensitivity and Specificity of the Maximally Effective Cut-off Score on Four Verbal Fluency Tasks

Task	Cut-off score	Sensitivity (%)	Specificity (%)
All DAT versus controls			
Category	<38	100	92
Letter	<31	88	84
First names	<16	94	86
Supermarket	<16	92	96
Mild dementia versus controls			
Category	<38	100	92
Letter	<32	81	83
First names	<18	90	83
Supermarket	<16	76	96

Note. The verbal fluency tasks included a category fluency task (animals, fruits, and vegetables), a letter fluency task (*F*, *A*, and *S*), a fluency for first names task, and the supermarket fluency task from the Mattis Dementia Rating Scale (Mattis, 1976). *N*s = 53 in the control group and 89 in the DAT group, 21 of whom were mildly demented (Mini-Mental State Examination ≥ 18). DAT = dementia of the Alzheimer type. Adapted from "A Comparison of Category and Letter Fluency in Alzheimer's Disease and Huntington's Disease" by A. U. Monsch, M. W. Bondi, N. Butters, D. P. Salmon, R. Katzman, and L. J. Thal, 1994, *Neuropsychology*, *8*, p. 29. Copyright 1994 by the American Psychological Association.

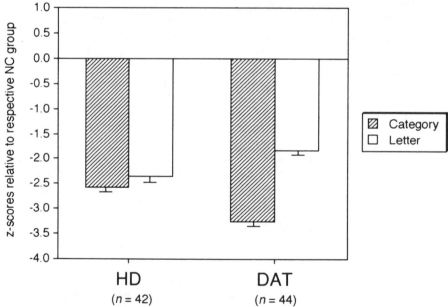

Figure 1. Standard scores of patients with dementia of the Alzheimer type (DAT) and Huntington's disease (HD) on the category and letter fluency tasks. NC = normal controls. From "A Comparison of Category and Letter Fluency in Alzheimer's Disease and Huntington's Disease" by A. U. Monsch, M. W. Bondi, N. Butters, D. P. Salmon, R. Katzman, and L. J. Thal, 1994, *Neuropsychology*, *8*, p. 26. Copyright 1994 by the American Psychological Association.

category to guide their responses on the category-fluency task, individuals with DAT appear to be deficient in their knowledge of the attributes that define the relevant semantic category or are unable to use this knowledge to locate specific category exemplars. When semantic organization is less salient or useful in the fluency task, as in the category of words that begin with a particular letter, patients with DAT show less impairment in relation to healthy older adults. Letter- and category-fluency performance would be affected equally if DAT patients' fluency deficit was due simply to an inability to retrieve information from semantic memory (as postulated for Huntington's disease patients).

Further evidence of the breakdown in the organization of semantic memory that is associated with DAT is provided by studies that examined the types of responses produced by these patients on a semantically based category-fluency task from the Dementia Rating Scale (Martin & Fedio, 1983; Troster, Salmon, McCullough, & Butters, 1989). In this fluency task, the subject must verbally generate items that can be found in a supermarket. The results of these studies reveal a disruption in the organization of DAT patients' semantic memory that is characterized by an initial loss of the most specific attributes of a semantic category with relative preservation of more general superordinate knowledge. In both studies, DAT patients generated significantly fewer specific items (e.g., carrots) per superordinate category (e.g., vegetables) than did normal older adults; they also generated a larger ratio of superordinate category names to total words produced. Thus, if the semantic representations of objects and categories are viewed as being organized in a hierarchical fashion with the most general aspects at the top and more specific features at the bottom, then DAT patients demonstrate a progressive "bottom-up" breakdown in the hierarchical organization of semantic knowledge and memory (Chertkow & Bub, 1990; Martin, 1987; Martin & Fedio, 1983; Troster, Salmon, McCullough, & Butters, 1989).

Impaired semantic memory in DAT patients is also evident in the numerous reports of these patients' deficits on tests of object naming (for a review see Hart, 1988). Studies examining the nature of the errors produced by DAT patients on confrontation-naming tasks demonstrate that they are more likely than normal older adults or patients with other dementing disorders to produce semantically related errors (Bayles & Tomoeda, 1983; Hodges et al., 1991; Huff, Corkin, & Growdon, 1986; Smith, Murdoch, & Chenery, 1989). For example, after performing a comprehensive classification of error types produced on a modified version of the Boston Naming Test, Hodges et al. (1991) found that DAT patients made a significantly greater proportion of semantically based errors (i.e., semantic-superordinate and semantic-associative errors) than did normal elderly individuals and patients with Huntington's disease, even though the DAT and Huntington's disease patients were matched for overall naming ability.

Patients with Huntington's disease performed like the normal elderly individuals but produced a significantly greater proportion of visually based errors. These results suggest that naming deficits in Huntington's disease initially involve primarily a disruption of perceptual analysis, whereas in DAT such naming impairments reflect a breakdown in semantic processes. The increased prevalence of semantic-superordinate errors in the naming performance of DAT patients is consistent with the bottom-up breakdown in their semantic knowledge that is proposed to explain their deficits on category-fluency tasks.

The influence of DAT patients' semantic memory impairment on their performance of tasks that are not typically viewed as tests of language or memory was demonstrated by Rouleau, Salmon, Butters, Kennedy, and McGuire (1992) in a study that was designed to examine visuoconstructive deficits in DAT and Huntington's disease patients. The visuoconstructive task that these investigators used required individuals to draw and copy clocks. In the command condition of this task, subjects were given a blank piece of paper and asked to simply "draw a clock, put in all the numbers and set the hands for 10 past 11." In the copy condition, subjects were asked to copy a drawing of a clock with the hands set at 10 past 11.

The results of the Rouleau et al. (1992) study revealed that although both patient groups were impaired in relation to normal elderly individuals in both task conditions, DAT patients were more impaired than were Huntington's disease patients in the command condition, but Huntington's disease patients were more impaired than were DAT patients in the copy condition. An explanation for this interaction was found in a qualitative analysis of the types of errors made on the task by the two patient groups (see Figure 2). Patients with Huntington's disease tended to make primarily graphic, visuospatial, and planning errors that occurred when they were spontaneously drawing or copying the clock. In contrast, DAT patients often made conceptual errors in the spontaneous condition that seem to reflect a loss, or a deficit in, accessing knowledge of the attributes, features, and meaning of a clock. This loss of semantic knowledge was evident in such conceptual errors as misrepresenting the clock by drawing a clock face without numbers or with an inappropriate use of numbers, and misrepresenting the time by failing to include the hands, inappropriately using the hands, or actually writing the time in the clock face. The conceptual errors that were evident in the DAT patients' spontaneous drawings were much less evident when the semantic memory demands of the task were reduced or eliminated by allowing them to copy a model clock.

CONCLUSION

As the knowledge of the neuropsychological characteristics of DAT has grown, it has become possible to identify a number of key neuropsy-

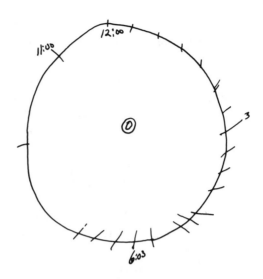

a) pt 2119: DAT (command)

b) pt 2232: DAT (command)

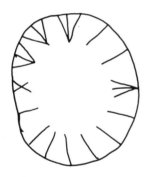

c) pt 2179: DAT (command)

d) pt 2179: DAT (copy)

Figure 2. Examples of conceptual errors in the clock drawings of patients with dementia of the Alzheimer type (DAT). Panels c and d represent a single DAT patient's (pt 2179) attempt to draw the clock to command (c) and to copy a model (d). From "Quantitative and Qualitative Analyses of Clock Drawings in Alzheimer's and Huntington's Disease" by I. Rouleau, D. P. Salmon, N. Butters, C. Kennedy, and K. McGuire, 1992, *Brain and Cognition, 18,* p. 77. Copyright 1992 by Academic Press.

chological measures that can effectively distinguish patients in the early stages of this disorder from normal elderly individuals. Among the more sensitive measures for identifying patients in the early stages of DAT are (a) delayed-recall and memory-savings scores that reflect these patients' inability to effectively store or consolidate new information, (b) intrusion errors that arise from an increased susceptibility to proactive interference,

(c) a severe and temporally graded retrograde amnesia, and (d) a severe deficit in category fluency—a measure that is indicative of a breakdown in the organization of semantic memory. As the disease progresses and cognitive functioning is further compromised, tests of learning, confrontation naming, problem solving, and visuospatial and constructional abilities become useful for staging moderately and severely impaired DAT patients.

It has also become evident that, although all dementias (including so-called "pseudodementias") are characterized by a general decline in numerous cognitive functions, the pattern of deficits exhibited in various disorders are quite different. As we have demonstrated in this review, it is possible to differentiate dementias with distinct etiologies and neuropathological changes by the unique neuropsychological test performances that they engender. One form of dementia (e.g., Alzheimer's disease) is characterized by ineffective consolidation in memory, rapid forgetting, severe retrograde amnesia, and significant language impairment, whereas another (e.g., Huntington's disease) may be characterized by ineffective retrieval, a mild remote memory loss, and intact language. These unique patterns of neuropsychological deficits can provide important diagnostic information, particularly in the early stages of a dementing disorder.

REFERENCES

Albert, M. L., Feldman, R. G., & Willis, A. L. (1974). The "subcortical dementia" of progressive supranuclear palsy. *Journal of Neurology, Neurosurgery and Psychiatry, 37,* 121–130.

Albert, M. S., Butters, N., & Brandt, J. (1981). Development of remote memory loss in patients with Huntington's disease. *Journal of Clinical Neuropsychology, 3,* 1–12.

Albert, M. S., & Moss, M. B. (1988). *Geriatric neuropsychology.* New York: Guilford Press.

American Psychiatric Association. (1987). *Diagnostic and statistical manual of mental disorders* (3rd ed., rev.). Washington, DC: Author.

Bayles, K. A., & Kaszniak, A. W. (1987). *Communication and cognition in normal aging and dementia.* Boston: Little-Brown.

Bayles, K. A., & Tomoeda, C. K. (1983). Confrontation naming impairment in dementia. *Brain and Language, 19,* 98–114.

Beatty, W. W., & Salmon, D. P. (1991). Remote memory for visuospatial information in patients with Alzheimer's disease. *Journal of Geriatric Psychiatry and Neurology, 4,* 14–17.

Beatty, W. W., Salmon, D. P., Butters, N., Heindel, W. C., & Granholm, E. L. (1988). Retrograde amnesia in patients with Alzheimer's disease or Huntington's disease. *Neurobiology of Aging, 9,* 181–186.

Becker, J. T., Huff, F., Nebes, R. D., Holland, A., & Boller, F. (1988). Neuropsychological function in Alzheimer's disease: Pattern of impairment and rates of progression. *Archives of Neurology, 45*, 263–268.

Blessed, G., Tomlinson, B. E., & Roth, M. (1968). The association between quantitative measures of dementia and of senile change in the cerebral grey matter of elderly subjects. *British Journal of Psychiatry, 114*, 797–811.

Bondi, M. W., Monsch, A. U., Butters, N., Salmon, D. P., & Paulsen, J. S. (1993). Utility of a modified version of the Wisconsin Card Sorting Test in the detection of dementia of the Alzheimer type. *Clinical Psychologist, 7*, 161–170.

Bondi, M. W., Salmon, D. P., & Butters, N. (1994). Neuropsychological features of memory disorders in Alzheimer's disease. In R. D. Terry, R. Katzman, & K. L. Bick (Eds.), *Alzheimer's disease* (pp. 41–63). New York: Raven Press.

Brandt, J., & Butters, N. (1986). The neuropsychology of Huntington's disease. *Trends in Neurosciences, 9*, 118–120.

Brandt, J., Folstein, S. E., & Folstein, M. F. (1988). Differential cognitive impairment in Alzheimer's disease and Huntington's disease. *Annals of Neurology, 23*, 555–561.

Bruyn, G. W., Bots, G., & Dom, R. (1979). Huntington's chorea: Current neuropathological status. In T. Chase, N. Wexler, & A. Barbeau (Eds.), *Advances in neurology: Vol. 23. Huntington's disease* (pp. 83–94). New York: Raven Press.

Buschke, H., & Fuld, P. A. (1974). Evaluating storage, retention, and retrieval in disordered memory and learning. *Neurology, 24*, 1019–1025.

Butters, N. (1984). The clinical aspects of memory disorders: Contributions from experimental studies of amnesia and dementia. *Journal of Clinical Neuropsychology, 6*, 17–36.

Butters, N., Granholm, E., Salmon, D., Grant, I., & Wolfe, J. (1987). Episodic and semantic memory: A comparison of amnesic and demented patients. *Journal of Clinical and Experimental Neuropsychology, 9*, 479–497.

Butters, N., Heindel, W., & Salmon, D. (1990). Dissociation of implicit memory in dementia: Neurological implications. *Bulletin of the Psychonomic Society, 28*, 359–366.

Butters, N., Salmon, D. P., Cullum, C. M., Cairns, P., Troster, A. I., Jacobs, D., Moss, M. B., & Cermak, L. S. (1988). Differentiation of amnesic and demented patients with the Wechsler Memory Scale–Revised. *Clinical Neuropsychologist, 2*, 133–144.

Butters, N., Salmon, D. P., & Heindel, W. C. (1990). Processes underlying the memory impairments of demented patients. In E. Goldberg (Ed.), *Contemporary neuropsychology and the legacy of Luria* (pp. 99–126). Hillsdale, NJ: Erlbaum.

Butters, N., Sax, D. S., Montgomery, K., & Tarlow, S. (1978). Comparison of the neuropsychological deficits associated with early and advanced Huntington's disease. *Archives of Neurology, 35*, 585–589.

Butters, N., Wolfe, J., Martone, M., Granholm, E., & Cermak, L. (1985). Memory disorders associated with Huntington's disease: Verbal recall, verbal recognition and procedural memory. *Neuropsychologia, 23*, 729–743.

Carlesimo, G. A., & Oscar-Berman, M. (1992). Memory deficits in Alzheimer's patients: A comprehensive review. *Neuropsychology Review, 3*, 119–169.

Chertkow, H., & Bub, D. (1990). Semantic memory loss in dementia of Alzheimer's type. *Brain, 113*, 397–417.

Christensen, H., Hadzi-Pavlovic, D., & Jacomb, P. (1991). The psychometric differentiation of dementia from normal aging: A meta-analysis. *Journal of Consulting and Clinical Psychology, 3*, 147–155.

Collins, A. M., & Loftus, E. F. (1975). A spreading activation theory of semantic processing. *Psychological Review, 82*, 407–428.

Corkin, S., Davis, K. L., Growdon, J. H., Usdin, E., & Wurtman, R. J. (1982). *Alzheimer's disease: A report of research and progress.* New York: Raven Press.

Craik, F. I. M., & Rabinowitz, J. C. (1984). Age differences in the acquisition and use of verbal information. In H. Bouma & D. G. Bouwhuis (Eds.), *Attention and performance X* (pp. 471–499). Hillsdale, NJ: Erlbaum.

Crystal, H. A., Horoupian, D. S., Katzman, R., & Jotkowitz, S. (1982). Biopsy-proven Alzheimer's disease presenting as a right parietal lobe syndrome. *Annals of Neurology, 12*, 186–188.

Cullum, C. M., Butters, N., Troster, A. I., & Salmon, D. P. (1990). Normal aging and forgetting rates on the Wechsler Memory Scale–Revised. *Archives of Clinical Neuropsychology, 5*, 23–30.

Cummings, J. L. (1990). *Subcortical dementia.* New York: Oxford University Press.

Cummings, J. L., & Benson, D. F. (1992). *Dementia: A clinical approach* (2nd ed.). Boston: Butterworth-Heinemann.

Delis, D. C., Kramer, J. H., Kaplan, E., & Ober, B. A. (1987). *The California Verbal Learning Test.* New York: Psychological Corporation.

Delis, D. C., Massman, P. J., Butters, N., Salmon, D. P., Kramer, J. H., & Cermak, L. (1991). Profiles of demented and amnesic patients on the California Verbal Learning Test: Implications for the assessment of memory disorders. *Psychological Assessment: A Journal of Clinical and Consulting Psychology, 3*, 19–26.

Drachman, D. A. (1977). Memory and cognitive function in man: Does the cholinergic system have a specific role? *Neurology, 27*, 783–790.

Folstein, M. F., Folstein, S. E., & McHugh, P. R. (1975). Mini-mental state: A practical way for grading the cognitive state of patients for the clinician. *Journal of Psychiatric Research, 12*, 189–198.

Folstein, S. E. (1989). *Huntington's disease: A disorder of families.* Baltimore: Johns Hopkins University Press.

Freedman, M., Rivoira, P., Butters, N., Sax, D. S., & Feldman, R. S. (1984). Retrograde amnesia in Parkinson's disease. *Canadian Journal of Neurological Science, 11*, 297–301.

Fuld, P. A. (1978). Differential diagnosis of dementias. In R. Katzman, R. D.

Terry, & K. L. Bick (Eds.), *Alzheimer's disease: Senile dementias and related disorders* (pp. 185–193). New York: Raven Press.

Fuld, P. A. (1983). Word intrusions as a diagnostic sign of Alzheimer's disease. *Geriatric Medicine Today, 2,* 33–41.

Fuld, P., Katzman, R., Davies, P., & Terry, R. D. (1982). Intrusions as a sign of Alzheimer dementia: Chemical and pathological verification. *Annals of Neurology, 11,* 155–159.

Haaland, K. Y., Linn, R. T., Hunt, W. C., & Goodwin, J. S. (1983). A normative study of Russell's variant of the Wechsler Memory Scale in a healthy elderly population. *Journal of Clinical and Consulting Psychology, 51,* 878–881.

Hart, R. P., Kwentus, J. A., Harkins, S. W., & Taylor, J. R. (1988). Rate of forgetting in mild Alzheimer-type dementia. *Brain and Cognition, 7,* 31–38.

Hart, R. P., Kwentus, J. A., Wade, J. B., & Taylor, J. R. (1988). Modified Wisconsin Card Sorting Test in elderly normal, depressed and demented patients. *Clinical Neuropsychologist, 2,* 49–56.

Hart, S. (1988). Language and dementia: A review. *Psychological Medicine, 18,* 99–112.

Hayden, M. R. (1981). *Huntington's chorea.* New York: Springer-Verlag.

Hodges, J. R., Salmon, D. P., & Butters, N. (1991). The nature of the naming deficit in Alzheimer's and Huntington's disease. *Brain, 114,* 1547–1558.

Hodges, J. R., Salmon, D. P., & Butters, N. (1993). Recognition and naming of famous faces in Alzheimer's disease: A cognitive analysis. *Neuropsychologia, 31,* 775–788.

Huff, F. J., Corkin, S., & Growdon, J. H. (1986). Semantic impairment and anomia in Alzheimer's disease. *Brain and Language, 28,* 235–249.

Hyman, B. T., Van Hoesen, G. W., Damasio, A., & Barnes, C. (1984). Alzheimer's disease: Cell-specific pathology isolates the hippocampal formation. *Science, 225,* 1168–1170.

Ivnik, R. J., Malec, J. F., Tangalos, E. G., Petersen, R. C., Kokmen, E., & Kurland, L. T. (1990). The Auditory Verbal Learning Test (AVLT): Norms for ages 55 years and older. *Psychological Assessment, 2,* 304–312.

Jacobs, D., Salmon, D. P., Troster, A. I., & Butters, N. (1990). Intrusion errors in the figural memory of patients with Alzheimer's and Huntington's disease. *Archives of Clinical Neuropsychology, 5,* 49–57.

Jacobs, D., Troster, A. I., Butters, N., Salmon, D. P., & Cermak, L. S. (1990). Intrusion errors on the Visual Reproduction test of the Wechsler Memory Scale and the Wechsler Memory Scale–Revised: An analysis of demented and amnesic patients. *Clinical Neuropsychologist, 4,* 177–191.

Kaszniak, A. W., Poon, L. W., & Riege, W. (1986). Assessing memory deficits: An information processing approach. In L. W. Poon (Ed.), *Handbook for clinical memory assessment of older adults* (pp. 168–188). Washington, DC: American Psychological Association.

Katzman, R. (1986). Alzheimer's disease. *New England Journal of Medicine, 314,* 964–973.

Katzman, R., Brown, T., Thal, L. J., Fuld, P. A., Aronson, M., Butters, N., Klauber, M. R., Wiederholt, W., Pay, M., Renbing, X., Ooi, W. L., Hofstetter, R., & Terry, R. D. (1988). Comparison of rate of annual change of mental status score in four independent studies of patients with Alzheimer's disease. *Annals of Neurology, 24,* 384–389.

Kemper, S., LaBarge, E., Ferraro, R., Cheung, H., Cheung, H., & Storandt, M. (1993). On the preservation of syntax in Alzheimer's disease: Evidence from written sentences. *Archives of Neurology, 50,* 81–86.

Kempler, D., Curtiss, S., & Jackson, C. (1987). Syntactic preservation in Alzheimer's disease. *Journal of Speech and Hearing Research, 30,* 343–350.

Knopman, D. S., & Ryberg, S. (1989). A verbal memory test with high predictive accuracy for dementia of the Alzheimer type. *Archives of Neurology, 46,* 141–146.

Kopelman, M. D. (1989). Remote and autobiographical memory, temporal context memory and frontal atrophy in Korsakoff and Alzheimer patients. *Neuropsychologia, 27,* 437–460.

Kramer, J. H., Levin, B. E., Brandt, J., & Delis, D. C. (1988). Differentiation of Alzheimer's, Huntington's, and Parkinson's disease patients on the basis of verbal learning characteristics. *Neuropsychology, 3,* 111–120.

Martin, A. (1987). Representation of semantic and spatial knowledge in Alzheimer's patients: Implications for models of preserved learning in amnesia. *Journal of Clinical and Experimental Neuropsychology, 9,* 191–124.

Martin, A., Browers, P., Cox, C., & Fedio, P. (1985). On the nature of the verbal memory deficit in Alzheimer's disease. *Brain and Language, 25,* 323–341.

Martin, A., & Fedio, P. (1983). Word production and comprehension in Alzheimer's disease: The breakdown in semantic knowledge. *Brain and Language, 19,* 124–141.

Massman, P. J., Delis, D. C., Butters, N., Dupont, R. M., & Gillin, J. C. (1992). The subcortical dysfunction hypothesis: Neuropsychological validation in a subgroup of patients. *Journal of Clinical and Experimental Neuropsychology, 14,* 687–706.

Masur, D. M., Fuld, P. A., Blau, A. D., Thal, L. J., Levin, H. S., & Aronson, M. K. (1989). Distinguishing normal and demented elderly with the selective reminding test. *Journal of Clinical and Experimental Neuropsychology, 11,* 615–630.

Mattis, S. (1976). Mental status examination for organic mental syndrome in the elderly patient. In L. Bellack & T. Karasu (Eds.), *Geriatric psychiatry* (pp. 77–120). New York: Grune & Stratton.

McHugh, P. R., & Folstein, M. F. (1975). Psychiatric syndromes in Huntington's disease. In D. F. Benson & D. Blumer (Eds.), *Psychiatric aspects of neurologic disease* (pp. 267–285). New York: Grune & Stratton.

Miller, E. (1971). On the nature of the memory disorder in presenile dementia. *Neuropsychologia, 9,* 75–81.

Monsch, A. U., Bondi, M. W., Butters, N., Paulsen, J. S., Salmon, D. P., Brugger,

P., & Swenson, M. R. (1994). A comparison of category and letter fluency in Alzheimer's disease and Huntington's disease. *Neuropsychology, 8,* 25–30.

Monsch, A. U., Bondi, M. W., Butters, N., Salmon, D. P., Katzman, R., & Thal, L. J. (1992). Comparisons of verbal fluency tasks in the detection of dementia of the Alzheimer type. *Archives of Neurology, 49,* 1253–1258.

Moss, M. B., & Albert, M. S. (1988). Alzheimer's disease and other dementing disorders. In M. S. Albert & M. B. Moss (Eds.), *Geriatric neuropsychology* (pp. 145–178). New York: Guilford Press.

Moss, M. B., Albert, M. S., Butters, N., & Payne, M. (1986). Differential patterns of memory loss among patients with Alzheimer's disease, Huntington's disease and alcoholic Korsakoff's syndrome. *Archives of Neurology, 43,* 239–246.

Nebes, R. D. (1989). Semantic memory in Alzheimer's disease. *Psychological Bulletin, 106,* 377–394.

Nebes, R. D. (1992). Cognitive dysfunction in Alzheimer's disease. In F. I. Craik & T. A. Salthouse (Eds.), *Handbook of cognitive aging* (pp. 373–446). Hillsdale, NJ: Erlbaum.

Ober, B. A., Koss, E., Friedland, R. P., & Delis, D. C. (1985). Processes of verbal memory failure in Alzheimer-type dementia. *Brain and Cognition, 4,* 90–103.

Ortof, E., & Crystal, H. A. (1989). Rate of progression of Alzheimer's disease. *Journal of the American Geriatric Society, 37,* 511–514.

Rouleau, I., Salmon, D. P., Butters, N., Kennedy, C., & McGuire, K. (1992). Quantitative and qualitative analyses of clock drawings in Alzheimer's and Huntington's disease. *Brain and Cognition, 18,* 70–87.

Sagar, H. J., Cohen, N. J., Sullivan, E. V., Corkin, S., & Growdon, J. H. (1988). Remote memory function in Alzheimer's disease and Parkinson's disease. *Brain, 111,* 525–539.

Salmon, D. P., & Butters, N. (1992). Neuropsychologic assessment of dementia in the elderly. In R. Katzman & J. W. Rowe (Eds.), *Principles of geriatric neurology* (pp. 144–163). Philadelphia: F. A. Davis.

Salmon, D. P., Kwo-on-Yuen, P. F., Heindel, W. C., Butters, N., & Thal, L. J. (1989). Differentiation of Alzheimer's disease and Huntington's disease with the Dementia Rating Scale. *Archives of Neurology, 46,* 1204–1208.

Salmon, D. P., Thal, L. J., Butters, N., & Heindel, W. C. (1990). Longitudinal evaluation of dementia of the Alzheimer type: A comparison of 3 standardized mental status examinations. *Neurology, 40,* 1225–1230.

Schacter, D. (1987). Implicit memory: History and current status. *Journal of Experimental Psychology: Learning, Memory, and Cognition, 13,* 501–517.

Shindler, A. G., Caplan, L. R., & Heir, D. B. (1984). Intrusions and perseverations. *Brain and Language, 23,* 148–158.

Smith, S. R., Murdoch, B. E., & Chenery, H. J. (1989). Semantic abilities in dementia of the Alzheimer type: 1. Lexical semantics. *Brain and Language, 36,* 314–324.

Storandt, M., Botwinick, J., Danziger, W. L., Berg, L., & Hughes, C. P. (1984). Psychometric differentiation of mild senile dementia of the Alzheimer type. *Archives of Neurology, 41*, 497–499.

Terry, R. D., & Katzman, R. (1983). Senile dementia of the Alzheimer type. *Annals of Neurology, 14*, 497–506.

Terry, R. D., & Katzman, R. (1992). Alzheimer's disease and cognitive loss. In R. Katzman & J. Rowe (Eds.), *Principles of geriatric neurology* (pp. 207–265). Philadelphia: F. A. Davis.

Terry, R. D., Peck, A., DeTeresa, R., Schechter, R., & Horoupian, D. S. (1981). Some morphometric aspects of the brain in senile dementia of the Alzheimer type. *Annals of Neurology, 10*, 184–192.

Thal, L. J., Grundman, M., & Golden, R. (1986). Alzheimer's disease: A correlational analysis of the Blessed Information–Memory–Concentration Test and the Mini-Mental State Exam. *Neurology, 36*, 262–264.

Tomlinson, B. E., Blessed, G., & Roth, M. (1970). Observations on the brains of demented old people. *Journal of Neurological Sciences, 11*, 205–242.

Troster, A., Butters, N., Salmon, D. P., Cullum, C. M., Jacobs, D., Brandt, J., & White, R. (1993). Diagnostic utility of savings scores: Differentiating Alzheimer's and Huntington's diseases with the Logical Memory and Visual Reproduction tests. *Journal of Clinical and Experimental Neuropsychology, 15*, 773–788.

Troster, A. I., Jacobs, D., Butters, N., Cullum, C. M., & Salmon, D. P. (1989). Differentiating Alzheimer's disease from Huntington's disease with the Wechsler Memory Scale–Revised. *Clinics in Geriatric Medicine, 5*, 611–632.

Troster, A. I., Salmon, D. P., McCullough, D., & Butters, N. (1989). A comparison of the category fluency deficits associated with Alzheimer's and Huntington's disease. *Brain and Language, 37*, 500–513.

Vitaliano, P. P., Breen, A. R., Russo, J., Albert, M., Vitiello, M. V., & Prinz, P. N. (1984). The clinical utility of the Dementia Rating Scale for assessing Alzheimer patients. *Journal of Chronic Diseases, 37*, 743–753.

Wechsler, D. (1945). A standardized memory scale for clinical use. *Journal of Psychology, 19*, 87–95.

Wechsler, D. (1987). *Wechsler Memory Scale–Revised*. New York: Psychological Corporation.

Weingartner, H., Sitaram, N., & Gillin, J. C. (1979). The role of cholinergic nervous system in memory consolidation. *Bulletin of the Psychonomic Society, 13*, 9–11.

Welsh, K., Butters, N., Hughes, J., Mohs, R., & Heyman, A. (1991). Detection of abnormal memory decline in mild cases of Alzheimer's disease using CERAD neuropsychological measures. *Archives of Neurology, 48*, 278–281.

Welsh, K., Butters, N., Hughes, J., Mohs, R., & Heyman, A. (1992). Detection and staging of dementia in Alzheimer's disease: Use of the neuropsychological measures developed for the Consortium to Establish a Registry for Alzheimer's Disease (CERAD). *Archives of Neurology, 49*, 448–452.

Whitehouse, P. J., Price, D. L., Struble, R. G., Clark, A. W., Coyle, J. T., & DeLong, M. R. (1982). Alzheimer's disease and senile dementia: Loss of neurons in the basal forebrain. *Science, 215,* 1237–1239.

Wilson, R. S., Bacon, L. D., Fox, J. H., & Kaszniak, A. W. (1983). Primary and secondary memory in dementia of the Alzheimer type. *Journal of Clinical Neuropsychology, 5,* 337–344.

Wilson, R. S., Kaszniak, A. W., & Fox, J. H. (1981). Remote memory in senile dementia. *Cortex, 17,* 41–48.

Zola-Morgan, S., & Squire, L. R. (1990). The primate hippocampal formation: Evidence for a time-limited role in memory storage. *Science, 250,* 288–290.

4

ASSESSMENT OF DEPRESSION IN OLDER ADULTS: A GUIDE FOR PRACTITIONERS

FORREST R. SCOGIN

Service providers who work with older adults will undoubtedly encounter clients for whom depression is suspected or apparent. Proper diagnosis and treatment require assessment of the depressive syndrome for severity and comorbidity.

In this chapter, I review some of the issues involved in assessing depression in older adults, including sources of confusion in the presenting complaints of older adults, techniques that have proven useful in the assessment process, and recommendations for evaluation in clinical practice. I begin with an overview of the diagnostic categories, which will orient this discussion, and pose the following question: Should the same diagnostic criteria be applied to younger and older adults? (Hint: the answer is *yes* and *no*.)

AGING, PHYSICAL HEALTH, AND DEPRESSIVE SYMPTOMS

The most agreed-on criteria for the depressive disorders are those provided by the system of the revised third edition of the *Diagnostic and*

Statistical Manual of Mental Disorders (*DSM-III-R*; American Psychiatric Association, 1987). The diagnosis of *major depression*, the most pervasive (although not the most prevalent) of the disorders among older adults, requires that five of nine symptoms have been present during a 2-week period. These nine symptoms are: depressed mood, markedly diminished interest in activities, significant weight loss or gain, insomnia or hypersomnia, psychomotor agitation or retardation, fatigue or loss of energy, feelings of worthlessness or guilt, diminished ability to think or concentrate, and suicidal ideation.

Assessment of most of these symptoms in older adults can be problematic. Normal differences between younger and older persons can either obscure real depressive symptoms or be judged to be symptoms when they are not. For the sake of brevity, I discuss only three symptoms: two from the *DSM-III-R* list (sleep patterns and fatigue) and one that is more commonly associated with depression (changes in libido).

Sleep patterns undergo change in the later years; in particular, older adults experience increased nighttime awakening (Prinz, Dustman, & Emmerson, 1990). For the younger adult, sleep disturbance in a nondepressed person is considerably less common. Thus, complaints of sleep disturbance by a younger adult have strong diagnostic indications, whereas the same complaint by an older adult has potentially less diagnostic utility. It is particularly important to establish some temporal relation between sleep and mood changes among elders. This is not to say that sleep disturbances are not a part of the depressive syndrome among older adults, only that careful questioning is necessary in differentiating sleep changes due to aging or depression. For example, a query as to whether the sleep changes were present well before the onset of other depressive symptoms or whether they occurred concurrently with the depressive syndrome begins to disentangle these relations. Another question that I have found to be useful is whether the degree of sleep disturbance varies with the person's mood.

Fatigue is another indicant of depression that is less sensitive among older adults (Gallagher, 1986). Aging per se does not lead to loss of energy, but a host of physical conditions that are age-related can result in increased complaints of fatigability. For example, arthritic conditions can make movement more painful and tiresome. Fatigability related to depression in the physically robust older adult is probably pathonomic; however, for less fit elders, the complaints of fatigability should be beyond that expected from their health status. This is sometimes a difficult clinical judgment. The converging picture is that somatic symptoms associated with the depression syndrome can prove difficult to parcel into effects associated with aging, physical health, or depression.

Another often-used marker of depression is also worthy of mention in this context. Diminished interest in sex or loss of libido, although not a *DSM-III-R* criterion, is often a question used in self-report or interview-based assessments of depression. There is probably a quantitative, although not necessarily qualitative, decrease in sexual activity among older adults (Botwinick, 1984, chapter 6). Like sleep, another sensitive biological response system, changes in sexuality should be temporarily linked to other depressive syndrome indicants. I have asked questions such as "Have you noticed changes in your interest in sex that have occurred along with the other symptoms you are experiencing?" or "Sometimes when people are depressed they become less interested in sex. Have you noticed changes like that?"

Depressionlike symptoms may result from any of several medical conditions such as thyroid dysfunction, cerebrovascular accident, and cancer. In such instances, depressive symptoms are typically the result of physiological derangements, although the sequelae of these conditions can also produce primary depression. In this presentation, I mention only a few of the more frequently encountered organic mood disorder conditions. Interested readers are referred to Kathol (1985) for a more comprehensive review of this topic.

Disruption of thyroid function can produce symptoms of decreased energy and increased apathy that can easily be mistaken for depression. Cardiovascular conditions can also produce symptoms of depression, and postcerebrovascular accident depression is not uncommon (Stern & Bachman, 1991). Furthermore, treatment with antihypertensive medications can also produce depressive reactions.

The depression symptoms that are presented by an older adult patient and the interacting effects of aging, physical health, and depression can produce significant puzzlement in the clinician. Two important aids in assessing depression among elders are a medical evaluation, preferably by a geriatrician, and the taking of a medical history. As for the medical evaluation, a number of scenarios can be encountered. In some cases, the patient may have been referred by a physician who has eliminated to the extent possible all medical explanations for the depression and has requested evaluation and/or treatment from a psychological perspective. In other cases, the patient has come by nonmedical referral routes. In these cases, the clinician should suggest that the patient obtain a medical examination that includes evaluation of conditions that may have contributed to the development of their depressive symptoms. Not uncommonly, a patient will indicate that they have recently been medically evaluated and found to be free of conditions that might produce depressive symptoms. In still another scenario, the clinician may specifically refer a patient to a geriatrician and pose diagnostic questions concerning their depressive symptoms. Put simply, the clinician should look for a declaration that the patient's depressive symptoms do not appear to be a manifestation of a medical disorder.

As far as the medical history is concerned, the clinician should be interested in any lifetime acute or chronic conditions such as hypertension, diabetes, orthopedic impairments, or neurological disorders that may affect the client's functioning. Included in this medical history should be inquiries about current and past pharmaceutical use. Information obtained from the medical history should help determine the need for further medical evaluation.

EPIDEMIOLOGY OF DEPRESSION AMONG OLDER ADULTS

In the assessment of any disorder, it is important to have an appreciation of the prevalence and incidence of that disorder. Such information establishes an informal base rate that aids in diagnostic decision making. Gatz and Pearson (1988) identified epidemiological information as essential in clinical geropsychological practice for this reason. I briefly review the epidemiology of depressive disorders among older adults.

The most detailed epidemiological study of mental disorders among citizens of the United States was that undertaken by the National Institute of Mental Health (NIMH); it is referred to as the Epidemiological Catchment Area (ECA) study (Myers et al., 1984). Although certainly not beyond criticism, the data from the ECA study are frequently cited in establishing rates of disorders as a function of sex and age. According to Myers et al., the 6-month prevalence of major depression among those 65 years of age and older was approximately 2%. The rate for dysthymic disorder was approximately 1.5%.

Although a 2% prevalence rate certainly represents a significant number of persons and an enormous degree of suffering, many specialists on aging were surprised to find that this prevalence rate was the lowest of any of the adult age groups. For example, for adults 25–44 years old, the prevalence of major depression was approximately 4%.

The reconciliation of this surprising result of relatively low rates of formally diagnosed depression comes from studies that have found that the prevalence of clinically significant depressive symptoms that do not meet diagnostic criteria is around 20% among community-dwelling elders (Blazer, Hughes, & George, 1987). Although these depressive symptoms do not meet diagnostic criteria, the distress they produce certainly warrants clinical attention in many cases. These dysphoric persons are at risk for developing major depression (Rohde, Lewinsohn, & Seeley, 1990) and probably account for a sizeable portion of visits to physician offices for "physical problems" for which biological causes are not found.

This brief foray into epidemiology returns me to the question that was posed at the beginning of this section. Should different criteria be used in diagnosing depression among elders? The symptoms that currently comprise the criteria for major depression seem to be valid markers for depression experienced by elders, provided that the clinician exercises caution in disentangling aging, health, and treatment-related causes. The problem seems to be that the current system (i.e., *DSM-III-R*) does not identify a substantial number of older persons experiencing clinically significant depressive disorders other than through the largely meaningless category called *depressive disorder not otherwise specified*. Thus, the prevailing criteria do not provide a categorical classification that captures most of the older adults who are experiencing depressive difficulties. This may change with the proposed revisions in the fourth edition of the *Diagnostic and Statistical Manual of Mental Disorders* (*DSM-IV*; American Psychiatric Association, in press).

POSSIBLE *DSM-IV* CHANGES

At least two possible changes in *DSM-IV*, which is scheduled for publication in May 1994, could affect the diagnosis of depressive disorders among elders. As noted previously, a significant number of older adults experience depressive symptoms that do not meet criteria for an episode of major depression but that are clearly impairing to the individual. The Task Force on DSM-IV (1991) considered the adoption of a *minor depression* category for those circumstances in which a person experiences significant depressive symptoms that do not meet the criteria for major depression. The minor depression category should be useful in diagnosing depression in older adults, given the phenomenology of their depressive episodes. A prudent question might be "What real effect will this have on the individual?" because older adults experience their symptoms regardless of the shifting nomenclature. The importance of this category is that it acknowledges the need to treat what heretofore has been designated "subclinical" depression. In that elders seem to experience this variant of the depressive spectrum more frequently, this alteration may result in a larger number of persons receiving services for an apparently treatable disorder.

Another change considered by the Task Force on DSM-IV (1991) that may affect elders is the creation of a *mixed anxiety–depression disorder*. This diagnosis would apply to those individuals who have symptoms of both anxiety and depression but which are insufficient in number or severity to meet the diagnostic criteria except in combination. However, the combined anxiety–depression symptoms do produce clinically significant impairment. Anxiety disorders such as phobias are included; they are the most common disorders according to the ECA study (Myers et al., 1984). It is possible that subsyndromal variants of this spectrum of disorder are also quite common among elders. The mixed anxiety–depression category will likely provide a diagnostic "niche" for a number of distressed but heretofore underserved elders.

In summary, the epidemiological data indicate that rates of major depression are relatively low, although certainly significant, and that there are substantial numbers of older persons who are dysphoric and experience clinically significant depressive symptoms. The *DSM-IV* system may better recognize that depression exists on a severity continuum and that elders tend to experience depressive symptoms in the mild-to-moderate range of that continuum.

ASSESSMENT OF DEPRESSION

How can service providers most effectively and efficiently assess depression among their older patients? I pose the question in this way because I want to make it clear from the outset that my presentation is oriented to the provider rather than to the researcher. What would be necessary or desirable for research is often beyond what is needed for quality clinical work. Protocol-driven depression assessment is high in internal validity but routinely something I do not use in clinical work with elders.

Self-Report Assessment

There has been more research on the self-report assessment of depression among elders than on the other modes of evaluation. There are a variety of reasons for this, one of which is that there are a plethora of instruments on which to conduct reliability and validity investigations. A nonexhaustive list includes the Zung Self-Rating Depression Scale (SDS; Zung, 1965), the Center for Epidemiological Studies Depression Scale (Radloff, 1977), the Inventory for Diagnosing Depression (Zimmerman & Coryell, 1988), the Symptoms Checklist 90R (Derogatis, 1977), and the Brief Symptom Inventory (Derogatis & Spencer, 1983). Each investigator seems to have his or her favorite instrument, and most of these instruments are useful assessment tools. I focus on two: the Beck Depression Inventory (BDI; Beck, Ward, Mendelson, Mock, & Erbaugh, 1961) and the Geriatric Depression Scale (GDS; Yesavage et al., 1983). These two scales have been extensively evaluated with respect to older adults, and I can recommend them from personal experience. It is important to note that my review of the literature turned up little information on the assessment of depression among the oldest old (85 years and older). The utility of depression assessment techniques with this group would be a topic worthy of investigation.

Beck Depression Inventory

The BDI is undoubtedly the most widely used self-report depression inventory. In a review of the psychometric properties of the BDI, Beck,

Steer, and Garbin (1988) noted that over 1,000 research studies have used the BDI. Several of these were conducted with older adults.

The BDI is organized around 21 depression symptoms such as sadness, guilt, weight loss, and suicidal ideation. Within each symptom, respondents rate the severity of their experience of that symptom on a 4-point scale by endorsing statements that describe escalating seriousness. The BDI can typically be completed in 5–10 min. In addition to brevity, cutoff scores have been established for probable nondepression (0–9), mild-to-moderate depression (10–18), moderate-to-severe depression (19–29), and severe depression (30–73). For even greater brevity, Beck and Beck (1972) developed a 13-item short form. Both versions have demonstrated acceptable reliability and validity with older adults.

Gallagher, Nies, and Thompson (1982) found the 21-item BDI to evidence acceptable reliability with older nondepressed volunteers as well as depressed outpatients. In their study, test–retest and internal consistency values suggested that the BDI was probably useful as a research tool and as a screening instrument in clinical settings. Gallagher, Breckenridge, Steinmetz, and Thompson (1983) reached much the same conclusion in a study of 102 elders who had sought outpatient psychological treatment.

Norris, Gallagher, Wilson, and Winograd (1987) evaluated the BDI with older male medical outpatients. These investigators noted that medical outpatients are a population with a relatively high rate of depression but one that is at risk for having their depression unidentified. Sixty-eight participants were clinically interviewed for depressive disorder and then completed the BDI (as well as the GDS, which is reviewed later in this chapter). Using a cutoff score of 10 and *DSM-III-R* diagnosis as the criterion, Norris et al. found that the BDI correctly identified 84% of the cases, with sensitivity of 89% and specificity of 82%. With a cutoff score of 17, correct identification was 84%, with sensitivity of 50% and specificity of 92%. For screening purposes, the lower cutoff score is clearly desirable.

Rapp, Parisi, Walsh, and Wallace (1988) extended the investigation of the utility of the BDI with elders by obtaining estimates of sensitivity and specificity with medical inpatients. Diagnoses of major depression according to Research Diagnostic Criteria (RDC) interviews (Spitzer, Endicott, & Robbins, 1978) were the criterion in judging the efficiency of the BDI for screening. Using the conventional cutoff score of 10, sensitivity was 83% and specificity was 65%. As a reminder, *sensitivity* refers to the proportion of currently identified depressed persons (in this case, according to RDC interviews); *specificity* refers to the proportion of correctly identified nondepressed persons.

Rapp et al. (1988) also calculated predictive power estimates, a procedure advocated by some as more informative regarding the diagnostic efficiency of an instrument (Baldessarini, Finkelstein, & Arana, 1983; Widiger, Hunt, Frances, Clarkin, & Gilmore, 1984). The *predictive power of a positive test* (PPP = true positives/[true positives + false positives] × 100) indicates, in this case, the probability that a score on the BDI that is greater than the cutoff identifies a person diagnosed by the RDC as evidencing major depression. The *predictive power of a negative test* (PPN = true negatives/[true negatives + false negatives] × 100) indicates the probability that a score on the BDI that is less than the cutoff identifies a nondepressed person according to the RDC interview. With the conventional cutoff score of 10, the PPP was 30% and the PPN was 95%. As Rapp et al. noted, the former indicates that a positive test score by itself was not a very good predictor of diagnosed depression. I return to this point in a later section of this chapter.

Rapp et al. (1988) also analyzed the efficacy of two subscales of the BDI, the psychological-items portion (Items 1–14) and the somatic-items portion (Items 15–21). This seemed particularly important given the medical inpatient population of their study. They found, interestingly, that the psychological subscale demonstrated better overall performance (sensitivity = 75%, specificity = 92%, PPP = 63%, and PPN = 95%) than any of the other scales when using a cutoff score of 5. This finding reiterates the complicating nature of somatic depressive symptoms in the diagnosis of depression among elders.

In a related study, Bolla-Wilson and Blecker (1989) found that older adults had significantly higher scores on the somatic-items portion (Items 15–21) of the BDI than did younger adults. This was surprising in that the total scores for the two groups did not differ, nor did the mean scores for the psychological-items portion (Items 1–14). These investigators recommended that screening instruments that exclude somatic items be used when screening for depression among elders. This recommendation can be followed by examining responses to BDI Items 1–14 and using the cutoff score of 5 that was suggested by Rapp et al. (1988).

There has been less examination of the 13-item short form of the BDI in assessing depression among older adults. The available information, however, suggests that it is also a useful screening tool. Foelker, Schewchuk, and Niederehe (1987) examined the internal consistency of the short-form BDI and found Cronbach's alpha coefficients of .74 and .80 for two community-dwelling nondepressed older samples.

Scogin, Hamblin, Beutler, and Corbishley (1988) investigated the liability and validity of the 13-item BDI with 61 elders who evidenced major depression and 57 nonpatient older volunteers. The depressed sample was administered the short-form BDI and the Hamilton Rating Scale for Depression (HRSD; Hamilton, 1967) before and after depression treatment. The volunteers were administered the short-form BDI on only one occasion. The alpha coefficient for the combined sample (*n* = 118) was .90, with coefficients of .85 for the volunteers and .79 for the depressed individuals. These values are comparable to those reported by Foelker et al. (1987) and

Gallagher et al. (1982) with the 21-item BDI. Sensitivity and specificity using a cutoff score of 4 or greater was also examined. Sixty (98%) of the 61 depressed patients were correctly identified; 37 of 57 (65%) of the nondepressed group were correctly identified. Raising the cutoff score to 5 improved specificity to 77%, and sensitivity remained high at 97%. In addition, sensitivity to change in depression was examined by computing correlations between residualized change scores for the HRSD and the short-form BDI. The alpha coefficient was .40, which is statistically significant yet rather low. The relative emphasis on somatic items in the HRSD and the relative deemphasis on somatic items in the BDI may partly account for this finding. To date, there have been no efforts, to my knowledge, to tease apart the somatic and nonsomatic items of the short-form BDI to determine their relative efficiency.

In summary, the BDI possesses a number of positive characteristics: It has been evaluated considerably, with largely positive outcomes; it is relatively brief; and it is easily administered and scored. As for negatives, I offer the following: In assessing depression among elders with mild and moderate cognitive impairment, the multiple choice format of the BDI can be confusing. For example, I have observed some respondents to have forgotten the first option by the time they have read the third option. This observation was empirically evaluated by Olin, Schneider, Eaton, Zeman-sky, and Pollock (1992). They tallied the number of multiple endorsements on the BDI, which they took to be indicative of confusion over the format. Fifty older adults completed the BDI and the GDS; multiple-item endorsement was observed in 46% of the BDIs, whereas only 8% occurred with the GDS. This tendency was even more marked in depressed respondents than in nondepressed respondents. Similarly, Dunn and Sacco (1989) found that completion rates were higher for the GDS than for the SDS. Olin et al. concluded, quite sensibly, that clinicians who use the BDI with older adults should attempt to ensure minimal multiple responses to items, which may function to decrease reliability.

Geriatric Depression Scale

The GDS is also a widely used and well-researched self-report depression instrument. It is unique in at least one aspect; as the name implies, it was developed specifically for use with older adults. Two additional features of the GDS address issues raised earlier in this chapter. First, the 30 items of the GDS deemphasize the somatic symptoms of depression. This elimination was not capricious, because the developers of the GDS found that somatic items (e.g., sleep disturbance, weight loss, gastrointestinal symptoms) did not show acceptable item-to-total score correlations in their initial scale construction. The second feature of the GDS that bears mention is the *yes–no* response format. Olin et al. (1992) found fewer multiple endorsements with this format compared with the multiple choice format.

In the initial validation study, Yesavage et al. (1983) had 100 depressed and nondepressed subjects complete the GDS and the SDS; the subjects were also interviewed with the HRSD. Cronbach's alpha coefficient was .94, which suggests high internal consistency. Convergent validity was examined by correlating scores from the GDS and the HRSD; the obtained correlation was .83, which suggests high convergence. Yesavage et al. also suggested a cutoff score of 10 on this instrument; scores of 11 and greater were considered to be indicative of depression. The efficiency of the cutoff score has been examined in a number of subsequent studies (e.g., Norris et al., 1987; Rapp et al., 1988).

Norris et al. (1987) examined the utility of the GDS with 68 older male medical outpatients. With DSM-III-R depressive disorder diagnosis as the criterion and 10 as the cutoff score, correct identification was 77%. Sensitivity and specificity were 89% and 73%, respectively.

Rapp et al. (1988), in the same study reviewed earlier on the BDI, also examined the efficiency of the GDS with 150 older medical inpatients. Using the conventional cutoff score, these investigators found sensitivity to be 70% and specificity to be 89% (PPP = 53% and PPN = 94%). They concluded that the GDS (and the BDI psychological items) were efficient screening instruments for medical inpatients.

Parmelee, Lawton, and Katz (1989) evaluated the GDS among institutionalized aged. Subjects in the study were 806 persons who resided in a nursing home and a congregate apartment complex. Internal consistency was high (alpha = .91), although these researchers found rather low sensitivity using the conventional score of 10 as the cutoff. They noted that most of the false negatives occurred in identifying minor depression, and they suggested that clinicians interpret GDS scores liberally when screening. Perhaps most important, Parmelee et al. found the GDS to demonstrate acceptable psychometric properties among residents who evidenced mild-to-moderate cognitive impairment. As noted earlier, this is the group that is most likely to encounter difficulties with the response format of traditional depression inventories.

Olin et al. (1992), in addition to evaluating the propensity for multiple-item endorsement on the BDI and GDS, also evaluated the utility of the GDS in their older adult outpatient population. Participants were diagnosed as evidencing either major depression or no current DSM-III-R Axis I disorder. Using this as the criterion, the GDS demonstrated 96% sensitivity and 96% specificity (PPP = 96% and PPN = 96%) with the conventional cutoff score. Olin et al. noted that these values are somewhat higher than those reported in previous investigations and may suggest that the GDS functions more efficiently with outpatients.

Like the BDI, a shorter form of the GDS has also been developed. Sheikh and Yesavage (1986) selected the 15 questions from the 30-item GDS that were most highly correlated with depressive symptoms in earlier validation studies. Thirty-five subjects then completed the long and short forms of the GDS; the forms were significantly correlated ($r = .84$). In a more detailed investigation, Alden, Austin, and Sturgeon (1989) examined the correlation between the two forms in 81 older adults. Two weeks elapsed between the randomly ordered administration of the two instruments. The correlation between the two forms was significant ($r = .66$). Alden et al. noted that this correlation is not high enough to consider the short form as an equivalent of the 30-item GDS. To my knowledge, studies of the sensitivity and specificity of the short form have not yet been conducted.

In summary, the GDS has a number of desirable characteristics for a screening instrument: It is brief, well tolerated by respondents, and psychometrically sound with a variety of populations. As to negatives, I offer the following: If the clinician strongly desires that a screening instrument tap the somatic symptoms of depression, then the GDS will obviously not meet this need. A second, albeit somewhat minor, drawback that I have experienced with use of the GDS are complaints by respondents that the yes–no format is limiting; that is, that they can answer neither yes nor no to, for example, the inquiry "Are you basically satisfied with your life?" In general, however, I believe the simpler format is advantageous.

The review, to this point, suggests that self-report instruments, particularly the BDI and GDS, are useful for screening for depression among older adults. It is important to emphasize the screening nature of these instruments. When possible, administration of a "screener" should be followed by a diagnostic or clinical interview. If such a two-step procedure is possible, then it may be advisable to set cutoff scores lower on the BDI and GDS to afford almost complete sensitivity.

Before turning to a review of interview-based assessments of depression, I want to mention that self-report inventories are not particularly well suited to identifying dysthymic disorder or for capturing a lifetime history of depressive disorder. To wit, Stukenberg, Dura, and Kiecolt-Glaser (1990) found the short form of the BDI identified fewer than half of the dysthymic cases in their sample of community-dwelling older adults. The use of another instrument, such as the Inventory to Diagnose Depression–Lifetime Version (Zimmerman & Coryell, 1987), may be better suited for screening when such information is needed.

Interview-Based Assessment of Depression

Like self-report instruments, there are a number of interview-based assessment tools available. I review only a few instruments in two broad categories: interviews that are designed to yield diagnostic information and those that are primarily designed to yield depression severity information. There are the two major dimensions on which depression is usually assessed: (a) Do the symptoms meet the criteria for a diagnosis (or diagnoses) of a depressive disorder? and (b) How severe is the depression? These are overlapping but not isomorphic assessment goals.

Diagnostic Interviews

Instruments that map onto *DSM-III-R* (or *DSM-IV*) criteria are of most value, given that these are the most frequently used depression guidelines. Two currently popular instruments that do so are the Structured Clinical Interview for DSM-III-R (SCID; Spitzer, Williams, Gibbon, & First, 1992) and the Diagnostic Interview Schedule (DIS; Robins & Helzer, 1985). Both instruments are *DSM-III-R*-oriented, both provide information on lifetime and current psychiatric disorders, and both have been used extensively in clinical research. Unfortunately, they both are also time-consuming, require extensive training to properly administer, and typically assess many more disorders than the clinician may be interested in when providing services to an individual. For example, the DIS has over 200 questions and includes inquiries on most major Axis I and Axis II disorders. These instruments are appropriate for clinical trials and epidemiological surveys but are much less desirable for clinical practice. It is useful, however, to become familiar with the types of questions posed in these instruments. For example, the DIS inquiry concerning lifetime dysthymia—"Have you had 2 years or more in your life when you felt depressed or sad most days, even if you felt OK sometimes?"—is succinct yet thorough.

Another advantage of using interviews such as the SCID or the DIS in the assessment process is that it affords subtyping of major depression into melancholic or nonmelancholic types. Gallagher-Thompson et al. (1992) found that the *DSM-III-R* definition of melancholic (endogenous) depression among older patients was reliably coded by raters. Interestingly, the melancholic subtype was not associated with greater severity ratings, as has often been the case with younger patients. Nonetheless, the subtyping of depression may have some bearing on the type of treatment modality chosen (e.g., psychosocial treatment, pharmacotherapy, or some combination), although there has been too little research with depressed elders on this topic to make strong matching prescriptions.

Determining Severity

Diagnostically oriented structured interviews provide information on the severity of the depressive disorders only indirectly, because the DIS and SCID are based on the categorical approach of *DSM-III-R*. In many circumstances, a quantitative estimate of the severity of depression is desired in either assessment or treatment. For example, in tracking progress in the treatment of depression, it is useful to the client and therapist to be able to plot scores over time. The classic instrument for estimating depression severity from an interview is the HRSD. This instrument is used extensively as an outcome measure in depression treatment studies, including the major trials that have been conducted with older adults (e.g., Beutler et al., 1987; Thompson, Gallagher, & Breckenridge, 1987). The HRSD has 17- and 21-item versions, with symptoms rated as to severity. For example, the items on "feelings of guilt" range from 0 (absent) to 4 (hears accusatory or denunciatory voices and/or experiences threatening visual hallucinations). Guidelines for using the HRSD have been developed by, among others, Williams (1988). Cutoff scores have also been developed for the HRSD. Using the 21-item version, the Department of Psychology research team at the University of Alabama (Tuscaloosa) gives a score of 10 or greater to indicate at least mild depression among older and younger participants. Studies that have screened for major depression have often used a score of 17 as an entry criterion (e.g., Beutler et al., 1987). Scores of 17 or greater on the HRSD almost always result in a patient meeting *DSM-III-R* criteria.

Despite the extensive history of use, the HRSD has a number of limitations. First, the HRSD is heavily weighted toward somatic symptoms of depression (e.g., gastrointestinal complaints, fatigability, changes in libido). As noted earlier, these symptoms can be difficult to attribute to the depressive syndrome among elders. Considerable clinician skill is required to reliably administer the HRSD. Gallagher (1986) suggested that, on average, about 20 supervised interviews with older adults are necessary before achieving acceptable reliability. Is it worth the struggle to learn this somewhat difficult instrument? Put differently, does the HRSD add anything in terms of assessment efficiency over that derived from a self-report instrument? Rapp, Smith, and Britt (1990) evaluated this possibility by comparing an extracted 17-item version of the HRSD to several popular self-report instruments in a group of older medical patients. They concluded that the HRSD has adequate internal consistency, interrater reliability, concurrent validity, convergent validity, and discriminant validity to warrant its use as an interview-based assessment of depression severity with older medical patients. In addition, Rapp et al. found that the HRSD had superior overall performance, in terms of sensitivity and specificity, to the self-report instruments. These investigators recommended a cutoff score of 12 on this version of the HRSD to achieve strong sensitivity and specificity.

Stukenberg et al. (1990) examined the utility of the HRSD with community-dwelling elders. They found that the HRSD did not increase the efficiency of diagnosing depression over that obtained by administering self-report inventories (e.g., the BDI). Thus, for nonclinical samples, the HRSD interview may not be cost efficient. However, for patients for whom completion of a self-report inventory is problematic (e.g., cognitively impaired, hospitalized), a structured interview for depression may aid validity.

The preceding may sound a bit paradoxical. A structured interview like the HRSD is probably useful, but it is difficult to administer reliably. This dilemma led Christine Jamison and me to develop an interview-based assessment of geriatric depression that surmounted some of the problems associated with the HRSD. We crafted the Geriatric Depression Rating Scale (GDRS; Jamison & Scogin, 1992) to combine the format of the HRSD for severity rating purposes with the content of the GDS, thus deemphasizing the somatic items that can be problematic. The GDRS has 35 items, with 6 added to conform to the RDC for major depression (Spitzer et al., 1978). Althought the GDRS is still in development, we have conducted one study of its psychometric properties. Sixty-eight older adults (25 from a Veterans Affairs hospital, 24 from an outpatient depression treatment study, and 19 community-dwelling voluteers) were assessed for depression severity using the HRSD, GDS, and GDRS. Cronbach's alpha for the GDRS was .92, which suggests acceptable internal consistency. Concurrent validity estimates with the HRSD, BDI, and GDS were .83, .69, and .84, respectively. Sensitivity and specificity using various cutoff scores were examined. Optimal performance was observed with a cutoff score of 20 or greater, which suggests the presence of at least mild-to-moderate depression severity (sensitivity = 82% and specificity = 82%). These efficiency estimates compare favorably with the HRSD. Although there is clearly no psychometric superiority for the GDRS in relation to the HRSD, I believe it will require less experience and training to administer reliably.

To conclude this section on the interview-based assessment of depression among elders, I offer this confession: In my outpatient clinical assessments of older adults, I do not administer a HRSD, a GDRS, or a SCID. My hunch is that most practitioners do not do this either unless they are following a research protocol. I believe that familiarization and preferably experience with instruments like the HRSD, however, affords one greater skill in conducting a nonstructured clinical interview—the standard for practice-based assessment.

USE OF COLLATERALS IN THE ASSESSMENT OF DEPRESSION

For some older clients, it is advantageous, even necessary, to gather information about them from family, friends, or others who are familiar with them. This is especially true for the cognitively impaired or hospitalized elder for whom self-report is difficult. Information that is relevant to the assessment of depressive syndromes such as the course and history of symptoms may be provided by a collateral source.

Several instruments have been developed for the purpose of assessing depression in these circumstances. For example, the Cornell Scale for Depression in Dementia (CSDD; Alexopoulos, Abrams, Young, & Shamoian, 1988) provides a quantitative estimate of depressive severity. In the validation study, interviews were conducted with 83 patients and a nursing staff member who was familiar with them using a 19-item scale. The items on the scale emphasized observable signs of depression such as sadness, agitation, sleep difficulties, and lack of energy. The CSDD was found to have acceptable interrater reliability and internal consistency. Furthermore, it demonstrated sensitivity to RDC-based depression diagnoses. As Alexopoulos et al. noted, it will be useful to validate this scale with community-dwelling demented persons whose collateral source would probably not be professionally trained.

Another comparable scale is the NIMH Dementia Mood Assessment Scale (Sunderland et al., 1988). Seventeen of the 24 items measure depression severity, and 7 concern dementia severity. Sunderland et al. noted that information from the nursing staff or family is required for scoring this instrument. Available data suggest acceptable concurrent validity.

TRADITIONAL ASSESSMENT BATTERIES

To this point, the procedures and instruments reviewed have been rather specialized. For many practitioners (particularly those working in outpatient settings), the use of the aforementioned techniques and instruments would be in addition to a standard assessment battery. The modal battery would probably include a test of intelligence or cognitive function, a personality inventory such as the revised Minnesota Multiphasic Personality Inventory (MMPI-2), a projective technique, and a clinical interview. The strengths and weaknesses of this hypothetical assessment battery in appraising depression among older persons should be mentioned; however, I comment on the personality and projective portions only.

The MMPI-2 is a useful tool for assessing personality and psychopathology among elders. For example, Butcher et al. (1991) concluded that special, age-related norms were not needed for assessing older men with MMPI-2. They did find, however, that older men ($M = 61.2$ years) had higher scores on the D or 2 scale than did younger men ($M = 41.7$ years). Butcher et al. suggested, as is consistent with the tenor of this chapter, that the use of items in the D scale that reflect somatic complaints may account for this difference. The actual magnitude of difference between the two age groups was not clinically meaningful. Thus, the D scale is probably a valid, though not optimal, self-report measure of depression severity among elders. To assess depression by administering the MMPI-2 is probably overzealous, however, to say nothing of the problems associated with asking a depressed older adult to complete the 567 questions of the entire inventory. For a broadly based assessment of personality and psychopathology, the MMPI-2 or a similar instrument is a powerful tool and recommended; for the assessment of depression alone, it is not.

As for projectives, almost no research has been conducted on their use in the assessment of depression among older adults. Hayslip and Lowman (1986) concluded that clinicians should use "extreme caution" in making clinical use of the Rorschach with older adults. I suggest the same be said for the Thematic Apperception Test, another popular projective technique.

SUGGESTED ASSESSMENT STRATEGIES

My recommendations for the assessment of depression among older adults involve a multitiered approach. This perspective is quite similar to that put forth by Futterman, Thompson, and Gallagher-Thompson (1993).

For referral questions that ask the clinician to assess the presence or absence of a depressive syndrome or for patients for whom the clinician is treating and for whom he or she wishes to evaluate depression severity, the following is suggested.

1. Screen using a self-report instrument such as the BDI or the GDS with a cutoff score set low to maximize sensitivity. Few false negatives will occur, and false positives can be identified in Step 2. The GDS may be advantageous for cognitively impaired respondents, whereas the BDI includes somatic symptoms of depression that may be important in some assessment circumstances.

2. If the older patient scores greater than the cutoff score on the self-report screener, then use a clinical interview that focuses at least in part on depression for diagnostic confirmation. A semistructured, DSM-III-R (or DSM-IV) keyed set of questions for establishing major depression, dysthymic disorder, depressive disorder not otherwise specified, and adjustment disorder with depressed features is recommended. The DIS or the SCID provide useful frameworks for this sort of diagnostic interview. To gather even more detailed information, the HRSD or the GDRS can be administered to provide a quantitative severity rating.

SUMMARY

The assessment of depression in older adults can prove to be vexing. The difficulties emerge in disentangling depressive symptoms, primarily of the somatic variety, from the effects of normal aging processes, medical conditions, and cognitive impairments. Several self-report and clinician-rated instruments have been evaluated and proven useful in the evaluation of depressive symptoms among older adults. Included in this category are the BDI, the GDS, and the HRSD. The utility of these instruments with adults who are 85 years of age and older is a topic worthy of future investigation because the evaluation of depression in this age group will become increasingly important.

REFERENCES

Alden, D., Austin, C., & Sturgeon, R. (1989). A correlation between the Geriatric Depression Scale long and short forms. *Journal of Gerontology: Psychological Sciences, 44*, 124–125.

Alexopoulos, G. S., Abrams, R. C., Young, R. C., & Shamoian, C. A. (1988). Cornell Scale for Depression in Dementia. *Biological Psychiatry, 23*, 271–284.

American Psychiatric Association. (1987). *Diagnostic and statistical manual of mental disorders* (3rd ed., rev.). Washington, DC: Author.

American Psychiatric Association. (in press). *Diagnostic and statistical manual of mental disorders* (4th ed.). Washington, DC: Author.

Baldessarini, R. J., Finkelstein, S., & Arana, G. W. (1983). The predictive power of diagnostic tests and the effect of prevalence of illness. *Archives of General Psychology, 40*, 569–573.

Beck, A. T., & Beck, R. W. (1972). Screening depressed patients in family practice: A rapid technic. *Postgraduate Medicine, 52*, 81–85.

Beck, A. T., Steer, R. A., & Garbin, M. G. (1988). Psychometric properties of the Beck Depression Inventory: Twenty-five years of evaluation. *Clinical Psychology Review, 8*, 77–100.

Beck, A. T., Ward, C. H., Mendelson, M., Mock, J., & Erbaugh, J. (1961). An inventory for measuring depression. *Archives of General Psychiatry, 4*, 561–571.

Beutler, L. E., Scogin, F., Kirkish, D., Schretlen, D., Corbishley, A., Meredith, K., Potter, R., Hamblin, D., & Levenson, A. I. (1987). Group cognitive therapy and alprazolam in the treatment of depression in elderly adults. *Journal of Consulting and Clinical Psychology, 55*, 550–556.

Blazer, D., Hughes, D. C., & George, L. K. (1987). The epidemiology of depression in an elderly community population. *Gerontologist, 27*, 281–287.

Bolla-Wilson, K., & Blecker, M. L. (1989). Absence of depression in elderly adults. *Journal of Gerontology: Psychological Sciences, 44*, 53–55.

Botwinick, J. (1984). *Aging and human behavior* (3rd ed.). New York: Springer.

Butcher, J. N., Aldwin, C. M., Levenson, M. R., Ben-Porath, Y. S., Spiro, A., & Bosse, R. (1991). Personality and aging: A study of the MMPI-2 among older adults. *Psychology and Aging, 6*, 361–370.

Derogatis, L. R. (1977). *SCL-90R administration, scoring, and procedures manual.* Baltimore: Johns Hopkins University School of Medicine, Clinical Psychometrics Unit.

Derogatis, L. R., & Spencer, P. M. (1983). *BSI manual: I. Administration and procedures.* Baltimore: Johns Hopkins University School of Medicine, Clinical Psychometric Unit.

Dunn, V. K., & Sacco, W. P. (1989). Psychometric evaluation of the Geriatric Depression Scale and the Zung Self-Rating Depression Scale using an elderly community sample. *Psychology and Aging, 4,* 125–126.

Foelker, G. A., Jr., Schewchuk, R. M., & Niederehe, G. (1987). Confirmatory factor analysis of the short form Beck Depression Inventory in elderly community samples. *Journal of Clinical Psychology, 43,* 111–118.

Futterman, A., Thompson, L., & Gallagher-Thompson, D., (1993). *Depression in later life: Epidemiology, assessment, etiology and treatment.* Unpublished manuscript.

Gallagher, D. (1986). Assessment of depression by interview methods and psychiatric rating scales. In L. W. Poon (Ed.), *Handbook for clinical memory assessment of older adults* (pp. 202–212). Washington, DC: American Psychological Association.

Gallagher, D., Breckenridge, J., Steinmetz, J., & Thompson, L. (1983). The Beck Depression Inventory and Research Diagnostic Criteria: Congruence in an older population. *Journal of Consulting and Clinical Psychology, 51,* 945–946.

Gallagher-Thompson, D., Futterman, A., Hanley-Peterson, P., Zeiss, A., Ironson, G., & Thompson, L. W. (1992). Endogenous depression in the elderly: Prevalence and agreement among measures. *Journal of Consulting and Clinical Psychology, 60,* 300–303.

Gallagher, G., Nies, G., & Thompson, L. W. (1982). Reliability of the Beck Depression Inventory with older adults. *Journal of Consulting and Clinical Psychology, 50,* 152–153.

Gatz, M., & Pearson, C. G. (1988). Ageism revised and the provision of psychological services. *American Psychologist, 43,* 181–189.

Hamilton, M. (1967). Development of a rating scale for primary depressive illness. *British Journal of Social and Clinical Psychology, 6,* 278–296.

Hayslip, B., Jr., & Lowman, R. L. (1986). The clinical use of projective techniques with the aged: A critical review and synthesis. In T. L. Brink (Ed.), *Clinical gerontology: A guide to assessment and intervention* (pp. 63–94). New York: Haworth Press.

Jamison, C., & Scogin, F. (1992). Development of an interview-based geriatric depression rating scale. *International Journal of Aging and Human Development, 35,* 193–204.

Kathol, R. G. (1985). Depression associated with physical disease. In E. F. Beckham & W. R. Leber (Eds.), *Handbook of depression: Treatment, assessment, and research* (pp. 745–762). Homewood, IL: Dorsey Press.

Myers, J. K., Weissman, M. M., Tischler, G. L., Holzer III, C. E., Leaf, P. J., Orvaschel, H., Anthony, J. C., Boyd, J. H., Burke, J. D., Jr., Kramer, M., & Stoltzman, R. (1984). Six-month prevalence of psychiatric disorders in three communities. *Archives of General Psychiatry, 41,* 959–967.

Norris, J. T., Gallagher, D., Wilson, A., & Winograd, C. H. (1987). Assessment of depression in geriatric medical outpatients: The validity of two screening measures. *Journal of the American Geriatrics Society, 35,* 989–995.

Olin, J. T., Schneider, L. S., Eaton, E. E., Zemansky, M. F., & Pollock, V. E. (1992). The Geriatric Depression Scale and the Beck Depression Inventory as screening instruments in an older adult outpatient population. *Psychological Assessment, 4,* 190–192.

Parmelee, P. A., Lawton, M. P., & Katz, I. R. (1989). Psychometric properties of the Geriatric Depression Scale among the institutionalized aged. *Psychological Assessment, 1,* 331–338.

Prinz, P. N., Dustman, R. E., & Emmerson, R. (1990). Electrophysiology and aging. In J. E. Birren & K. W. Schaie (Eds.), Handbook of the psychology of aging (3rd ed., pp. 135–149). San Diego: Academic Press.

Radloff, L. (1977). The CES-D Scale: A self-report depression scale for research in the general population. *Applied Psychological Measurement, 1,* 385–401.

Rapp, S. R., Parisi, S. A., Walsh, D. A., & Wallace, C. E. (1988). Detecting depression in elderly medical inpatients. *Journal of Consulting and Clinical Psychology, 56,* 509–513.

Rapp, S. R., Smith, S. S., & Britt, M. (1990). Identifying comorbid depression in elderly medical patients: Use of the extracted Hamilton Depression Rating Scale. *Psychological Assessment, 2,* 243–247.

Robins, L. N., & Helzer, J. E. (1985). *Diagnostic Interview Schedule: Version III-A.* St. Louis, MO: Washington University School of Medicine.

Rohde, P., Lewinsohn, D. M., & Seeley, J. R. (1990). Are people changed by the experience of having an episode of depression? A further test of the scar hypothesis. *Journal of Abnormal Psychology, 99,* 264–271.

Scogin, F., Hamblin, D., Beutler, L., & Corbishley, A. (1988). Reliability and validity of the short-form Beck Depression Inventory with older adults. *Journal of Clinical Psychology, 44,* 853–857.

Sheikh, J. I., & Yesavage, J. A. (1986). Geriatric Depression Scale (GDS): Recent evidence and development of a shorter version. In T. L. Brink (Ed.), *Clinical gerontology: A guide to assessment and intervention* (pp. 165–173). New York: Haworth Press.

Spitzer, R. L., Endicott, J., & Robbins, E. (1978). Research Diagnostic Criteria: Rationale and reliability. *Archives of General Psychiatry, 35,* 773–782.

Spitzer, R. L., Williams, J. B. W., Gibbon, M., & First, M. (1992). The Structured Clinical Interview for DSM-III-R (SCID): History, rationale, and description. *Archives of General Psychiatry, 49,* 624–629.

Stern, R. A., & Bachman, D. L. (1991). Depressive symptoms following stroke. *American Journal of Psychiatry, 148,* 351–356.

Stukenberg, K. W., Dura, J. R., & Kiecolt-Glaser, J. K. (1990). Depression screening scale validation in an elderly, community-dwelling population. *Psychological Assessment, 2,* 134–138.

Sunderland, T., Alterman, I. S., Yount, D., Hill, J. L., Tariot, P. N., Newhouse, P. A., Mueller, F. A., Mellow, A. M., & Cohen, R. M. (1988). A new scale for the assessment of depressed mood in demented patients. *American Journal of Psychiatry, 148*, 955–959.

Task Force on DSM-IV. (1991). *DSM-IV options book: Work in progress(9/1/91)*. Washington, DC: American Psychiatric Association.

Thompson, L. W., Gallagher, D., & Breckenridge, J. S. (1987). Comparative effectiveness of psychotherapies for depressed elders. *Journal of Consulting and Clinical Psychology, 55*, 385–390.

Widiger, T. A., Hunt, S. W., Frances, A., Clarkin, J. F., & Gilmore, M. (1984). Diagnostic efficiency and DSM-III. *Archives of General Psychiatry, 41*, 1005–1012.

Williams, J. (1988). A structured interview guide for the Hamilton Depression Rating Scale. *Archives of General Psychiatry, 45*, 742–747.

Yesavage, J. A., Brink, T. L., Rose, T. L., Lum, O., Huang, V., Adey, M., & Leirer, V. O. (1983). Development and validation of a geriatric depression screening scale: A preliminary report. *Journal of Psychiatric Research, 17*, 37–49.

Zimmerman, M., & Coryell, W. (1987). The inventory to diagnose depression, lifetime version. *Acta Psychiatrica Scandinavica, 75*, 495–499.

Zimmerman, M., & Coryell, W. (1988). The validity of a self-report questionnaire for diagnosing major depressive disorder. *Archives of General Psychiatry, 45*, 738–740.

Zung, W. W. K. (1965). A self-rating depression scale. *Archives of General Psychiatry, 12*, 63–70.

5

DIFFERENTIAL DIAGNOSIS OF DEMENTIA AND DEPRESSION

ALFRED W. KASZNIAK and GINA DITRAGLIA CHRISTENSON

A continuing problem for physicians and other health care professionals involves the diagnosis of older adults who present with concomitant signs of cognitive impairment and depression. In such cases, a determination must be made concerning whether the patient is experiencing cognitive difficulty secondary to a mood disorder (e.g., major depressive disorder) or whether the patient has developed a depressive syndrome secondary to a dementing illness, such as Alzheimer's disease (AD). Complicating differential diagnosis is the fact that what appear to be depressive symptoms may actually reflect cognitive and/or behavioral aspects of the dementing illness itself.

Our goals in this chapter are (a) to provide an overview of current research and clinical literature concerning the differential diagnosis of dementia and depression in older adults and (b) to describe the contributions of neuropsychological assessment to clinical diagnosis. We make recommendations, on the basis of research data and clinical experience, for selecting assessment procedures. We conclude the chapter with brief case presentations that illustrate the clinical application of such procedures.

DIAGNOSTIC ACCURACY, TREATMENT IMPLICATIONS, AND THE CONSEQUENCES OF DIAGNOSTIC ERROR

In the past, inaccurate diagnoses of dementia in the general medical population had been reported to range from 10% to over 50% (Gurland & Toner, 1983; National Institute on Aging Task Force, 1980). Many of these misdiagnoses were false negative errors (failing to diagnose the syndrome of dementia when it is present), and many false negative errors involved physicians who had inadequately assessed cognitive functioning in their older medical patients (McCartney, 1986). Clinical psychologists also appear to have experienced significant difficulty in recognizing the indicators of possible neurological disorder, including dementing illness, in their patients (Sbordone & Rudd, 1986). More recent evidence suggests that accuracy in the diagnosis of dementia has improved. Multidisciplinary evaluations of older patients who are suspected of dementia using current diagnostic criteria (McKhann et al., 1984) have provided better diagnostic accuracy than in the past (Cummings & Benson, 1986; Wade et al., 1987). For example, correct diagnosis of AD, as validated against autopsy or biopsy criteria, has recently been reported to occur in 70–100% of purported cases (Kukull et al., 1990b; Martin et al., 1987; Molsa, Paljarvi, Rinne, Rinne, & Saks, 1985; Morris, McKeel, Falling, Torach, & Berg, 1988; Sulkava, Haltia, Paetan, Wikstrom, & Palo, 1983), although clinicopathological agreement varies depending on the pathological diagnostic criteria used (Tierney et al., 1988). Investigators have argued that this apparent improvement has resulted primarily from the application of more recently developed specific criteria (see later discussion) for the diagnosis of dementing illnesses such as AD (Kawas, 1990). Some caution needs to be exercised in interpreting available clinicopathological diagnostic accuracy studies, because cases of depression (with or without significant cognitive impairment) appear to be markedly underrepresented in the samples investigated. Increasingly, false positive errors in the diagnosis of dementia, particularly overdiagnosis of AD in patients with combined cognitive and affective symptoms, are becoming a concern (Gatz & Pearson, 1988; Heston & Mastri, 1982). For example, Garcia, Reding, and Blass (1981) reported a 25% rate of false positive dementia diagnoses (as judged against longitudinal follow-up criteria) in their study of 100 older adults who had been referred to a specialized outpatient dementia clinic. Most of these misdiagnosed patients proved to be suffering from depression.

It has long been recognized that memory complaints by an older individual may be associated with depression or other psychiatric disorders (Emery, 1988). Kiloh (1961) originally used the term *pseudodementia* to describe cases in which significant cognitive impairment seemed to be resolved with treatment of a depression or other psychiatric disorder. However, because the degree of cognitive impairment can be relatively severe (e.g., McCallister & Price, 1982), some have argued that there is nothing "pseudo" about the dementia, and alternative terms such as *dementia syndrome of depression* (Folstein & McHugh, 1978) and *depression-related cognitive dysfunction* (Stoudemire, Hill, Gulley, & Morris, 1989) have been proposed. Available data have indicated that approximately 20% of older depressed patients show cognitive deficits that are sufficiently severe as to merit the application of such labels (La Rue, D'Elia, Clark, Spar, & Jarvik, 1986).

Although some investigators (e.g., Bieliauskas, 1993) have suggested that problems in differential diagnosis have been overrated, most agree that patients who present with dementia syndrome of depression can be difficult to diagnose (La Rue, 1992). Across different studies, it has been estimated that between 1% and 31% of patients who are diagnosed as having a progressive dementing illness might actually be depressed and have associated memory deficits (for a review see Katzman, Lasker, & Bernstein, 1988). Mistakenly diagnosing an irreversible dementing illness in a depressed individual with potentially reversible cognitive impairment may result in confinement to a long-term care facility, where the individual may deteriorate. Furthermore, if left untreated, such patients may exhibit immobility, fecal impaction, incontinence, and clouding of consciousness (Klerman, 1983), as well as continued symptoms of depression and risk of suicide. Failure to treat depression is all the more tragic because depression in older adults often responds to treatment with antidepressant medication, psychotherapy, and/or electroconvulsive therapy (for reviews see Benedict & Nacoste, 1990; Koenig & Blazer, 1992; Salzman & Nevis-Olesen, 1992).

Conversely, costs are clearly associated with misdiagnosing depression as a progressive dementing illness. In a review of the literature, Siegel and Gershon (1986) concluded that 25–30% of older patients who are initially referred for evaluation and treatment of depression are ultimately diagnosed as having a progressive dementing illness. As we review later, estimates of diagnostic accuracy (as judged against the criteria of longitudinal course) for older adults meeting specific criteria for a diagnosis of depression have varied, which possibly reflects methodological differences between studies. Inappropriate treatment for nonexistent depression in a patient with a progressive dementia not only represents unnecessary expense, but treatment with antidepressant medications having anticholinergic properties (e.g., imipramine) may exacerbate memory impairment (Benedict & Nacoste, 1990; Harris, Gierz, & Lohr, 1989).

Although there has historically been an "either/or" approach to the differential diagnosis of dementia and depression in older patients, it is now well recognized that AD and depression often coexist. In a recent review, Teri and Wagner (1992) noted that the reported prevalence of depressive syndromes in AD ranges from 0% to 86%, with most studies reporting rates in the 17–29% range. The broad range of prevalence estimates likely reflects both sampling differences across studies and the difficulties of diagnosing depression in a demented individual. Once an individual has been diagnosed as having probable AD, symptoms of depression may go unrecognized. Behavioral and cognitive changes that are associated with the course of a primary dementing illness may, in fact, mask a depressive syndrome. In addition, discrepancies between patient and caregiver reports of AD patients' depression-related symptoms, as discussed later, complicate assessment. Because patients with coexisting depression and AD can expect to benefit from treatment of their depression (see Teri & Wagner, 1992), failure to diagnose and treat depression in an AD patient may result in unnecessary emotional, physical, and/or social discomfort. Patients with coexistent depression and AD are more likely to exhibit delusions (Rabins, Merchant, & Nestadt, 1984), various behavioral problems such as restlessness and agitation (Reifler, Larson, & Teri, 1987), and impairment of instrumental activities of daily living (Pearson, Teri, Reifler, & Raskind, 1989) than are AD patients without depression.

Although patients with coexistent AD and depression will remain demented after pharmacological and/or electroconvulsive treatment of their depression, many show improvement in mood, functional abilities, and even some aspects of cognition (Greenwald et al., 1989; Reifler, Larson, Teri, & Poulsen, 1986; Reynolds et al., 1987). Note that these studies of the efficacy of pharmacological and electroconvulsive treatments in patients with coexistent AD and depression have been uncontrolled clinical trials. The only controlled, random-assignment, double-blind clinical trial (Reifler et al., 1989; Teri et al., 1991) compared a placebo (inert pills plus weekly meetings with a psychiatrist and research nurse) with imipramine in 28 depressed and 33 nondepressed AD patients. In this study, imipramine- and placebo-treated patients showed comparable reductions in depression, with nondepressed AD patients in the imipramine condition showing mild cognitive decline (which did not occur in the placebo condition). Thus, specific efficacy of pharmacological treatment for depression in AD remains to be demonstrated. One nonpharmacological intervention study of behavior therapy techniques (taught to patients and their family caregivers) with depressed AD patients showed significant reduction in depression severity, increased pleasant activity frequency and duration, reduced frequency of problem behavior, and reduced caregiver depression (Teri & Gallagher, 1991; Teri & Uomoto, 1991). Additional research concerning the specific and comparative efficacy of pharmacological and behavioral interventions for depression in AD is clearly warranted. However, evidence to date encourages diagnostic efforts in identification of depression among AD (and possibly other) dementia patients.

Overall, the risks of misdiagnosis, and the potential benefits of accurate diagnosis, make strong arguments for the importance of careful diagnostic evaluation. As we discuss in the remainder of this chapter, psychological (particularly neuropsychological) assessment has an important role to play in the differential diagnosis of dementia and depression in older adults. However, we emphasize that differential diagnosis in this area is a fundamentally interdisciplinary endeavor, with physicians and other health care providers also playing necessary roles. Complex interactions between medical illnesses, medications (both psychotropic and nonpsychotropic), age-related changes in pharmacokinetics and pharmacodynamics, and a variety of psychological and social factors influence the occurrence and nature of both cognitive and affective symptoms in older adults (see Cummings & Benson, 1992; Depression Guideline Panel, 1993; Koenig & Blazer, 1992). This complexity requires the cooperative interaction of various medical and mental health practitioners if the diagnostic and treatment needs of older adults are to be adequately served.

DEMENTIA AND DEPRESSION: DIAGNOSTIC CRITERIA, PREVALENCE, AND SYMPTOM OVERLAP

As described by Butters, Salmon, and Butters (chapter 3 in this book), the term *dementia* is used to describe the general syndrome of acquired and intellectual impairment caused by brain dysfunction. The syndrome of dementia involves persistent impairment of two or more of the following domains of psychological functioning: memory, language, visuospatial skills, judgment or abstract thinking, and emotion or personality (Bayles & Kaszniak, 1987; Cummings & Benson, 1992; Kaszniak, 1986). Because of methodological difficulties in operationally defining criteria for the presence of dementia (particularly when the severity of impairment is mild), and because of difficulties in adequately sampling from the various environments in which persons with dementia may live (e.g., home, hospitals, nursing homes, other institutions), the actual prevalence of dementia is unknown. In studies of dementia in various countries, prevalence rates have ranged from 2.5% to 24.6% for persons over the age of 65 years (for a review see Ineichen, 1987), with variability between studies likely reflecting differences in dementia definitions, sampling techniques, and sensitivity of instruments used to identify cases. Average prevalence estimates across studies suggest that approximately 6% of persons over the age of 65 years have severe dementia, with an additional 10–15% having mild-to-moderate dementia (Cummings & Benson, 1992). The prevalence of dementia is clearly age related, doubling approximately every 5 years after age 65 (Jorm, Korten, & Henderson, 1987). As would be expected, the prevalence of dementia is considerably higher among nursing home and hospital residents than among those living within the community (for reviews see Kramer, 1986; Smyer, 1988).

Dementia can be associated with more than 70 different causes of brain dysfunction (Haase, 1977; Katzman, 1986). Across most published investigations of the relative prevalence of different causes of dementia, AD accounts for the largest proportion of all causes, varying from a low of 22% to a high of 70% of all patients studied (Cummings & Benson, 1992). However, in some community surveys (particularly, although not exclusively, those in Japan and China), multi-infarct dementia (MID; a type of dementia associated with cerebrovascular disease) has been found to be more common than AD (Folstein, Anthony, Parhad, Duffy, & Gruenberg, 1985; Li, Shen, Chen, Zhao, & Li, 1989; Rorsman, Hagnell, & Lanke, 1986; Shibayama, Kasahara, & Kobayashi, 1986). Whether such differences in relative prevalence estimates reflect actual regional and international disparities or methodological variation across studies remains unclear. Despite these differences in the results of epidemiological investigations, there is consensual agreement that AD and vascular dementia (VaD) are the most common causes of age-associated dementia (Roman, 1991). Available evidence supports the conclusion that AD and VaD are the most frequent diagnoses of patients who are referred for comprehensive assessment because of memory complaints (Thal, Grundman, & Klauber, 1988). Therefore, when we examine research concerning differential diagnosis in this chapter, we focus on these two most prevalent causes of dementia among older adults, with a particular emphasis on AD. To clarify approaches to, and problems surrounding, the differential diagnosis of dementia and depression, it is first necessary to specify commonly accepted diagnostic criteria for the most prevalent dementing illnesses (i.e., AD and VaD), as well as for depression. The following subsections provide a brief overview of these diagnostic criteria.

Alzheimer's Disease

In North America, the most commonly used diagnostic criteria for AD are those found within the revised third edition of the *Diagnostic and Statistical Manual of Mental Disorders* (*DSM-III-R*; American Psychiatric Association, 1987), therein termed *primary degenerative dementia of the Alzheimer's type*. In order for this diagnosis to be made, the following *DSM-III-R* criteria must be met: (a) presence of dementia (see the following discussion); (b) an insidious onset and progressive course of deterioration; and (c) exclusion of all other possible causes of dementia by history, physical examination, and laboratory tests. The *DSM-III-R* criteria for dementia require evidence of memory impairment and at least one of the following: impairment in abstract thinking or judgment, personality changes, and/or other disturbance of higher cortical function (e.g., aphasia, apraxia, agnosia, visuoconstructive deficit). In addition, the impairment must significantly interfere with everyday functioning and must not occur exclusively during the course of delirium. Finally, there must be evidence of an organic factor (or factors) that has been judged to be etiologically related to the disturbance or (in the absence of such evidence) the reasonable presumption of an organic etiology, as supported by the systematic elimination of other potential nonorganic mental disorders (e.g., depression) that could account for the disturbance.

The *DSM-III-R* criteria for dementia are not substantially different from those of the *DSM-III* (American Psychiatric Association, 1980). The *DSM-III* dementia criteria have shown both acceptable interclinician reliability (Kukull et al., 1990a) and reasonable sensitivity and specificity, compared with neuropathological and long-term follow-up criteria (Kukull et al., 1990b). In an effort to improve on the sensitivity and specificity of dementia diagnoses, primarily for the purpose of providing consistent definitions for comparisons across therapeutic trials, the Work Group on the Diagnosis of Alzheimer's Disease that was established by the National Institute of Neurological and Communicative Disorders and Stroke and the Alzheimer's Disease and Related Disorders Association (NINCDS-ADRDA; McKhann et al., 1984) published inclusion and exclusion criteria for diagnoses of *definite, probable,* and *possible* AD. The criteria for probable and possible AD are summarized in Table 1. For an NINCDS-ADRDA diagnosis of definite AD to be made, all criteria for probable AD must be met, and there must be histopathological evidence of the microscopic pathology of AD (i.e., particular anatomic distribution and sufficient accumulation of neuritic plaques and neurofibrillary tangles; see Khachaturian, 1985) obtained from an autopsy or biopsy. Given the invasive nature and consequent risk of biopsies, a diagnosis of definite AD is seldom made during a patient's life.

As noted by Kawas (1990), compared with the *DSM-III-R* criteria, the NINCDS-ADRDA criteria differ (a) in not requiring that memory necessarily be one of the two impaired areas of cognitive functions, (b) in requiring formal mental status and neuropsychological testing evidence of cognitive dysfunction (and providing examples of suitable tests), (c) in not requiring specific evidence of deterioration in social or occupational functioning (hence presumably increasing sensitivity to milder dementia severity), and (d) in not requiring the exclusion of other *DSM-III-R* diagnoses, such as depression, to make a diagnosis of AD. This final difference is obviously of particular relevance to the present focus, given the aforementioned evidence for coexistent AD and depression. Clinicopathological studies (for a review see Kawas, 1990) have documented excellent validity for the NINCDS-ADRDA criteria. For example, both Morris et al. (1988), who used autopsy histopathological criteria, and Martin et al. (1987), who used biopsy histopathological criteria, found 100% diagnostic accuracy.

TABLE 1
National Institute of Neurological and Communicative Disorders and Stroke and the Alzheimer's Disease and Related Disorders Association Workgroup[a] Criteria for Diagnoses of Probable and Possible Alzheimer's Disease (AD)

A clinical diagnosis of *probable* AD is made when

1. Dementia is established by clinical examination and documented by performance on the Mini-Mental State Examination (Folstein, Folstein, & McHugh, 1975), the Blessed Dementia Scale (Blessed, Tomlinson, & Roth, 1968), or a similar mental status examination, *and*
2. Confirmed by neuropsychological testing, documenting deficits in two or more areas of cognition, *and*
3. Characterized by a history of progressive worsening of memory and other cognitive deficits, *with*
4. No disturbance in level of consciousness, *and*
5. Symptom onset between the ages of 40 and 90 years, most typically after age 65, *and*
6. There is an absence of systemic disorders or other brain diseases that of themselves could account for the progressive deficits.

The diagnosis of probable AD is further supported by evidence (i.e., from neuropsychological reexamination) of progressive deterioration of specific cognitive functions, impairment in activities of daily living, a family history of similar disorders, and results of particular laboratory tests (e.g., a normal lumbar puncture, normal pattern or nonspecific changes in the electroencephalogram, evidence of cerebral atrophy on computerized tomographic scanning).

The clinical diagnosis of *possible* AD is made when

1. The syndrome of dementia is present, *and*
2. There is an absence of other neurological, psychiatric, or systemic disorders that are sufficient to cause the dementia, *but*
3. There are present variations from criteria for probable AD in the onset, presentation, or clinical course.

Possible AD may also be diagnosed when there is a systemic or brain disease that is sufficient to produce a dementia, but which (for various reasons) is not considered to be the cause of the patient's dementia.

[a]McKhann et al., 1984.

However, both studies used a small number of highly select research subjects, and therefore, generalization from these studies should be limited. Furthermore, although the NINCDS-ADRDA criteria allow for the diagnosis of AD in a patient with coexistent depression, the criteria are not specific concerning the differentiation of such patients from those with the dementia syndrome of depression, and as of this writing, clinicopathological validity studies of the criteria applied to such patient groups are unavailable.

Vascular Dementia

Until recently, there had been no standard or generally accepted criteria for the diagnosis of dementia related to vascular disease. The *DSM*

III-R provides criteria for one type of VaD—MID—which require that the patient: (a) meet the criteria for presence of dementia; (b) have a history of a stepwise (rather than smoothly gradual) course and a "patchy" distribution of deficits (i.e., impairment in some cognitive functions, but not others) early in the course of illness; (c) present focal neurological signs and symptoms; and (d) provide evidence from physical examination, laboratory tests, and/or history of significant cerebrovascular disease that is judged to be etiologically related to the disturbance. These criteria are quite similar to those proposed by Hachinski and colleagues (Hachinski, Lassen, & Marshall, 1974; Hachinski et al., 1975) in their original description of MID. Rosen, Terry, Fuld, Katzman, and Peck (1980), who used a modification of the clinical rating scale that was suggested by Hachinski and colleagues for identifying MID, correctly differentiated 5 AD patients from 11 MID or mixed MID and AD patients (as defined by autopsy histopathological criteria). Loeb and Gandolfo (1983) also provided evidence for the validity of the Hachinski MID criteria, on the basis of computed tomography evidence that is consistent with multiple cerebrovascular infarcts.

To some extent, MID has become synonymous with all dementias of vascular etiology (Roman et al., 1993), although the *DSM-III-R* and Hachinski criteria (Hachinski et al., 1974, 1975) best match those signs and symptoms that are seen in patients with multiple (typically medium-to-large vessel) cortical infarcts (Cummings & Benson, 1992; La Rue, 1992). However, it is clear that dementia syndromes can also be associated with multiple lacunar infarcts of the subcortical gray matter as well as multiple small-vessel infarctions of either the cortex or subcortical white matter (see Cummings & Benson, 1992; Roman et al., 1993). These other vascular dementias often do not fit the pattern described by diagnostic criteria for MID. To consolidate the different clinical presentations of dementia and typical laboratory findings that are associated with this range of ischemic cerebrovascular disease, clinicians and investigators from the State of California Alzheimer's Disease Diagnostic and Treatment Centers (Chui et al., 1992) recently proposed specific criteria for diagnosing ischemic vascular dementia. Even more recently, the Neuroepidemiology Branch of the National Institute of Neurological Disorders and Stroke (NINDS) organized an international workshop, with support from the Association Internationale pour la Recherche et l'Enseignement en Neurosciences (AIREN), and subsequently published research criteria for diagnosing VaD (Roman et al., 1993). These criteria were intended to encompass cases of dementia resulting from ischemic and hemorrhagic brain lesions, as well as those from cerebral ischemic–hypoxic lesions (e.g., those due to cardiac arrest). Similar to the NINCDS-ADRDA criteria for AD, the NINDS-AIREN criteria provide for the diagnoses of *probable*, *possible*, and *definite* VaD, as well as subcategorization of the specific types of vascular lesions (as determined by clinical, radiological, and neuropathological features). A summary of the criteria for probable and possible VaD is provided in Table 2.

A diagnosis of definite VaD requires that the patient meet criteria for probable VaD, plus histopathological evidence of cerebrovascular disease obtained from autopsy or biopsy, an absence of neurofibrillary tangles and neuritic plaques exceeding those expected for age, and an absence of other histopathological or clinical disorders that are capable of producing dementia. As with the NINCDS-ADRDA criteria for the diagnosis of definite AD, the risks that are associated with brain biopsy generally preclude a diagnosis of definite VaD being made during a patient's life. Finally, note that the NINDS-AIREN criteria specify that the term *AD with cerebrovascular disease* (CVD) should be used to classify patients who meet the NINCDS-ADRDA criteria for possible AD and who also show clinical and/ or brain imaging evidence of relevant CVD.

Depression

Within North America, the most generally accepted criteria for the identification and classification of depression are those contained within the *DSM-III-R*. As noted by Scogin (chapter 4 in this book), the *DSM-III-R* uses a specific nomenclature and a hierarchical organization scheme to differentiate between mood syndromes, mood episodes, and mood disorders. A *mood syndrome* is defined by the co-occurrence of a particular mood and associated symptoms for a specified length of time. A *mood episode* is a mood syndrome with an etiology that cannot be attributed to a known organic factor (such as AD) or to a nonmood psychotic disorder (such as schizophrenia). A *mood disorder* is defined by the pattern of episodes. There are two major categories of syndromes—manic and depressive—and two major categories of disorders—bipolar and depressive.

The *DSM-III-R* criteria for a *major depressive syndrome* include either depressed mood or loss of interest or pleasure, and four of the following associated symptoms: change in appetite or weight; insomnia or hypersomnia; observed psychomotor agitation or retardation; fatigue or loss of energy; feelings of worthlessness or guilt; concentration or decision-making difficulties; and suicidal attempts, ideation, or recurrent thoughts of death. In addition, the constellation of symptoms must represent a change from previous levels of functioning and must have been present during the same 2-week period. For a major depressive episode to be identified, it must also be established that an "organic" factor (i.e., presence of a diagnosable disorder of presumed neurological etiology, such as AD) did not initiate and is not maintaining the symptoms. The presence of a nonmood psychotic disorder must also be ruled out. A major depressive disorder is diagnosed only in those cases for which there has been at least one major depressive episode and no history of a manic or hypomanic episode. Thus, by *DSM-*

TABLE 2
Neuroepidemiology Branch of the National Institute of Neurological Disorders and Stroke and the Association Internationale pour la Recherche et l'Enseignement en Neurosciences Workshop[a] Criteria for Diagnoses of Probable and Possible Vascular Disease (VaD)

The clinical diagnosis of *probable* VaD is made when

1. Dementia is present, defined by (a) cognitive decline from a previously higher level of functioning, (b) impairment of memory and two or more other cognitive domains (preferably established by clinical examination and documented by neuropsychological testing (c) sufficient severity as to interfere with activities of daily living, and (d) is not due to the physical (i.e., sensorimotor) effects of stroke alone, *and*
2. The patient does not show disturbance of consciousness, delirium, psychosis, severe aphasia, sensorimotor impairment sufficient to preclude neuropsychological testing, systemic disorders, or other brain diseases (e.g., Alzheimer's disease) that could account for the cognitive deficits, *and*
3. Cerebrovascular disease is present, defined by (a) the presence of focal neurological signs (e.g., hemiparesis, sensory deficit, hemianopia, dysarthria, lower facial weakness, Babinski sign), (b) evidence of relevant features consistent with cerebrovascular disease on brain imaging (e.g., computed tomography, magnetic resonance imaging) including ". . . multiple large-vessel infarcts or a single strategically placed infarct (angular gyrus, thalamus, basal forebrain, or posterior cerebral artery or anterior cerebral artery territories), as well as multiple basal ganglia and white matter lacunes or extensive periventricular white matter lesions, or combinations thereof" (Roman et al., 1984, p. 257), *and*
4. A relationship is established between the dementia and the cerebrovascular disease, inferred from one or more of the following: (a) onset of dementia within 3 months after a recognized stroke; (b) abrupt deterioration in cognitive functioning; or (c) fluctuating, stepwise progression of cognitive deficits.

The diagnosis of probable VaD is further supported by (a) the early presence of a gait disturbance (small-step gait, or magnetic, apraxic–ataxic, or parkinsonian gait); (b) a history of unsteadiness and frequent falls; (c) early urinary urgency, frequency, and other urinary symptoms not explained by urologic disease; (d) pseudobulbar palsy; and (e) mood and personality changes, abulia, depression, emotional incontinence, or other subcortical deficits including psychomotor retardation and abnormal executive function.

The clinical diagnosis of *possible* VaD is made when

1. The patient meets criteria for the presence of dementia, with focal neurological signs, *but*
2. In whom brain imaging studies to confirm cerebrovascular disease are missing, *or*
3. When there is an absence of clear temporal relationship between dementia and stroke, *or*
4. In patients with subtle onset and variable course (improvement or plateau) of cognitive deficits and evidence of relevant cerebrovascular disease.

[a]Roman et al., 1993.

III-R criteria, neither a major depressive episode nor a major depressive disorder can be diagnosed in an individual with AD. A depressive syndrome, as determined by the just-listed criteria, may be identified in persons with AD.

It is clear that a depressive syndrome may manifest in a variety of ways, depending on the combination of symptoms present. Several reviews of the literature have, in fact, suggested that the population of individuals with depressive syndromes may not be homogeneous in their symptom profiles. There has been speculation that older adults may have a generally more heterogeneous display of depressive symptoms compared with middle-aged adults (Benedict & Nacoste, 1990). Of particular interest is the observation that older individuals may be more likely to endorse somatic complaints and less likely to explicitly admit to dysphoric mood (see Benedict & Nacoste, 1990; Kaszniak & Allender, 1985; Salzman & Shader, 1979). Because both patient and clinician may be more concerned about concurrent medical conditions, depressive symptoms may be overlooked in older persons. Depression in older age often coexists with multiple chronic diseases and disabilities, which complicate diagnosis and treatment, and may directly contribute to the pathogenesis of depressive symptoms. Because a number of chronic diseases and disabilities in older adults may interfere with performance on cognitive tasks (see Storandt, chapter 2 in this book), the differential diagnosis of depression and dementia in such patients is complex. Although the prognosis for depressed older individuals who are hospitalized with medical illness may be poorer than for those without medical illness, depressive symptoms respond to treatment in many of these patients (see Folks & Kinney, 1991; Koenig & Blazer, 1992). Heterogeneity in the symptom presentation of depression in older adults also appears to be influenced by age of depression onset. Elderly depressed patients with an older age of onset, compared with those elderly with younger age of depression onset, have shown more frequent neuroimaging abnormalities, more frequent neuropsychological impairment, and less frequent family histories of affective illness, among other differences (for a review see Caine, Lyness, & King, 1993).

Despite continuing research, no specific biological marker for the screening of depression in older adults has been identified. The dexamethasone suppression test (DST), which is based on the hyperactivity of the hypothalamic–pituitary–adrenal axis that is known to occur in severe depression, lacks sufficient specificity, with a number of physical illnesses (particularly infectious disease), other psychiatric disorders, weight loss, and certain medications producing false positive test results (Koenig & Blazer, 1992). Although controversial (see Weiner, 1989), there is also some evidence (Rosenbaum et al., 1984) for a higher prevalence of positive DSTs in nondepressed healthy persons over the age of 65 years compared with younger adults, which suggests that the DST may be generally less specific in the elderly. Other potential biological markers for depression, including platelet tritiated imipramine binding and platelet membrane fluidity, remain experimental tools awaiting demonstrations of specificity for depression in older adults (see Allen & Blazer, 1991).

The clinical interview thus remains the mainstay for evaluation and diagnosis of depression in older adults (National Institutes of Health, 1991). The *DSM-III-R* provides some guidelines for obtaining relevant interview information and observations for a given patient. More specific guidance is provided by the protocol of the Structured Clinical Interview for DSM-III-R (SCID; Spitzer, Williams, Gibbon, & First, 1990), which is designed to assist clinicians in making *DSM-III-R* diagnoses. When depression syndrome diagnoses are arrived at through use of the Diagnostic Interview Schedule (DIS; National Institute of Mental Health, 1979; Robins, Helzer, Croughan, & Ratcliff, 1981), a predecessor of the SCID, interdiagnostician concordance (diagnostic reliability) is acceptably high when assessing both younger and older adults (Blazer, Hughes, & George, 1987; Helzer et al., 1985; Robins, 1985). In applying the *DSM-III-R* criteria for a major depressive syndrome, however, the clinician should remember that many of the somatic and behavioral symptoms listed in the criteria may actually occur as part of the normal aging process (see Kaszniak & Allender, 1985) or may be related to physical conditions or diseases that are common among older persons (Klerman, 1983). These include changes in sleep pattern, appetite changes, fatigue, behavioral slowing or agitation, and complaints of diminished ability to think or concentrate. In addition, many drugs that are taken by elderly individuals for common medical conditions may either induce depression, aggravate pre-existing depression, or produce depressionlike symptoms (Klerman, 1983; Salzman, 1992). Polypharmacy is common among older individuals and further complicates the picture because drug interactions may also produce depression or depressionlike symptoms (Salzman, 1992). These same concerns, of course, apply to other interview protocols and criteria for the assessment of depression, such as the Hamilton Rating Scale for Depression (HRSD; Hamilton, 1967). Because 9 of the 17 HRSD items concern somatic symptoms, scores can be significantly elevated by the presence of physical illness in older adults (Gallagher, Slife, Rose, & Okarma, 1982).

Initial screening for depression-related symptoms can be facilitated through the use of brief self-report questionnaires. Reviews that compare older adult normative, reliability, and validity data for self-report depression screening instruments are available (e.g., Fry, 1986; Gallagher, 1986a; Kaszniak & Allender, 1985; Yesavage, 1986). Reviews of the aging-specific literature for particular instruments include those concerned with the Center for Epidemiologic Studies Depression Scale (Radloff & Teri, 1986), the Zung Self-Rating Depression Scale (Zung & Zung, 1986), the Beck Depression Inventory (Gallagher, 1986b), the Geriatric Depression Scale (GDS;

Sheikh & Yesavage, 1986), and the Depression Adjective Check List and Multiple Affect Adjective Check List (Lubin & Rinck, 1986). The availability of reliability and validity data that is specific for older adults allows for informed choices about which instruments are best suited for a particular assessment question. Unfortunately, depression scale reliability and validity data for the oldest old (i.e., those 85 years old and older) are generally not available (see Weiss, Nagel, & Aronson, 1986).

Dementia Syndrome of Depression

As noted earlier, the cardinal feature of the dementia syndrome of depression is ". . . clinically significant cognitive disturbance that coincides with a depressive episode and that remits or improves substantially when depressive symptoms abate" (La Rue, 1992, p. 281). Persons with depression and severe cognitive impairment, as discussed later, are likely to be a heterogeneous group, with some having the dementia syndrome of depression and others having dementing illness, such as AD or VaD, with coexistent depression.

CONCOMITANT DEPRESSION AND COGNITIVE IMPAIRMENT IN OLDER ADULTS: SOURCES OF DIFFERENTIAL DIAGNOSTIC DIFFICULTY

As already noted in our discussion of diagnostic accuracy, differentiating older adults with dementing illness, such as AD or MID, from those with depression, or from those with coexistent dementia and depression is difficult. Major contributors to this difficulty include the association of memory complaints with both normal aging and depressive symptoms, overlapping clinical signs and symptoms, problems in the identification of depression in cognitively impaired persons, and ambiguity concerning long-term prognosis. The following subsections briefly discuss each of these contributors, focusing on features that assist in differentiation, wherever possible.

Association of Memory Complaints With Normal Aging and With Depression

Research using questionnaires to assess the subjective frequency of everyday memory failures has shown older adults to complain of memory difficulty more frequently than do younger adults (Perlmutter, 1978; Zelinski, Gilewski, & Thompson, 1980). However, correlations between these subjective estimates and performance on verbal memory tests for normal older adults have varied. Some studies have reported significant correlations between subjective complaint and performance on some, but not all, memory tasks (Hulicka, 1982; Riege, 1982; Zelinski et al., 1980). Other studies have failed to find relationships at greater than chance expectations (Gilewski, 1983; Larrabee & Levin, 1986; Perlmutter, 1978; Zarit, Cole, & Guider, 1981). In a study of a small group ($N = 17$) of independently living "young" old adults, complaints of everyday memory difficulty were not predictive of either concurrent memory test performance or worsened health or cognitive functioning an average of 27 months later (Reisberg & Ferris, 1982). As reviewed by Gilewski and Zelinski (1986), memory complaint questionnaires used in studies of older adults have shown test–retest reliability coefficients from .22 to .64 and internal consistency coefficients from .61 to .93.

Thus, older adults' complaints of memory difficulty, even when assessed with carefully constructed questionnaires, may not be reliable or valid predictors of objective memory task performance. However, as Gilewski and Zelinski (1986) suggested, comparing memory complaint with objective memory task performance may provide important information to assist in differential diagnosis. Available research supports the conclusion that depressed older adults tend to complain about memory difficulty, even though they may show no memory performance deficits (Gilewski, 1983; Kahn, Zarit, Hilbert, & Niederehe, 1975; Larrabee & Levin, 1986). Furthermore, memory complaints have been shown to decrease as depressed older adults improve over the course of treatment for their depression (Popkin, Gallagher, Thompson, & Moore, 1982). Conversely, AD patients show clear memory performance impairment but subjectively overestimate their memory ability (McGlynn & Kaszniak, 1991; Reisberg, Gordon, McCarthy, Ferris, & de Leon, 1985).

Sign–Symptom Overlap and Problems in Identifying Depression in Cognitively Impaired Older Adults

Considerable difficulties are encountered in assessing for depression in older adults with known or suspected cognitive impairment. For example, memory difficulty, agitation, disrupted sleep–wake cycle, and personality changes such as apathy and increased dependency are classical symptoms of AD that may be mistaken for depressive signs of poor concentration, decreased interest, changes in psychomotor activity, sleep disturbance, and fatigue (for reviews see Kaszniak, Sadeh, & Stern, 1985; Raskind & Peskind, 1992; Rubin, Zorumski, & Burke, 1988). In a somewhat-recent study, depression-related symptoms (decreased interest, decreased concentration and energy, and psychomotor activity changes) were reported significantly more often in mild AD patients than in age-matched normal controls; however, over a 34-month period, a major depressive syndrome was not diagnosed in any of the participating subjects (Rubin, 1990). Thus, depression-related symptoms may be common in the early stages of AD and may occur in the absence of the full syndrome of clinical depression (cf. Burke, Rubin, Morris, & Berg, 1988; Merriam, Aronson, Gaston, Wey, & Katz, 1988). Although the difficulty that is associated with differential diagnosis of normal aging phenomena, major depressive disorder, and primary degenerative dementia of the Alzheimer type has been acknowledged in the *DSM-III-R*, the prescribed guidelines for differential diagnosis are based on subjective interpretation of qualitative differences in the relative "prominence" of presenting symptoms (American Psychiatric Association, 1987, pp. 106, 220, and 221). Moreover, the *DSM-III-R* fails to provide sufficient criteria for the dual diagnosis of AD and depressive syndrome (Burns, 1991). This problem is currently being addressed by groups who are working on the fourth edition of the *DSM* (*DSM-IV*, American Psychiatric Association, in press; see Tucker et al., 1992; Popkin & Tucker, 1992).

The use of standard screening instruments for the assessment of depression requires particular caution when applied to patients who are suspected of having a dementing illness. Reisberg et al. (1986) pointed out that many items of the HRSD "are clearly inappropriate for the Alzheimer's patients with impaired cognitive and functional abilities" (p. 5). Similarly, Cummings (1989) cautioned that "overreliance on mood-independent ancillary symptoms may lead to overdiagnosis of depression in demented patients" (p. 237). One self-report depression screening instrument, the GDS (Brink et al., 1982; Yesavage et al., 1983), appears to have advantages over other available scales, in that it was developed specifically for use with older adults. The GDS is a 30-item questionnaire with clearly and simply phrased items and a *yes–no* response format, which takes only 8–10 min to administer. The item content focuses on mood and mood-related symptoms and excludes those somatic items that may reflect physical illness in the elderly. A score of 11 or greater is taken as an indication of possible depression. The GDS has been shown to be reliable and valid for the assessment of depression in elderly outpatients, inpatients, and individuals who reside in nursing homes (Lesher, 1986; Parmelee, Lawton, & Katz, 1989; Scogin, 1987; Yesavage et al., 1983). Some investigators have reported no differential reliability or validity of the GDS observed for AD patients compared with that for cognitively intact institutional residents (Parmelee & Katz, 1990; Yesavage, Rose, & Lapp, 1981), whereas others have reported less favorable sensitivity and specificity (Burke, Houston, Boust, & Rosaforte, 1989; Kafonek et al., 1989). Additional research investigating variables affecting the reliability and validity of the GDS when used with AD or other dementia patients is clearly needed.

Although the GDS may have merit as a screening instrument for depression in older adults with suspected memory impairment, the possibility of false negative results must be considered. Results of a number of studies have indicated that, compared with patient self-report, collateral sources (i.e., spouses and other relatives) and trained clinical observers consistently rate significantly higher frequencies of depression-related symptoms in mildly demented AD patients (Burke et al., 1988; Knesevich, Martin, Berg, & Danziger, 1983; Mackenzie, Robiner, & Knopman, 1989; Miller, 1980; Rubin, 1990; Teri & Wagner, 1991). Thus, AD patients may endorse fewer depression-related symptoms than do their clinicians or caregivers. This may reflect the impaired awareness of illness and deficits that appears to accompany AD (McGlynn & Kaszniak, 1991; Kaszniak, Di-Traglia, & Trosset, 1993); it may also reflect the possibility that accurate reporting of the frequency and severity of depression-related symptoms requires an intact ability to understand the question posed and to recall events within a given period (Burke et al., 1988; Teri & Wagner, 1992). However, it also remains possible that discrepancies between depression-related symptoms reported by AD patients and their collateral sources could be due, in some cases, to an overreporting of symptoms by the caregivers. Consistent with this possibility, Mackenzie et al. (1989) reported that family members tended to report that a patient was depressed when they were uncertain of the patient's current mood or need for treatment and that discrepant reports occurred more often in cases for which patients had a prior history of psychiatric illness and treatment. Burke et al. (1988) suggested that collateral sources may be more sensitive to or have a "heightened awareness" of depression-related symptoms that occur in AD and that they may be more likely to overreport them.

Given the possibilities of both patient and caregiver bias in reporting depression-related symptoms, depression screening in patients who are suspected of dementia should optimally include information from both patient self-report and caregiver report, in addition to direct clinician observation of patient behavior. Among those instruments that are appropriate for obtaining caregiver report of AD patient depression-related symptoms, the recently developed Columbia University Scale for Psychopathology in Alzheimer's Disease (CUSPAD; Devanand et al., 1992) appears most promising. The CUSPAD is a brief (requiring 10–25 min to administer to an informant) semistructured instrument that can be administered by a trained lay interviewer. In development of the CUSPAD, particular emphasis was placed on the use of follow-up questions (e.g., regarding frequency, persistence, and qualitative features of reported symptoms) to help establish operational definitions for the presence of depression and other symptoms of psychopathology in AD. Devanand et al. reported high interrater (i.e., between a trained lay interviewer and a research psychiatrist) reliability for the CUSPAD, as well as divergent validity for the depression- and other-scale items. Another promising new instrument is the Cornell Scale for

Depression in Dementia (CSDD; Alexopoulos, Abrams, Young, & Shamoian, 1988), which is a 19-item scale requiring a trained clinician to obtain information from both patient and informant. Additional research is needed to establish the psychometric properties of the CSDD and the relationship of both the CSDD and CUSPAD depression measures to other indices of depression.

Once the possibility of depression in a patient who is suspected of memory impairment has been established through screening with the GDS, CUSPAD, and/or CSDD, the patient should receive more comprehensive evaluation and potential treatment of depression. The differentiation of patients with depression complicating AD or other dementing illness from those with the dementia syndrome or depression remains difficult, even with comprehensive evaluation. Various clinicians and investigators have suggested patient history and behavioral features that may be useful in making this differentiation (see Table 3), although the validity of such guidelines remains to be clearly established. There is clearly overlap between the diagnostic groups for several of these features (e.g., patient complaint of deficit, emotional reaction to illness, valuation of accomplishments), particularly when dementia-syndrome-of-depression patients are compared with those AD patients with very mild dementia. This list of features should therefore be viewed as assisting in raising or lowering the suspicion of dementia syndrome of depression, rather than in confirming diagnosis.

Overlap between depression and dementia is also seen in performance on standardized intellectual and neuropsychological tests. Psychomotor

TABLE 3
History and Behavioral Features That Are Helpful in Differentiating
Alzheimer's Disease From Dementia Syndrome of Depression

Measure	Alzheimer's disease	Dementia syndrome of depression
Symptom duration at time of seeking medical attention	Long	Short
Previous psychiatric history	Unusual	Usual
Progression of symptoms	Slow	Rapid
Patient complaint of deficit	Variable	Abundant
Emotional reaction	Variable	Marked distress
Patient valuation of accomplishments	Variable	Minimized
Behavior congruent with cognitive deficits	Usual	Unusual
Delusions	Mood independent	Mood congruent
Mood disorder	Environmentally responsive	Persistent

Note. See Cummings, 1989; Emery, 1988; Kaszniak, 1987, 1990; Kaszniak, Saden, & Stern, 1985; La Rue, 1992; LaRue, Dessonville, & Jarvik, 1985; Wells, 1979.

slowing in depression contributes to lower scores on any cognitive task for which speed of performance enters into scoring. As a result, depressed older adults may score in a range similar to that for mildly demented AD patients on such tasks (Hart, Kwentus, Wade, & Hamer, 1987). Overlap between the memory task (untimed) performance of depressed and mildly demented older adults has also been described. As reviewed by Niederehe (1986), the research literature concerned with memory and other cognitive functioning in depressed middle-aged and older adults has yielded contradictory results. Some studies report depression and cognitive impairment to be significantly associated, whereas other studies find few significant differences between depressed patients and healthy controls. There is also controversy concerning the question of whether cognitive impairment is more likely in older depressed patients than in younger depressed patients. Many clinicians (e.g., Wells, 1983) believe symptoms that mimic dementia occur more often in older depressed patients, and there is some empirical evidence to support this belief (Cavanaugh & Wettstein, 1983; Donnelly, Waldman, Murphy, Wyatt, & Goodwin, 1980). However, Niederehe, who administered various memory tests to younger and older (20–45-year-olds vs. 55–80-year-olds) depressed and healthy women, reported a general lack of the Age × Depression interactions that would have been expected if older depressives were more susceptible to memory impairment than were younger depressives. Other studies (e.g., La Rue, Goodman, & Spar, in press; La Rue, Spar, & Hill, 1986) have also failed to find significant age differences between cognitively intact and cognitively impaired depressed older adults. Age alone is thus not a reliable predictor of cognitive dysfunction in depression. Reviews of the literature on depression and memory in older age (La Rue, 1992; Niederehe, 1986; Raskin, 1986) have suggested that higher probability of memory impairment is related to inpatient status, greater severity of depression (particularly when symptoms include delusions, severe anxiety, or agitation), poor premorbid social competence, and low premorbid intelligence.

Compared with AD patients, those with dementia syndrome of depression (as determined by coexistent depression and cognitive impairment, with improved cognitive functioning in response to treatment with antidepressant medication) have been found to show more severe depressive symptoms but milder cognitive deficits and fewer problems with everyday activities, such as finding one's way around familiar neighborhoods (Reynolds et al., 1988). Specific patterns of, and qualitative features within, neuropsychological test performance (as reviewed later) have also been reported to differentiate AD from dementia-syndrome-of-depression patients. However, the results of long-term follow-up investigations of dementia-syndrome-of-depression patients suggest the need to clinically interpret such group differences cautiously.

Ambiguity in the Long-Term Prognosis of Patients With Symptoms of Both Dementia and Depression

The long-term prognosis for patients with concomitant dementia and depression remains unclear. Some investigators (e.g., Rabins et al., 1984) have reported stable (i.e., over a 2-year follow-up) improvement in mood and cognitive functioning in patients who met diagnostic criteria for both dementia and depression and were treated for their depression. Others (e.g., Kral & Emery, 1989) have reported that most (89%) patients with evidence of concomitant depression and dementia, who were successfully treated for depression, eventually develop a progressive dementia syndrome when followed over very long intervals (i.e., 18 years). Further complicating matters is the possibility that dementia may initially present as depression, without marked cognitive deficit, in some cases. Reding, Haycox, and Blass (1985), in a 3-year follow-up study, showed that 16 (57%) of 28 depressed patients, who were not initially thought to be demented, went on to develop frank dementia. Retrospective analysis of other data obtained on these patients suggested the following risk factors for the development of dementia in depressed older adults: older age; evidence of cerebrovascular, extrapyramidal, or spinocerebellar disease; confusion or somnolence in response to low doses of tricyclic antidepressant medication; or more than two errors on a brief mental status questionnaire. In a similar study, Nussbaum, Kaszniak, Allender, and Rapcsak (1991) found that 8 of 35 (23%) patients, who were initially diagnosed as depressed but not demented, showed a significant decline in mental status over an average 18-month follow-up. Compared with those depressed patients who did not decline, the deteriorating patients had more frequently abnormal electrocardiograms and neuroradiological imaging results at the time of initial examination, although performance on a battery of neuropsychological tests did not reliably differentiate the groups. Thus, even those elderly patients with initial improvement of mood and cognitive functioning after treatment of their depression may go on to develop a progressive dementia. Although some demographic and clinical features (e.g., older age, evidence of cardiovascular or cerebrovascular disease, and brain imaging abnormalities) may be associated with the development of dementia in depressed older adults, the relative strength of the predictive validity for such features is unknown. The lack of predictive validity for the neuropsychological battery that was used in the Nussbaum et al. (1991) study suggests that guidelines for interpretation of neuropsychological test results in differential diagnosis of patients with coexistent symptoms of dementia and depression (such as those described later) must be used cautiously. Periodic reevaluation of patients presenting with concomitant memory impairment and depression, even after apparent improvement of cognitive deficits when depressive symptoms abate, appears indicated.

NEUROPSYCHOLOGICAL TEST PERFORMANCE OF PATIENTS WITH DEPRESSION

As noted earlier, depressed patients often complain of memory and other cognitive (e.g., concentration) difficulty and may also show some evidence of impairment on neuropsychological testing. Except for those more severely depressed older patients who qualify for a diagnosis of dementia syndrome of depression, cognitive deficits are relatively mild for most depressed patients (for reviews of relevant studies see Johnson & Magaro, 1987; La Rue, 1992; Niederehe, 1986). As illustrated in a series of studies by Weingartner and his colleagues (see Weingartner, 1986), cognitive processes that are presumed to require greater effort are the ones generally most impaired in depression. In this context, effort is defined in terms of demands placed on a hypothetical limited capacity attentional system. Those tasks that make little attentional capacity demand are termed *automatic*, whereas those that require much attentional capacity are termed *effortful* (Hasher & Zacks, 1979). Craik and McDowd (1987) used performance decrement on a secondary reaction-time task to index attentional resource "cost." They showed that recall requires more processing resources (effort) than does recognition, for both younger and older adults. Recent data showing depressed older adults to be impaired (in relation to age-matched controls) on free recall, but not recognition memory testing, have therefore been interpreted as consistent with decreased effort of memory processing in depression (Blau & Ober, 1988; Nussbaum, Kaszniak, Swanda, & Allender, 1988). In contrast, mildly-to-moderately demented AD patients show deficits in both recall and recognition memory (Corkin, 1982; Wilson, Kaszniak, Bacon, Fox, & Kelly, 1982).

Comparison of recall and recognition memory task performance thus appears to be helpful in attempting to differentiate the memory impairments of mildly demented AD patients from those of patients with depression. It also appears that qualitative analysis of error patterns in recognition memory task performance may be helpful. Niederehe (1986) reported no significant overall difference in verbal recognition memory performance due to age (younger vs. older adults) or diagnosis (presence vs. absence of depression). However, both the young and old depressed groups showed conservative decision criteria (i.e., a disproportionate number of false negative errors) compared with nondepressed subjects. Furthermore, this "cautious" response style appeared to be greater among the older subjects. Other investigators (Corwin, Peselow, & Dash, 1988; Miller & Lewis, 1977) have found similar evidence for a conservative response bias in older adult depressed patients. In contrast, AD patients have been reported to show an abnormally liberal response bias with both verbal (Branconnier, Cole, Spera, & De Vitt, 1982) and pictorial recognition memory tasks (Snodgrass & Corwin, 1988). Snodgrass and Corwin provided an excellent review and comparison of different theoretic models of yes–no recognition memory task performance and associated indices of discrimination and response bias. The California Verbal Learning Test (CVLT; Delis, Freeland, Kramer, & Kaplan, 1988; Delis, Kramer, Kaplan, & Ober, 1987) contains both free-recall and recognition memory tasks and provides for calculation of response bias. Although further research is needed, a recent investigation (Massman, Delis, Butters, Dupont, & Gillin, 1992) suggests that the CVLT has clinical validity for the differentiation of AD patients from depressed patients.

As already noted, some data indicate that depressed patients learn and remember less than do normal controls only under conditions that demand effortful processing. However, depressed individuals might show normal storage, as reflected by rate of forgetting, once initial learning of new information is equated to that of controls. In contrast, mildly demented AD patients might be expected to show abnormally rapid forgetting, even under conditions in which initial learning is optimized. This expectation is based on (a) the marked damage that occurs early in the course of AD to the hippocampal formation and its connections to the cortex (Hyman, Van Hoesen, Damasio, & Barnes, 1984; Hyman, Van Hoesen, Kromer, & Damasio, 1986) and (b) previous demonstrations of abnormally rapid forgetting in patients with amnesic syndromes that are secondary to bilateral hippocampal damage (e.g., Squire & Cohen, 1984). Indeed, AD patients have demonstrated more rapid forgetting of words (over a 15-s–2-min interval) after several learning trials than other patients whose memory deficits are not thought to be caused by hippocampal damage (Moss, Albert, Butters, & Payne, 1986).

Hart, Kwentus, Taylor, and Harkins (1987) directly tested rate-of-forgetting differences between age-matched depressed older adults, mildly demented AD patients, and normal controls. Rate of forgetting line drawings of common objects (tested through a yes–no recognition procedure) was examined, after the groups had been equated for acquisition by variation of stimulus exposure time. Depressed and AD patients both showed learning impairments, but only the AD group showed rapid forgetting in the first 10 min after learning to criterion. Hart et al. interpreted these data as suggesting that deficient consolidation contributes to memory impairment in AD, but not in depression. Their results are of particular clinical interest because the depressed and AD patients performed similarly on most of a set of commonly used neuropsychological tests.

Thus, even when mildly demented AD patients and depressed older adults cannot be differentiated on the basis of initial learning ability, examination of rate of forgetting might be helpful. Note, however, that AD patients may not reveal evidence of rapid forgetting when they are not equated to normals for initial learning (Becker, Boller, Saxton, & McGonigle-Gibson, 1987) or when rate of forgetting is evaluated over the interval of 10 min to 1 week after initial learning (Kopelman, 1985). Future research will need to resolve issues concerning the intervals over which forgetting is measured. Additional research on the impact of stimulus exposure time (or other ways of equating initial learning) on rate of forgetting (cf. Martone, Butters, & Trauner, 1986) is needed before the diagnostic validity of rate of forgetting can be uncritically accepted.

Standardized memory assessment instruments that allow a distinction to be made between the hypothetical memory processes of storage and retrieval have also been shown to have some validity in distinguishing dementia from depression. One such instrument is the Buschke Selective Reminding Test (SRT; Buschke, 1973; Buschke & Fuld, 1974). AD patients obtain lower scores than do age-matched controls on SRT measures of storage and retrieval from long-term memory (Weingartner et al., 1981). Hart, Kwentus, Taylor, and Hamer (1987) found that depressed older adults, although impaired in relation to controls on a recall measure from the SRT, could be differentiated from AD patients on the basis of storage and recognition memory measures. Another test that allows a similar distinction between storage and retrieval is the Fuld Object Memory Evaluation (OME; Fuld 1981, 1984). The OME has been shown to be a better discriminator of depressed versus demented older adults than are various other commonly used memory tests (La Rue, D'Elia, Clark, Spar, & Jarvik, 1986).

NEUROPSYCHOLOGICAL ASSESSMENT AND DIFFERENTIATION OF OLDER ADULTS WITH THE DEMENTIA SYNDROME OF DEPRESSION

The research literature concerning the neuropsychological test performance of dementia-syndrome-of-depression patients remains small and difficult to interpret because of various methodological problems (e.g., criterion confounds, in which the same cognitive tests are used to identify and classify patients and to examine performance patterns between groups). As already noted, the dementia syndrome of depression likely represents a heterogeneous mixture of patients. Some of these patients may have a combination of a primary dementing illness (e.g., AD or VaD) and depression and will remain cognitively impaired after effective treatment of their depression. Others would appear to have cognitive impairment that is secondary to their depression and will show improvement of both cognition and affect after effective treatment. However, even among this second group, some patients, when followed over a number of years, may manifest a clear progressive dementia. Thus, it is not surprising to find that depressed patients form clusters of intact and different patterns of impaired performance on various neuropsychological tests, such as the CVLT (Massman et al., 1992). In various reviews of the research literature that is relevant to the differentiation of dementia from depression (e.g., Cummings, 1989; Emery, 1986; Kaszniak, 1987, 1990; Kaszniak et al., 1985; La Rue, 1992; La Rue, Dessonville, & Jarvik, 1985), attempts have been made to determine those quantitative and qualitative aspects of neuropsychological test performance that may be helpful in this diagnostic task. Those features most frequently identified by these investigators are listed in Table 4.

As with those historical and behavioral features that are listed in Table 3, the neuropsychological test features summarized in Table 4 should be viewed as guidelines for increasing or decreasing suspicion of a patient having AD versus the dementia syndrome of depression, rather than as providing definitive diagnoses. Also note that those features that are listed in Table 4 apply only to comparisons of dementia syndrome of depression with AD patients. Those with different dementia etiologies, such as VaD, may appear quite different from AD patients on various neuropsychological tests. Recent research suggests that differentiating dementia-syndrome-of-depression patients from those with VaD caused by subcortical infarctions or from those with other subcortical dementias may be particularly difficult. For example, Massman et al. (1992) found that, among a group of depressed patients, the CVLT revealed a subgroup that showed the same pattern of deficits as that shown by patients with Huntington's disease, which is typically regarded as a prototypical subcortical dementing illness (see chapter 3 in this book).

Despite continuing research efforts, it remains quite difficult to distinguish dementia-syndrome-of-depression patients from AD and VaD pa-

TABLE 4
Qualitative Features in Neuropsychological Test Data That Are Helpful in Differentiating Alzheimer's Disease From Dementia Syndrome of Depression

Measure	Alzheimer's disease	Dementia syndrome of depression
Recognition memory	Impaired	Relatively intact
False positive recognition memory errors	Greater	Fewer
"Don't know" errors (controversial)	Unusual	Usual
Performance on "automatic" encoding tasks	Impaired	Intact
Effort in attempting to perform tasks	Good	Poor
Performance on tasks of similar difficulty	Consistent	Variable
Semantic organization	Unhelpful	Helpful
Prompting	Less helpful	Helpful
Awareness of impairment	Impaired	Intact

Note. See Cummings, 1989; Emery, 1988; Kaszniak, 1990; La Rue, 1992; LaRue, Dessonville, & Jarvik, 1985; Wells, 1979.

tients, particularly when dementia severity is relatively mild. Clearly, additional longer term longitudinal studies allowing investigation of potential predictive validity of neuropsychological and other clinical assessment measures are needed. Until such additional data become available, the clinician is well advised to proceed cautiously in contributing to this important, although difficult, diagnostic problem.

REFERENCES

Alexopoulos, G. S., Abrams, R. C., Young, R. C., & Shamoian, C. A. (1988). Cornell scale for depression in dementia. *Biological Psychiatry, 23*, 271–284.

Allen, A., & Blazer, D. G. (1991). Mood disorders. In J. Sadavoy, L. W. Lazarus, & L. F. Jarvik (Eds.), *Comprehensive review of geriatric psychiatry* (pp. 337–351). Washington, DC: American Psychiatric Press.

American Psychiatric Association. (1980). *Diagnostic and statistical manual of mental disorders* (3rd ed.). Washington, DC: Author.

American Psychiatric Association. (1987). *Diagnostic and statistical manual of mental disorders* (3rd ed., rev.). Washington, DC: Author.

American Psychiatric Association. (in press). *Diagnostic and statistical manual of mental disorders* (4th ed.). Washington, DC: Author.

Bayles, K. A., & Kaszniak, A. W. (1987). *Communication and cognition in normal aging and dementia.* Boston: College-Hill/Little, Brown.

Becker, J. T., Boller, F., Saxton, J., & McGonigle-Gibson, K. L. (1987). Normal rates of forgetting of verbal and non-verbal material in Alzheimer's disease. *Cortex, 23*, 59–72.

Benedict, K. B., & Nacoste, D. B. (1990). Dementia and depression: A framework for addressing difficulties in differential diagnosis. *Clinical Psychology Review, 10*, 513–537.

Bieliauskas, L. A. (1993). Depressed or not depressed? That is the question. *Journal of Clinical and Experimental Neuropsychology, 15*, 119–134.

Blau, E., & Ober, B. A. (1988). The effect of depression on verbal memory in older adults. *Journal of Clinical and Experimental Neuropsychology, 10*, 81.

Blazer, D., Hughes, D. C., & George, L. K. (1987). The epidemiology of depression in an elderly community population. *Gerontologist, 27*, 281–287.

Blessed, G., Tomlinson, B. E., & Roth, M. (1968). The association between quantitative measures of dementia and of senile change in the cerebral grey matter of elderly subjects. *British Journal of Psychiatry, 114*, 797–811.

Branconnier, R. J., Cole, J. O., Spera, K. F., & De Vitt, D. R. (1982). Recall and recognition as diagnostic indices of malignant memory loss in senile dementia: A Bayesian analysis. *Experimental Aging Research, 8*, 189–193.

Brink, T. L., Yesavage, J. A., Lum, O., Hursema, P. H., Adey, M., & Rose, T. L. (1982). Screening tests for geriatric depression. *Clinical Gerontologist, 1*, 37–43.

Burke, W., Houston, M., Boust, S., & Rosaforte, W. (1989). Use of the Geriatric Depression Scale in dementia of the Alzheimer's type. *Journal of the American Geriatrics Society, 37*, 856–860.

Burke, W. J., Rubin, E. H., Morris, J., & Berg, L. (1988). Symptoms of "depression" in senile dementia of the Alzheimer's type. *Alzheimer's Disease and Associated Disorders, 2*, 356–362.

Burns, A. (1991). Affective symptoms in Alzheimer's disease. *International Journal of Geriatric Psychiatry, 6*, 371–376.

Buschke, H. (1973). Selective reminding for analysis of memory and learning. *Journal of Verbal Learning and Verbal Behavior, 12*, 543–550.

Buschke, H., & Fuld, P. A. (1974). Evaluating storage, retention, and retrieval in disordered memory and learning. *Neurology, 24*, 1019–1025.

Caine, E. D., Lyness, J. M., & King, D. A. (1993). Reconsidering depression in the elderly. *American Journal of Geriatric Psychiatry, 1*, 4–20.

Cavanaugh, S., & Wettstein, R. M. (1983). The relationship between severity of depression, cognitive dysfunction, and age in medical inpatients. *American Journal of Psychiatry, 140*, 495–496.

Chui, H. C., Victoroff, J. I., Margolin, D., Jagust, W., Shankle, R., & Katzman, R. (1992). Criteria for the diagnosis of ischemic vascular dementia proposed by the State of California Alzheimer's Disease Diagnostic and Treatment Centers. *Neurology, 42*, 473–480.

Corkin, S. (1982). Some relationships between global amnesias and the memory impairments in Alzheimer's disease. In S. Corkin, K. L. Davis, J. H. Growdon, E. Usdin, & R. L. Wurtman (Eds.), *Alzheimer's disease: A report of progress in research* (pp. 149–164). New York: Raven Press.

Corwin, J., Peselow, E., & Dash, S. (1988). Effects of depression on response bias, and explicit and implicit memory tasks [abstract]. *Journal of Clinical and Experimental Neuropsychology, 10*, 81.

Craik, F. I. M., & McDowd, J. M. (1987). Age differences in recall and recognition. *Journal of Experimental Psychology: Learning, Memory, and Cognition, 13*, 474–479.

Cummings, J. L. (1989). Dementia and depression: An evolving enigma. *Journal of Neuropsychiatry and Clinical Neurosciences, 1*, 236–242.

Cummings, J. L., & Benson, D. F. (1986). Dementia of the Alzheimer type: An inventory of diagnostic clinical features. *Journal of the American Geriatrics Society, 34*, 12–19.

Cummings, J. L., & Benson, D. F. (1992). *Dementia: A clinical approach* (2nd ed.). Boston: Butterworth-Heinemann.

Delis, D. C., Freeland, J., Kramer, J. H., & Kaplan, E. (1988). Integrating clinical assessment with cognitive neuroscience: Construct validation of the California Verbal Learning Test. *Journal of Consulting and Clinical Psychology, 56*, 123–130.

Delis, D. C., Kramer, J. H., Kaplan, E., & Ober, B. A. (1987). *The California verbal learning test—Research edition.* New York: Psychological Corporation.

Depression Guideline Panel. (1993). *Depression in primary care: Vol. 1. Detection and diagnosis. Clinical Practice Guideline, No. 5* (AHCPR Publication No. 93-0550). Rockville, MD: U.S. Department of Health and Human Services, Public Health Service, Agency for Health Care Policy and Research.

Devanand, D. P., Miller, L., Richards, M., Marder, K., Bell, K., Mayeux, R., & Stern, Y. (1992). The Columbia University scale for psychopathology in Alzheimer's disease. *Archives of Neurology, 49,* 371–376.

Donnelly, E. F., Waldman, I. N., Murphy, D. L., Wyatt, R. J., & Goodwin, F. K. (1980). Primary affective disorder: Thought disorder in depression. *Journal of Abnormal Psychology, 89,* 315–319.

Emery, V. O. B. (1988). *Pseudodementia: A theoretical and empirical discussion.* Cleveland, OH: Western Reserve Geriatric Education Center.

Folks, D. G., & Kinney, F. C. (1991). Consultation-liason in the general hospital. In J. Sadavoy, L. W. Lazarus, & L. F. Jarvik (Eds.), *Comprehensive review of geriatric psychiatry* (pp. 565–581). Washington, DC: American Psychiatric Press.

Folstein, M. F., Anthony, J. C., Parhad, I., Duffy, B., & Gruenberg, E. M. (1985). The meaning of cognitive impairment in the elderly. *Journal of the American Geriatrics Society, 33,* 228–235.

Folstein, M. F., Folstein, S., & McHugh, P. R. (1975). Mini-mental state: A practical method for grading the cognitive state of patients for the clinician. *Journal of Psychiatric Research, 12,* 189–198.

Folstein, M. F., & McHugh, P. R. (1978). Dementia syndrome of depression. *Aging, 7,* 87–93.

Fry, P. S. (1986). *Depression, stress, and adaptations in the elderly: Psychological assessment and intervention.* Rockville, MD: Aspen Systems.

Fuld, P. A. (1981). *The Fuld object memory evaluation.* Chicago: Stoelting Instrument Company.

Fuld, P. A. (1984). Test profile of cholinergic dysfunction and of Alzheimer-type dementia. *Journal of Clinical Neuropsychology, 6,* 380–392.

Gallagher, D. (1986a). Assessment of depression by interview methods and psychiatric rating scales. In L. W. Poon (Ed.), *Handbook for clinical memory assessment in older adults* (pp. 202–212). Washington, DC: American Psychological Association.

Gallagher, D. (1986b). The Beck Depression Inventory and older adults: Review of its development and utility. *Clinical Gerontologist, 5,* 149–163.

Gallagher, D., Slife, B., Rose, T., & Okarma, T. (1982). Psychological correlates of immunologic disease in older adults. *Clinical Gerontologist, 1,* 51–58.

Garcia, C. A., Reding, M. J., & Blass, J. P. (1981). Overdiagnosis of dementia. *Journal of the American Geriatrics Society, 29,* 407–410.

Gatz, M., & Pearson, C. G. (1988). Ageism revised and the provision of psychological services. *American Psychologist, 43,* 184–188.

Gilewski, M. J. (1983). Self-reported memory functioning in young-old and old-old age: Structural models of predictive factors (Doctoral dissertation, University of Southern California, 1983). *Dissertation Abstracts International, 43,* 4170B.

Gilewski, M. J., & Zelinski, E. M. (1986). Questionnaire assessment of memory complaints. In L. W. Poon (Ed.), *Handbook for clinical memory assessment of older adults* (pp. 93–107). Washington, DC: American Psychological Association.

Greenwald, B. S., Kramer-Ginsberg, E., Marin, D. B., Laitman, L. B., Hermann, C. K., Mohs, R. C., & Davis, K. L. (1989). Dementia with coexistent major depression. *American Journal of Psychiatry, 11,* 1472–1478.

Gurland, B., & Toner, J. (1983). Differentiating dementia from nondementing conditions. In R. Mayeux & W. G. Rosen (Eds.), *The dementias* (pp. 1–17). New York: Raven Press.

Haase, G. R. (1977). Diseases presenting as dementia. In C. E. Wells (Ed.), *Dementia* (2nd ed., pp. 27–67). Philadelphia: F. A. Davis.

Hachinski, V. C., Iliff, L. D., Zilhka, E., Du Boulay, G. H., McAllister, V. L., Marshall, J., Russell, R. W., & Symon, L. (1975). Cerebral blood flow in dementia. *Archives of Neurology, 32,* 632–637.

Hachinski, V. C., Lassen, N. A., & Marshall, J. (1974). Multi-infarct dementia, a cause of mental deterioration in the elderly. *Lancet, 2,* 207–210.

Hamilton, M. (1967). Development of a rating scale for primary depressive illness. *British Journal of Social and Clinical Psychology, 6,* 278–296.

Harris, M. J., Gierz, M., & Lohr, J. B. (1989). Recognition and treatment of depression in Alzheimer's disease. *Geriatrics, 44,* 26–30.

Hart, R. P., Kwentus, J. A., Taylor, J. R., & Hamer, R. M. (1987). Selective reminding procedure in depression and dementia. *Psychology and Aging, 2,* 111–115.

Hart, R. P., Kwentus, J. A., Taylor, J. R., & Harkins, S. W. (1987). Rate of forgetting in dementia and depression. *Journal of Consulting and Clinical Psychology, 55,* 101–105.

Hart, R. P., Kwentus, J. A., Wade, J. B., & Hamer, R. M. (1987). Digit symbol performance in mild dementia and depression. *Journal of Consulting and Clinical Psychology, 55,* 236–238.

Hasher, L., & Zacks, R. T. (1979). Automatic and effortful processes in memory. *Journal of Experimental Psychology: General, 108,* 356–388.

Helzer, J. E., Robins, L. N., McEvoy, L. T., Spitznagel, E. L., Stoltzman, R. K., Farmer, A., & Brockington, I. F. (1985). A comparison of clinical and Diagnostic Interview Schedule diagnoses. *Archives of General Psychiatry, 42,* 657–666.

Heston, L. L., & Mastri, A. R. (1982). Age at onset of Pick's and Alzheimer's dementia: Implications for diagnosis and research. *Journal of Gerontology, 37,* 422–424.

Hulicka, I. M. (1982). Memory functioning in late adulthood. In F. I. M. Craik & S. Trehub (Eds.), *Advances in the study of communication and affect: Vol. 8. Aging and cognitive processes* (pp. 331–351). New York: Plenum.

Hyman, B. T., Van Hoesen, G. W., Damasio, A. R., & Barnes, C. L. (1984). Alzheimer's disease: Cell-specific pathology isolates the hippocampal formation. *Science, 225*, 1168–1170.

Hyman, B. T., Van Hoesen, G. W., Kromer, L. J., & Damasio, A. R. (1986). Perforant pathway changes and the memory impairment of Alzheimer's disease. *Annals of Neurology, 20*, 472–481.

Ineichen, B. (1987). Measuring the rising tide: How many dementia cases will there be by 2001? *British Journal of Psychiatry, 150*, 193–200.

Johnson, M. H., & Magaro, P. A. (1987). Effects of mood and severity on memory processes in depression and mania. *Psychological Bulletin, 101*, 28–40.

Jorm, A. F., Korten, A. E., & Henderson, A. S. (1987). The prevalence of dementia: A quantitative integration of the literature. *Acta Psychiatrica Scandinavica, 76*, 465–479.

Kafonek, S., Ettinger, W., Roca, R., Kittner, S., Taylor, N., & German, P. (1989). Instruments for screening for depression and dementia in a long-term care facility. *Journal of the American Geriatrics Society, 37*, 29–34.

Kahn, R. L., Zarit, S. H., Hilbert, N. M., & Niederehe, G. (1975). Memory complaint and memory impairment in the aged. *Archives of General Psychiatry, 32*, 1569–1573.

Kaszniak, A. W. (1986). The neuropsychology of dementia. In I. Grant & K. M. Adams (Eds.), *Neuropsychological assessment of neuropsychiatric disorders* (pp. 172–220). New York: Oxford University Press.

Kaszniak, A. W. (1987). Neuropsychological consultation to geriatricians: Issues in the assessment of memory complaints. *Clinical Neuropsychologist, 1*, 35–46.

Kaszniak, A. W. (1990). Psychological assessment of the aging individual. In J. E. Birren & K. W. Schaie (Eds.), *Handbook of the psychology of aging* (3rd ed., pp. 427–445). San Diego, CA: Academic Press.

Kaszniak, A. W., & Allender, J. (1985). Psychological assessment of depression in older adults. In G. M. Chaisson-Stewart (Ed.), *Depression in the elderly: An interdisciplinary approach* (pp. 107–160). New York: Wiley.

Kaszniak, A. W., DiTraglia, G., & Trosset, M. W. (1993, February). *Self-awareness of cognitive deficit in patients with probable Alzheimer's disease.* Paper presented at the 21st annual meeting of the International Neuropsychological Society, Galveston, TX.

Kaszniak, A. W., Sadeh, M., & Stern, L. Z. (1985). Differentiating depression from organic brain syndromes in older age. In G. M. Chaisson-Stewart (Ed.), *Depression in the elderly: An interdisciplinary approach* (pp. 161–189). New York: Wiley.

Katzman, R. (1986). Alzheimer's disease. *New England Journal of Medicine, 314*, 964–973.

Katzman, R., Lasker, B., & Bernstein, N. (1988). Advances in the diagnosis of dementia: Accuracy of diagnosis and consequences of misdiagnosis of disorders causing dementia. In R. D. Terry (Ed.), *Aging and the brain* (pp. 17–62). New York: Raven Press.

Kawas, C. H. (1990). Early clinical diagnosis: Status of NINCDS-ADRDA criteria. In R. E. Becker & E. Giacobini (Eds.), *Alzheimer disease: Current research in early diagnosis*. Washington, DC: Taylor & Francis.

Khachaturian, Z. S. (1985). Diagnosis of Alzheimer's disease. *Archives of Neurology, 42*, 1097–1105.

Kiloh, L. G. (1961). Pseudo-dementia. *Acta Psychiatrica Scandinavica, 37*, 336–351.

Klerman, G. L. (1983). Problems in the definition and diagnosis of depression in the elderly. In L. D. Breslau & M. R. Haug (Eds.), *Depression and aging: Causes, care and consequences* (pp. 3–19). New York: Springer.

Knesevich, J. W., Martin, R. L., Berg, L., & Danziger, W. (1983). Preliminary report on affective symptoms in the early stages of senile dementia of the Alzheimer's type. *American Journal of Psychiatry, 140*, 233–234.

Koenig, H. G., & Blazer, D. G. (1992). Mood disorders and suicide. In J. E. Birren, R. B. Sloane, & G. D. Cohen (Eds.), *Handbook of mental health and aging* (2nd ed., pp. 379–407). San Diego, CA: Academic Press.

Kopelman, M. D. (1985). Rates of forgetting in Alzheimer-type dementia and Korsakoff's syndrome. *Neuropsychologia, 23*, 623–638.

Kral, V. A., & Emery, O. B. (1989). Long-term follow-up of depressive pseudo-dementia of the aged. *Canadian Journal of Psychiatry, 34*, 445–446.

Kramer, M. (1986). Trends of institutionalization and prevalence of mental disorders in nursing homes. In M. S. Harper & B. D. Lebowitz (Eds.), *Mental illness in nursing homes: Agenda for research* (DHHS Publication No. [ADM] 86-1459, pp. 7–26). Rockville, MD: National Institute of Mental Health.

Kukull, W. A., Larson, E. B., Reifler, B. V., Lampe, T. H., Yerby, M. S., & Hughes, J. P. (1990a). Interrater reliability of Alzheimer's disease diagnosis. *Neurology, 40*, 257–260.

Kukull, W. A., Larson, E. B., Reifler, B. V., Lampe, T. H., Yerby, M. S., & Hughes, J. P. (1990b). The validity of 3 clinical diagnostic criteria for Alzheimer's disease. *Neurology, 40*, 1364–1369.

Larrabee, G. L., & Levin, H. S. (1986). Memory self-ratings and objective test performance in a normal elderly sample. *Journal of Clinical and Experimental Neuropsychology, 8*, 275–284.

La Rue, A. (1992). *Aging and neuropsychological assessment*. New York: Plenum.

La Rue, A., D'Elia, L. F., Clark, E. O., Spar, J. E., & Jarvik, L. F. (1986). Clinical tests of memory in dementia, depression, and healthy aging. *Journal of Psychology and Aging, 1*, 69–77.

La Rue, A., Dessonville, C., & Jarvik, L. F. (1985). Aging and mental disorders. In J. E. Birren & K. W. Schaie (Eds.), *Handbook of the psychology of aging* (2nd ed., pp. 664–702). New York: Van Nostrand Reinhold.

La Rue, A., Goodman, S., & Spar, J. E. (in press). Risk factors for memory impairment in geriatric depression. *Neuropsychiatry, Neuropsychology, and Behavioral Neurology*.

La Rue, A., Spar, J., & Hill, C. (1986). Cognitive impairment in late-life depression: Clinical correlates and treatment implications. *Journal of Affective Disorders, 11,* 179–184.

Lesher, E. L. (1986). Validation of the Geriatric Depression Scale among nursing home residents. *Clinical Gerontologist, 4,* 21–28.

Li, G., Shen, Y. C., Chen, C. H., Zhao, Y. W., & Li, S. R. (1989). An epidemiological survey of age-related dementia in an urban area of Bejing. *Acta Psychiatrica Scandinavica, 79,* 557–563.

Loeb, C., & Gandolfo, C. (1983). Diagnostic evaluation of degenerative and vascular dementia. *Stroke, 14,* 399–401.

Lubin, B., & Rinck, C. M. (1986). Assessment of mood and affect in the elderly: The Depression Adjective Check List and the Multiple Affect Adjective Check List. *Clinical Gerontologist, 5,* 187–191.

Mackenzie, T. B., Robiner, W. N., & Knopman, D. S. (1989). Differences between patient and family assessments of depression in Alzheimer's disease. *American Journal of Psychiatry, 146,* 1174–1178.

Martin, E. M., Wilson, R. S., Penn, R. D., Fox, J. H., Clasen, R. A., & Jaroy, S. M. (1987). Cortical biopsy results in Alzheimer's disease: Correlation with cognitive deficits. *Neurology, 37,* 1201–1204.

Martone, M., Butters, N., & Trauner, D. (1986). Some analyses of forgetting of pictorial material in amnesic and demented patients. *Journal of Clinical and Experimental Neuropsychology, 8,* 161–178.

Massman, P. J., Delis, D. C., Butters, N., Dupont, R. M., & Gillin, J. C. (1992). The subcortical dysfunction hypothesis of memory deficits in depression: Neuropsychological validation in a subgroup of patients. *Journal of Clinical and Experimental Neuropsychology, 14,* 687–706.

McCallister, T. W., & Price, T. R. P. (1982). Severe depressive pseudodementia with and without dementia. *American Journal of Psychiatry, 139,* 626–629.

McCartney, J. R. (1986). Physician's assessment of cognitive capacity: Failure to meet the needs of the elderly. *Archives of Internal Medicine, 146,* 177–178.

McGlynn, S. M., & Kaszniak, A. W. (1991). When metacognition fails: Impaired awareness of deficit in Alzheimer's disease. *Journal of Cognitive Neuroscience, 3,* 183–189.

McKhann, G., Drachman, D., Folstein, M., Katzman, R., Price, D., & Stadlin, E. M. (1984). Clinical diagnosis of Alzheimer's disease: Report of the NINCDS-ADRDA work group under the auspices of the Department of Health and Human Services Task Force on Alzheimer's Disease. *Neurology, 34,* 939–944.

Merriam, A. E., Aronson, M. K., Gaston, P., Wey, S. L., & Katz, I. (1988). The psychiatric symptoms of Alzheimer's disease. *Journal of the American Geriatrics Society, 36,* 7–12.

Miller, E., & Lewis, P. (1977). Recognition memory in elderly patients with depression and dementia: A signal detection analysis. *Journal of Abnormal Psychology, 86,* 84–86.

Miller, N. E. (1980). The measurement of mood in senile brain disease: Examiner ratings and self-reports. In J. O. Cole & J. E. Barrett (Eds.), *Psychopathology in the aged* (pp. 97–118). New York: Raven Press.

Molsa, P. K., Paljarvi, L., Rinne, J. O., Rinne, U. K., & Saks, E. (1985). Validity of clinical diagnosis in dementia: A prospective clinicopathological study. *Journal of Neurology, Neurosurgery, and Psychiatry, 48*, 1085–1090.

Morris, J. C., McKeel, D. W., Falling, K., Torach, R. M., & Berg, L. (1988). Validation of clinical diagnostic criteria for Alzheimer's disease. *Annals of Neurology, 24*, 17–22.

Moss, M. B., Albert, M. S., Butters, N., & Payne, M. (1986). Differential patterns of memory loss among patients with Alzheimer's disease, Huntington's disease, and alcoholic Korsakoff's syndrome. *Archives of Neurology, 43*, 239–246.

National Institute on Aging Task Force. (1980). Senility reconsidered: Treatment possibilities for mental impairment in the elderly. *Journal of the American Medical Association, 244*, 259–263.

National Institutes of Health. (1991). *Consensus development conference statement: Diagnosis and treatment of depression in late life.* Washington, DC: Author.

National Institute of Mental Health. (1979). *The diagnostic interview schedule.* Washington, DC: National Institute of Mental Health, Center for Epidemiological Studies.

Niederehe, G. (1986). Depression and memory impairment in the aged. In L. W. Poon (Ed.), *Handbook for clinical memory assessment in older adults* (pp. 226–237). Washington, DC: American Psychological Association.

Nussbaum, P. D., Kaszniak, A. W., Allender, J., & Rapcsak, S. Z. (1991). Depression and cognitive deterioration in the elderly: A follow-up study [abstract]. *Journal of Clinical and Experimental Neuropsychology, 13*, 100–101.

Nussbaum, P. D., Kaszniak, A. W., Swanda, R. M., & Allender, J. (1988). Quantitative and qualitative aspects of memory performance in older depressed vs. probable Alzheimer's disease patients [abstract]. *Journal of Clinical and Experimental Neuropsychology, 10*, 63.

Parmelee, P. A., & Katz, I. R. (1990). Geriatric depression scale. *Journal of the American Geriatrics Society, 38*, 1379.

Parmelee, P. A., Lawton, M. P., & Katz, I. R. (1989). Psychometric properties of the Geriatric Depression Scale among the institutional aged. *Psychological Assessment: A Journal of Consulting and Clinical Psychology, 1*, 331.

Pearson, J., Teri, L., Reifler, B., & Raskind, M. (1989). Functional status and cognitive impairment in Alzheimer's disease patients with and without depression. *Journal of the American Geriatrics Society, 39*, 1117–1121.

Perlmutter, M. (1978). What is memory aging the aging of? *Developmental Psychology, 14*, 330–345.

Popkin, M. K., & Tucker, G. J. (1992). "Secondary" and drug-induced mood, anxiety, psychotic, catatonic, and personality disorders: A review of the literature. *Journal of Neuropsychiatry and Clinical Neurosciences, 4*, 369–385.

Popkin, S. J., Gallagher, D., Thompson, L. W., & Moore, M. (1982). Memory complaint and performance in normal and depressed older adults. *Experimental Aging Research, 8,* 141–145.

Rabins, P. V., Merchant, A., & Nestadt, G. (1984). Criteria for diagnosing reversible dementia caused by depression. *British Journal of Psychiatry, 144,* 488–492.

Radloff, L. S., & Teri, L. (1986). Use of the Center for Epidemiological Studies Depression Scale with older adults. *Clinical Gerontologist, 5,* 119–136.

Raskin, A. (1986). Partialling out the effects of depression and age on cognitive functions: Experimental data and methodologic issues. In L. W. Poon (Ed.), *Handbook for clinical memory assessment of older adults* (pp. 244–256). Washington, DC: American Psychological Association.

Raskind, M. A., & Peskind, E. R. (1992). Alzheimer's disease and other dementing disorders. In J. E. Birren, R. B. Sloane, & G. D. Cohen (Eds.), *Handbook of mental health and aging* (2nd ed., pp. 478–513). San Diego, CA: Academic Press.

Reding, M., Haycox, J., & Blass, J. (1985). Depression in patients referred to a dementia clinic: A three-year prospective study. *Archives of Neurology, 42,* 894–896.

Reifler, B. V., Larson, E., & Teri, L. (1987). An outpatient psychiatry assessment and treatment service. *Clinics in Geriatric Medicine, 3,* 203–209.

Reifler, B. V., Larson, E., Teri, L., & Poulsen, M. (1986). Dementia of the Alzheimer's type and depression. *Journal of the American Geriatric Society, 34,* 855–859.

Reifler, B. V., Teri, L., Raskind, M., Veith, R., Barnes, R., White, E., & McLean, P. (1989). Double-blind trial of imipramine in Alzheimer's disease patients with and without depression. *American Journal of Psychiatry, 146,* 45–49.

Reisberg, B., Borenstein, J., Franssen, E., Salob, S., Steinberg, S. G., Shulman, E., Ferris, S. H., & Georgotas, A. (1986). In H. J. Altman (Ed.), *Alzheimer's disease: Problems, prospects, and perspectives* (pp. 1–16). New York: Plenum.

Reisberg, B., & Ferris, S. H. (1982). Diagnosis and assessment of the older patient. *Hospital and Community Psychiatry, 33,* 104–110.

Reisberg, B., Gordon, B., McCarthy, M., Ferris, S. H., & de Leon, M. J. (1985). Insight and denial accompanying progressive cognitive decline in normal aging and Alzheimer's disease. In B. Stanley (Ed.), *Geriatric psychiatry: Ethical and legal issues* (pp. 37–79). Washington, DC: American Psychiatric Press.

Reynolds, C. F., Hoch, C. C., Kupfer, D. J., Buysse, D. J., Houck, P. R., Stack, J. A., & Campbell, D. W. (1988). Bedside differentiation of depressive pseudodementia from dementia. *American Journal of Psychiatry, 145,* 1099–1103.

Reynolds, C. F., Perel, J. M., Kupfer, D. J., Zimmer, B., Stack, J. A., & Hoch, C. C. (1987). Open-trial response to antidepressant treatment in elderly patients with mixed depression and cognitive impairment. *Psychiatry Research, 21,* 111–122.

Riege, W. H. (1982). Self-report and tests of memory aging. *Clinical Gerontologist, 1,* 23–36.

Robins, L. N. (1985). Epidemiology: Reflections on testing the validity of psychiatric interviews. *Archives of General Psychiatry, 42,* 918–924.

Robins, L. N., Helzer, J. E., Croughan, J., & Ratcliff, K. S. (1981). National Institute of Mental Health Diagnostic Interview Schedule: Its history, characteristics, and validity. *Archives of General Psychiatry, 38,* 381–389.

Roman, G. C. (1991). The epidemiology of vascular dementia. In A. Hartman, W. Kuschinsky, & S. Hoyer (Eds.), *Cerebral ischemia and dementia* (pp. 9–15). Berlin: Springer-Verlag.

Roman, G. C., Tatemichi, T. K., Erkinjuntti, T., Cummings, J. L., Masdeu, J. C., Garcia, J. H., Amaducci, L., Orgogozo, J. M., Brun, A., Hofman, A., Moody, D. M., O'Brien, M. D., Yamaguchi, T., Grafman, J., Drayer, B. P., Bennett, D. A., Fisher, M., Ogata, J., Kokmen, E., Bermejo, F., Wolf, P. A., Gorelick, P. B., Bick, K. L., Pajeau, A. K., Bell, M. A., DeCarli, C., Culebras, A., Korczyn, A. D., Bogousslavsky, J., Hartmann, A., & Scheinberg, P. (1993). Vascular dementia: Diagnostic criteria for research studies. Report of the NINDS-AIREN International Workshop. *Neurology, 43,* 250–260.

Rorsman, B., Hagnell, O., & Lanke, J. (1986). Prevalence and incidence of senile and multi-infarct dementia in the Lundby Study: A comparison between the time periods 1947–1957 and 1957–1972. *Neuropsychobiology, 15,* 122–129.

Rosen, W. G., Terry, R. D., Fuld, P. A., Katzman, R., & Peck, A. (1980). Pathologic verification of ischemic score in differentiation of dementias. *Annals of Neurology, 7,* 486–488.

Rosenbaum, A. H., Schatzberg, A. F., MacLaughlin, R. A., Snyder, K., Jiang, N., Ilstrup, D., Rothschild, A. J., & Kliman, B. (1984). The DST in normal control subjects: A comparison of two assays and the effects of age. *American Journal of Psychiatry, 141,* 1550–1555.

Rubin, E. H. (1990). Psychopathology of senile dementia of the Alzheimer type. In R. J. Wurtman, S. Corkin, J. H. Growdon, & E. Ritter-Walker (Eds.), *Advances in neurology: Vol. 51. Alzheimer's disease* (pp. 53–59). New York: Raven Press.

Rubin, E. H., Zorumski, C. F., & Burke, W. J. (1988). Overlapping symptoms of geriatric depression and Alzheimer-type dementia. *Hospital and Community Psychiatry, 39,* 1074–1079.

Salzman, C. (Ed.). (1992). *Clinical geriatric psychopharmacology* (2nd ed.). Baltimore: Williams & Wilkins.

Salzman, C., & Nevis-Olesen, J. (1992). Psychopharmacologic treatment. In J. B. Birren, R. B. Sloane, & G. D. Cohen (Eds.), *Handbook of mental health and aging* (2nd ed., pp. 722–762). San Diego, CA: Academic Press.

Salzman, C., & Shader, R. I. (1979). Clinical evaluation of depression in the elderly. In A. Raskin & L. F. Jarvik (Eds.), *Psychiatric symptoms and cognitive loss in the elderly: Evaluation and assessment techniques* (pp. 39–72). Washington, DC: Hemisphere.

Sbordone, R. J., & Rudd, M. (1986). Can psychologists recognize neurological disorders in their patients? *Journal of Clinical and Experimental Neuropsychology, 8,* 285–291.

Scogin, F. (1987). The concurrent validity of the Geriatric Depression Scale with depressed older adults. *Clinical Gerontologist, 7,* 23–31.

Sheikh, J. I., & Yesavage, J. A. (1986). Geriatric Depression Scale (GDS): Recent evidence and development of a shorter version. *Clinical Gerontologist, 5,* 165–173.

Shibayama, H., Kasahara, Y., & Kobayashi, H. (1986). Prevalence of dementia in a Japanese elderly population. *Acta Psychiatrica Scandinavica, 74,* 144–151.

Siegel, B., & Gershon, S. (1986). Dementia, depression, and pseudodementia. In H. J. Altman (Ed.), *Alzheimer's disease: Problems, prospects, and perspectives* (pp. 29–44). New York: Plenum.

Smyer, M. A. (1988). The nursing home community. In M. A. Smyer, M. D. Cohn, & D. Brannon (Eds.), *Mental health consultation in nursing homes* (pp. 1–23). New York: New York University Press.

Snodgrass, J. G., & Corwin, J. (1988). Pragmatics of measuring recognition memory: Applications to dementia and amnesia. *Journal of Experimental Psychology: General, 117,* 34–50.

Spitzer, R. L., Williams, J. B. W., Gibbon, M., & First, M. B. (1990). *Structured clinical interview for DSM-III-R (SCID).* Washington, DC: American Psychiatric Press.

Squire, L. R., & Cohen, N. J. (1984). Human memory and amnesia. In G. Lynch, J. L. McGaugh, & N. M. Weinberger (Eds.), *Neurobiology of learning and memory* (pp. 3–61). New York: Guilford Press.

Stoudemire, A., Hill, C., Gulley, L. R., & Morris, R. (1989). Neuropsychological and biomedical assessment of depression–dementia syndromes. *Journal of Neuropsychiatry and Clinical Neurosciences, 1,* 347–361.

Sulkava, R., Haltia, M., Paetan, A., Wikstrom, J., & Palo, J. (1983). Accuracy of clinical diagnosis in primary degenerative dementia: Correlation with neuropathological findings. *Journal of Neurology, Neurosurgery, and Psychiatry, 46,* 9–13.

Teri, L., & Gallagher, D. (1991). Cognitive–behavioral interventions for treatment of depression. *Gerontologist, 31,* 413–416.

Teri, L., Reifler, B. V., Raskind, M., Veith, R. C., Barnes, R., White, E., & McLean, P. (1991). Imipramine in the treatment of depressed Alzheimer's patients: Impact on cognition. *Journal of Gerontology, 46,* 372–377.

Teri, L., & Uomoto, J. (1991). Reducing excess disability in dementia patients: Training caregivers to manage patient depression. *Clinical Gerontologist, 10,* 49–63.

Teri, L., & Wagner, A. (1991). Assessment of depression in patients with Alzheimer's disease: Concordance among informants. *Psychology and Aging, 6,* 280–285.

Teri, L., & Wagner, A. (1992). Alzheimer's disease and depression. *Journal of Consulting and Clinical Psychology, 60,* 379–391.

Thal, L. J., Grundman, M., & Klauber, M. R. (1988). Dementia: Characteristics of a referral population and factors associated with progression. *Neurology, 38,* 1083–1090.

Tierney, M. C., Fisher, R. H., Lewis, A. J., Zorzitto, M. L., Snow, G. W., Reid, D. W., & Niewnstraten, P. (1988). The NINCDS-ADRDA work group criteria for the clinical diagnosis of probable Alzheimer's disease: A clinicopathologic study of 57 cases. *Neurology, 38,* 359–364.

Tucker, G. J., Caine, E. D., Folstein, M. F., Grant, I., Liptzin, B., & Popkin, M. K. (1992). Introduction to background papers for the suggested changes to DSM-IV: Cognitive disorders. *Journal of Neuropsychiatry and Clinical Neurosciences, 4,* 360–368.

Wade, J. P. H., Mirsen, T. R., Hachinski, V. C., Fisman, M., Lau, C., & Mirskey, H. (1987). The clinical diagnosis of Alzheimer's disease. *Archives of Neurology, 44,* 24–29.

Weiner, M. F. (1989). Age and cortisol suppression by dexamethasone in normal subjects. *Journal of Psychiatric Research, 23,* 163–168.

Weingartner, H. (1986). Automatic and effort-demanding cognitive processes in depression. In L. W. Poon (Ed.), *Handbook for clinical memory assessment in older adults* (pp. 218–225). Washington, DC: American Psychological Association.

Weingartner, H., Kaye, W., Smallberg, S. A., Ebert, M. H., Gilin, J. C., & Sitaram, N. (1981). Memory failures in progressive idiopathic dementia. *Journal of Abnormal Psychology, 90,* 187–196.

Weiss, I. K., Nagel, C. L., & Aronson, M. K. (1986). Applicability of depression scales to the old old person. *Journal of the American Geriatrics Society, 34,* 215–218.

Wells, C. E. (1979). Pseudodementia. *American Journal of Psychiatry, 136,* 895–900.

Wells, C. E. (1983). Differential diagnosis of Alzheimer's dementia: Affective disorder. In B. Reisberg (Ed.), *Alzheimer's disease: The standard reference* (pp. 193–198). New York: Free Press.

Wilson, R. S., Kaszniak, A. W., Bacon, L. D., Fox, J. H., & Kelly, M. P. (1982). Facial recognition memory in dementia. *Cortex, 18,* 329–336.

Yesavage, J. A. (1986). The use of self-rating depression scales in the elderly. In L. W. Poon (Ed.), *Handbook for clinical memory assessment of older adults* (pp. 213–217). Washington, DC: American Psychological Association.

Yesavage, J. A., Brink, T. L., Rose, T. L., Lum, O., Huang, V., Adey, M., & Leirer, V. O. (1983). Development and validation of a geriatric screening scale: A preliminary report. *Journal of Psychiatric Research, 17,* 37–49.

Yesavage, J. A., Rose, T. L., & Lapp, D. (1981). *Validity of the Geriatric Depression Scale in subjects with senile dementia.* Palo Alto, CA: Clinical Diagnostic and Rehabilitation Unit, Veterans Administration Medical Center.

Zarit, S. H., Cole, K. D., & Guider, R. L. (1981). Memory training strategies and subjective complaints of memory in the aged. *Gerontologist, 21,* 158–164.

Zelinski, E. M., Gilewski, M. J., & Thompson, L. W. (1980). Do laboratory tests relate to self-assessment of memory ability in the young and old? In L. W. Poon, J. L. Fozard, L. S. Cermak, D. Arenberg, & L. W. Thompson (Eds.), *New directions in memory and aging* (pp. 519–544). Hillsdale, NJ: Erlbaum.

Zung, W. W. K., & Zung, E. M. (1986). Use of the Zung Self-Rating Depression Scale in the elderly. *Clinical Gerontologist, 5*, 137–148.

6

CLINICAL ASSESSMENTS FOR LEGAL COMPETENCE OF OLDER ADULTS

THOMAS GRISSO

Clinicians are commonly asked to address questions of legal competence when they are evaluating or treating older persons. This will become even more common as the United States' population ages (Smyer, 1993). Many clinicians approach questions of legal competence with uncertainty. Even some familiarity with the relevant laws is not reassuring because legal definitions of incompetence often are vague or obscure. Their relation to clinical data regarding cognitive deficits of older persons is often quite unclear. If clinicians are unsure of these matters, then they will also be uncertain about the assessment methods that might be most appropriate for addressing legal questions of incompetence.

My purpose in this chapter is to provide some structure for thinking about legal competencies, so that clinicians can approach their work with more confidence when they receive requests for assessments that will be used by courts to make judgments about legal competence. I begin by

This chapter was prepared, in part, with support provided by the John D. and Catherine T. MacArthur Foundation, through its Network for Research on Mental Health and Law.

considering the reasons that questions of legal competence are so important in the lives of older people. I review some legal definitions of incompetence, primarily to point out the need for more differentiated evaluations for legal competence than was considered necessary only a few decades ago. I then describe four conceptual components of legal competence, which are used to identify the types of methods and data that should be included in clinical evaluations for legal competence of older persons.

WHY LEGAL COMPETENCE IS IMPORTANT

Every state provides by law for the assignment of a person to make decisions for older adults when they are considered to be incapable of making important decisions for themselves (Sales, Powell, & Van Duizend, 1982). This arises with greatest frequency in two broad circumstances.

The first arises when older adults' capacities have suddenly or progressively declined, such that they are having difficulties in either caring for their own everyday needs or making decisions about matters that are important for their welfare. In these cases, the older person may need a guardian: someone who is authorized to make decisions about everyday matters of the person's care. The guardian frequently is called a *conservator* when the decisions to be made are limited to the management of the person's property.

The other circumstance arises when the older person's medical condition requires an informed decision about treatment. If there are concerns that he or she may not have the capacity to make the decision (e.g., about surgery or medication) for purposes of informed consent, and if the older person has no previous guardian, then a surrogate decision maker may be appointed to make the treatment decision on behalf of the person.

One of the most critical aspects of U.S. society's provision of a guardian for an older person is the determination of legal competence. Other decisions are equally important, such as the choice of a guardian and determining the scope of guardianship. The determination of incompetence, however, is a threshold legal question that clears the way for the guardianship process.

The great importance of the legal competency question derives from the consequences of guardianship itself. Under the best of circumstances, these consequences are beneficial. The guardian makes decisions for the incompetent person (e.g., regarding conservation of financial assets, authorizing medical treatment, or deciding on a place of residence) that are in the person's best short- and long-term interests. Guardianship protects incompetent persons who might otherwise suffer the potentially life-threatening consequences of their own impaired decision making. This protection, however, has a cost. The legal power of the guardian is put in place at the expense of the ward's autonomy to decide.

At the center of this trade-off one finds the tension of two counter-vailing values, both of which are woven into the fabric of Western society: beneficence and autonomy. On the one hand is the recognition of social responsibility for the beneficent protection of some disabled individual from the potentially damaging consequences of choices that they might make. On the other hand is the desire to protect an individual's right to decide personal matters. Autonomy in decisions that affect oneself is a privilege that U.S. citizens enjoy as a matter of legal right to privacy and self-determination. Therefore, older persons' incapacities must weigh heavily on the side of beneficent protection in order to tilt the scales away from preservation of their right to autonomy.

Whether the scales will tip toward autonomy or beneficence—toward competence or incompetence as a legal status—is not decided by the older person's actual choice but rather by the person's capacity to make the choice. When older people's expressed choices seem bizarre or absurd, this might signal one to question whether or not they are capable of making the choice. But it is not a signal that they are incompetent. People are allowed to choose strange, even unwise, courses for their lives unless it is found that their decision-making capacities appear to be impaired.

Judges who must make determinations of competence, therefore, must consider the person's capacities to make decisions and to implement them. Judges often feel that they are not well prepared to assess these capacities themselves. Therefore, they seek information from others concerning the older person's abilities and disabilities, and they reason with the facts that are presented to them about the type, degree, and probable consequences of the disability manifested by the older person in question.

This is when health and mental health professionals enter into the picture. Clinicians do not determine that an older person is or is not legally competent; that is the job of the court. The clinician's role is to provide the court with clinical information with which the court can then reason about legal competence. Nevertheless, to offer courts meaningful assistance in these matters, clinicians must understand the law's definitions and con-cerns, so that they can focus their assessments on obtaining clinical infor-mation that is relevant to the fact finder.

LEGAL DEFINITIONS OF INCOMPETENCE

Until the most recent generation, most states' statutes that defined incompetence as a legal condition construed it as virtually synonymous with mental disease or disability. The language of these statutes often bore the colorful phrases of pre-Victorian British law, referring to attributions like lunacy, idleness, madness, improvidence, and of course, senility. An involuntary inpatient commitment for mental disorder carried with it an automatic presumption of incompetence; therefore, the older person's consent to treatment was unnecessary. In cases requiring court decisions, it was usually sufficient for the party seeking appointment of a guardian to produce an affidavit signed by a physician, most likely attesting in a single sentence that "I have examined the person and she is incompetent by reason of senility" (Horstman, 1975).

In the last few decades, however, demands have been placed on health and mental health professionals to produce much more differentiated assessments of older persons in evaluations for legal competence. These demands have resulted from several recent changes in the laws that courts must apply when deciding on a person's competence.

First, statutes in most states have adopted more specific definitions of incompetence. Global definitions have been replaced with statutes referring to various disorders, cognitive incapacities, functional deficits, and diverse antecedents and consequences of specific disabilities (Anderer, 1990). Although these new definitions often are more differentiated than the older ones, they are not necessarily clearer or self-explanatory. For example, Maryland's statute (Maryland Estates and Trusts Code Ann., 1974 & Suppl. 1974) defines the incompetent person as one who is:

> unable to provide for his daily needs sufficiently to protect his health or safety, because he lacks sufficient understanding or capacity to make or communicate responsible decisions concerning his person, including provisions for health care, food, clothing or shelter, because of any mental disability, senility or mental weakness or disease. (Sec. 13-101(d))

Such statutes do not spell out precisely the types of data that clinicians should obtain in their competence evaluations. But they do provide a more differentiated point of reference for weighing the competency question, and they make it clear that an evaluation that merely offers a diagnosis will no longer do. According to these newer definitions, it is not merely the diagnosis of a particular disorder that determines whether the person is legally incompetent. For example, an older person with dementia, even at a moderate stage of development, may still be found competent for certain types of decisions.

A second reason that clinicians' evaluations for legal competence have had to become more differentiated is an important trend toward narrowing the scope of the guardian's role. Traditionally, incompetence was considered an "all-or-none" status; when guardians were appointed, they made virtually all important decisions for the ward. Today, however, there is greater use of the concept of limited guardianship. Courts are being asked to determine more specifically the decisions that the older person is and is not capable of making, with the guardian's role being narrowed accordingly. For example, the guardian might be limited to making decisions about the management of the ward's investments involving significant capital, while the ward is allowed continued autonomy of choice regarding how he or she will use his or her financial assets (e.g., weekly allowance) for purposes of meeting day-to-day needs.

Limited guardianship has important implications for clinical evaluations that are intended to assist courts in legal competency cases. Courts are more often required to determine specifically those areas of daily life in which a person seems incapable of making decisions. Therefore, courts will no longer accept clinicians' opinions that refer globally to the person's ability to "manage financial assets" or "care for oneself." Greater differentiation is needed.

Third, the law once treated incompetence as though it was an enduring status; once declared incompetent, a person generally retained that status indefinitely. In contrast, modern legal views of incompetence recognize that an older person's incompetence status can change. If the older person's clinical condition changes such that his or her ability to make decisions improves, then the person's legal status as one who is competent to make decisions may be restored by the court. As noted later in this chapter, this has implications for assessments for legal competence, especially with regard to identifying the specific nature of the underlying clinical disability.

Finally, modern clinical evaluations for legal competence need to consider that many states have different incompetence definitions for different purposes. In addition to a guardianship statute that focuses generally on care for self and property, some states have a separate definition for competence related to voluntary mental hospitalization and still others for competence to accept or refuse treatment (e.g., psychoactive medication) after the individual is hospitalized. Older people in some states may be declared incompetent under as many as five different definitions found in separate sections of those particular states' codes (Allen, Ferster, & Weihofen, 1968; Sales et al., 1982). The consequence, of course, is that the nature of the clinician's evaluation for competence might have to vary in relation to these different legal definitions and purposes.

In this brief review of legal definitions of incompetence, I have emphasized the following general rules:

(a) Legal incompetence is not determined merely by the presence of a particular mental disorder. The older person may have a serious mental disorder, yet may be found competent. Legal questions now focus on the consequences of the disorder for the person's actual decision-making or other relevant functions.

(b) Legal incompetence is not an all-or-none status. An older person may be found incompetent for some decision-making purposes while being allowed to make autonomous decisions for other purposes.

(c) Legal incompetence is not conceptualized as "permanent." A person who has been found incompetent to make particular decisions at one time may later be found competent, depending on changes in the person's circumstances.

(d) There is no single legal definition of incompetence but several. Different definitions might apply for different circumstances and purposes for which the question is raised.

This brief review of legal definitions of incompetence shows that one cannot prescribe a set of assessment methods to use in all evaluations for legal competence. Clinicians are well aware of the general rule that one selects assessment methods on the basis of the specific assessment questions to be addressed. In the case of legal competence, those questions will vary from state to state; moreover, within states, they will vary for different legal purposes. The assessment methods, therefore, might also vary accordingly.

In the face of these uncertainties, clinicians can be prepared for competency assessments in two ways. They can be aware of the range of options at their disposal, and they should have a way to think through the demands of the particular competency assessment they are asked to perform.

The following discussions use a set of concepts that might help clinicians to organize their thinking about evaluations for legal competence. These four concepts represent essential components of legal competencies, called the *functional, causal, interactive,* and *judgmental* components. In the remainder of this chapter, I use these concepts to (a) explain the types of data that the clinician needs to collect for assessments related to legal competence, (b) review the types of assessment methods the clinician might use, and (c) identify standardized methods, when possible, for achieving these purposes and objectives.

The four concepts also provide a model that clinicians can use to think through the issues when they encounter competency assessment cases that are out of the ordinary or that present unique challenges. More detailed descriptions of these concepts have been presented previously (Grisso, 1986).

THE FUNCTIONAL COMPONENT OF LEGAL COMPETENCE

Every legal competence has a functional component. As noted in my review of legal definitions of incompetence, the law's fundamental concern in competence cases is the older person's functioning. *Functioning* is used here in a manner that distinguishes it from a clinical condition such as dementia or depression that underlies and may impair one's functioning. As I discuss later, diagnosing these conditions is important as well. Yet in most cases, no amount of evidence regarding such conditions will be sufficient to address the fundamental question that is at the heart of the inquiry about legal competence.

That fundamental question is addressed most appropriately by adequate description of the functional consequences of the person's clinical condition. To what extent can the person understand or do that which is relevant for making particular decisions or responding to his or her own needs? For example, how well does the older person perform in the domain of tasks that are actually required in order to care for oneself on a day-to-day basis? Can the person grasp what he or she is being told during the process of informed consent for the type of surgery that is being recommended? Can he or she make judgments about the value of purchases and record their costs?

Clinically, there are two fundamental ways to answer questions of this type: by inference and by relatively direct observation of the function in question. I call these the *inferential* and *functional* approaches.

Inferential Approach

In the inferential approach, the clinician assesses an underlying disorder and determines its effects as they are manifested in mental status exams or on neuropsychological measures of cognitive functioning. The clinician then makes inferences from these data regarding the probable capacity of the person to perform adequately those real-world tasks that are of concern to the court.

There is reason to believe that the process of using traditional neuropsychological assessment data to make inferences about everyday functioning of older persons has significant limitations. In a review of the literature over a decade ago, Heaton and Pendleton (1981) concluded that there was little empirical evidence about the relation between the results of neuropsychological tests and actual functioning in the domain of everyday demands of life. Today, not a great deal more is known about this relation (e.g., Searight & Goldberg, 1991). Moreover, the literature often confirms the notion that a person's ability to perform actual decision-making tasks is often not related to intellectual or neurological impairment (e.g., Kaplan, Strang, & Ahmed, 1988).

This is not to say that an inferential approach to the problem is never warranted; it is helpful in some cases. For example, imagine that an older person consistently manifests severe memory deficits for immediate or recent recall on neuropsychological examinations, such that cogent information presented only a minute or two before is not retained. By inference, this set of circumstances suggests serious limitations if the person were being asked to consent to medical treatment. One might expect that in a lengthy session involving informed consent, information presented to this older person early in the session would not be retained for processing along with information acquired later in the session. Similarly, patients who are so depressed that they cannot attend to a conversation or even respond to the mental status examiner are not likely to be able to engage in an informed consent process.

Inference may serve the clinician less well, however, in many other cases. For example, relatively normal performance on neuropsychological measures may be obtained for some patients with extensive prefrontal lobe damage, yet their judgment in everyday decisions may be significantly impaired (Stuss & Benson, 1986). In addition, the clinician may be accustomed to expecting serious memory problems in cases of dementia; yet there are published examples of persons whose dementia has not impaired their ability to retain information long enough to engage in a decision related to informed consent (Kaplan et al., 1988). Even inferences about persons with very poor intelligence are not straightforward; some individuals are able to perform a variety of important everyday tasks because they have been well learned, despite their limited intellectual capacity. Observations such as these led Salthouse (1990) to conclude that one of the greatest challenges in the field of psychology and aging is to better understand the discrepancy between the cognitive status of older adults based on neuropsychological measures and their successful functioning in everyday life.

On the other hand, the absence of a severe disorder may sometimes be misleading. For example, Fitten and Waite (1990) tested understanding of an informed consent disclosure for 25 older medically ill and hospitalized patients whose Mini-Mental Status Exam (see chapters 3 and 5 in this book) scores were in the normal range. All were considered competent by their physicians. Yet on a measure of actual understanding of informed consent material, one quarter of them scored below the lower 99.5% confidence limit of a non-ill control group matched with them for age and intelligence.

Whenever possible, therefore, it is preferable to include a functional assessment in the person's competency evaluation, rather than relying entirely on inference derived from neuropsychological measures. This requires ability to perform the everyday tasks, or to make specific types of decisions, that are in question.

Functional Approach

Clinicians have at their disposal some standardized methods for obtaining more direct information on functional abilities of the older person. These may be classified in two ways: according to the domain of abilities assessed and according to the way the data are obtained.

Domain of abilities

Some instruments assess simple functions—often called *activities of daily living* (ADLs)—that are associated with basic self-maintenance: for example, the ability to dress, feed, or bathe oneself (e.g., Kane & Kane,

1981; Katz, Ford, Moskowitz, Jackson, & Jaffee, 1963; Mahoney & Barthel, 1965). Other functional instruments assess a broader domain of abilities—often called *instrumental activities of daily living* (IADLs). These include the older person's capacity to manage decisions or actions of a more complex nature: for example, with transportation, communications, self-medication, and financial transactions (Fillenbaum & Smyer, 1981; Koyano, Shibata, Nakazato, Haga, & Suyama, 1991; Kuriansky & Gurland, 1976; Lawton, 1972; Lawton, Moss, Fulcomer, & Kleban, 1982; Loeb, 1983; Loewenstein et al., 1989; Mahurin, DeBettignies, & Pirozzolo, 1991; Pfeffer, Kurosaki, Harrah, Chance, & Filos, 1982; Tobacyk, Dixon, & Dixon, 1983; Williams et al., 1991).

The more basic domain of abilities assessed by ADL instruments tends to be helpful in making clinical decisions about nursing home versus semi-independent living arrangements. In contrast, instruments representing the more complex IADL domain are likely to be especially helpful in difficult assessments related to legal competence because they focus on the broader range of abilities with which courts are more often concerned.

Evidence of the courts' breadth of concerns in many competency cases involving older people was offered in a study by Anderten (1979; see Grisso, 1986, for a more detailed description of Anderten's unpublished study). Anderten performed a survey of judges, lawyers, older persons, and professionals in elder health care. The purpose was to determine the types of abilities that the respondents believed were important to consider in legal competency cases with older persons. From this project, Anderten arrived empirically at a domain of 15 components (e.g., Care for Medical Needs, Proper Diet, and Dealing With Emergencies) that went far beyond the domain represented by most ADL instruments.

Method of functional assessment

Standardized IADL measures also vary in the ways that they assess the functional abilities in question. Many of the IADL instruments have relied on health care professionals or relatives as informants regarding the older person's abilities, or they have simply asked the older person (e.g., "Can you manage your money without help?"). There is empirical evidence, however, for poor correspondence between self-report or collateral reports of an older person's abilities and more direct observations of actual functioning (Grisso, 1986; Sager et al., 1992; Searight, Dunn, Grisso, Margolis, & Gibbons, 1989; Weinberger et al., 1992).

This may occur for a variety of reasons. In some cases, the tasks in question may not have been required of the person in the past (e.g., making a decision about a risky and complex medical intervention for a life-threatening illness). Others' reports of the person's ability to do this, therefore, may be no more than guesses. In other cases, the reports offered by the older person may be of questionable reliability because of his or her desire to appear more-or-less capable in an attempt to preserve autonomy or to gain support. Similarly, relatives sometimes have self-serving motives for exaggerating or underreporting an older person's everyday abilities.

For these reasons, some standardized methods have taken an alternative approach. They ask the older person to actually demonstrate the capacity to perform the IADL abilities in question. For example, the just-mentioned survey by Anderten (1979) led her to develop an instrument called the Community Competence Scale (CCS) (Loeb [Anderten], 1983; described in Grisso, 1986). Her domain of 15 components was used to develop 180 items for several CCS subscales. Each item requires the older person to perform some function related to the subscale in question. For example, for Handling Emergencies, examinees are provided a telephone and asked to do what they would do if they needed help immediately. For Managing Money, they are given a blank check and asked to fill it out to a payee for a certain amount, then to subtract the amount from a facsimile of a checkbook balance page. All items are objectively scored according to well-defined criteria.

Considerable published research with the CCS during the 1980s provided reliability, construct validity, and normative data for its use with older and mentally ill persons (Caul, 1984; Christopher, Loeb, Zaretsky, & Jassani, 1988; D'Andrea, Goldberg, Searight, Gilner, & Katz, 1991; Dunn, Searight, Grisso, Margolis, & Gibbons, 1990; Goldberg et al., 1991; Grisso, 1986; Loeb, 1983; Schwartz & Barone, 1992; Searight & Goldberg, 1991; Searight, Oliver, & Grisso, 1983). The copyright for the CCS is owned by the Psychological Corporation, which currently plans to develop the instrument commercially as the Independent Living Scale. In the meantime, copyright laws do not allow author distribution of the CCS.

Three similar instruments, however, have been developed more recently and are available to clinicians. Loewenstein et al. (1989) published an instrument called the Direct Assessment of Functional Status (DAFS). Its domain of abilities is not as comprehensive as the CCS, but its procedure and scoring standards are similar. The DAFS requires actual demonstration of abilities associated with day-to-day instrumental functions, such as performing grooming functions, remembering items on a grocery list, and identifying street and roadway signs. Normative data are provided for groups of Alzheimer's disease patients, older depressed patients, and elderly controls.

Similarly, Edelstein, Nygren, Northrop, Staats, and Pool (1993) developed a procedure called the Hopemont Capacity Assessment Interview. Among other things, this procedure asks the older person to answer a number of questions about financial transactions. It includes, for example, a procedure in which the examinee actually uses coins to demonstrate the ability to handle money and make change.

Finally, Mahurin et al. (1991) published preliminary data on the Structured Assessment of Independent Living Skills (SAILS). It includes 50 tasks that are at the relatively "low end" of the IADL domain (e.g., zipping a jacket, using a telephone, picking up coins, unwrapping a Band-aid, responding to social greetings). Mahurin et al. reported normative data for control and Alzheimer disease groups, as well as relations of SAILS scores to various clinical measures of cognitive ability.

Special Assessment Methods for Decision-Making Capacities

Different methods may be needed to assess functional abilities associated with competence to consent to treatment. There are four types of abilities with which the law has been concerned when determining whether mentally ill or older people have the capacity to make treatment decisions for themselves. These are the abilities to (a) express a choice, (b) understand treatment information disclosed in an informed consent procedure, (c) appreciate the significance of the information for one's own circumstances (e.g., does not deny the existence or seriousness of one's illness), and (d) process the information rationally (Appelbaum & Grisso, 1988). A functional assessment for competence to consent to treatment should involve direct questioning of the person during the informed consent process, in order to assess these abilities.

Some structured methods for assessing these abilities are becoming available. They involve standardized presentation of information about a disorder and treatment, followed by questions to assess comprehension and/or reasoning regarding the information; often the methods allow responses to be objectively scored or rated. The Hopemont Capacity Assessment Interview by Edelstein et al. (1993), mentioned earlier, includes such a procedure, as does the Hopkins Competency Assessment Test, which was recently published by Janofsky, McCarthy, and Folstein (1992). Both the Edelstein and the Janofsky instruments have limited data that offer some standard with which to compare an individual case.

Grisso and Appelbaum (1992, 1993; Appelbaum & Grisso, 1992) developed several standardized research instruments for assessing an individual's capacity to make decisions about his or her treatment. They developed these measures for research to address a number of empirical questions about decisional capacities of mentally ill persons in general. The instruments are compatible for use with older persons as well, although current evidence for reliability and validity was developed with nonelderly mentally ill persons. The instruments simulate the content and process of a disclosure of information related to informed consent to treatment (especially for various forms of mental illness). They measure functioning related to the four standards noted earlier, using standardized questions and objective scoring criteria. The instruments are somewhat lengthy for routine clinical use, and a more clinically feasible tool is currently being developed based on these research instruments.

In summary, functional demonstrations of relevant abilities should be a fundamental part of any assessment related to a question of legal competence. This allows the clinician to describe clearly to the court the legally relevant functions that the older person has demonstrated. Once this is accomplished, however, there is yet a good deal more to be done with it, as a consideration of the remaining components of legal competence indicates.

THE CAUSAL COMPONENT OF LEGAL COMPETENCE

Most legal definitions of incompetence require that the performance deficits that the clinician has observed in a functional assessment must be related to a mental disorder. In other words, a mental disorder must be identified, and it must be shown how the disorder offers a causal explanation for any functional deficits the clinician has observed on legally relevant tasks.

Explaining functional deficits involves a twofold approach. First, can the types of functional deficits that the clinician has observed be related logically to evidence of specific underlying clinical conditions? Second, can other possible explanations for the apparent deficits be ruled out? I now examine why answers to these questions are important and how they can establish—and sometimes reduce—the significance of older persons' poor performance on functional tasks.

Remediable Functional Deficits

Imagine that the clinician has administered to an older person a standardized method for assessing this person's actual comprehension of some information about a proposed medical treatment. The clinician has presented information in a format something like an informed consent disclosure. To assess comprehension, the clinician has asked standardized questions that require the older person to paraphrase various types of information that the clinician has presented that would be important for the older person to consider if he or she were making a treatment decision. The older person has performed poorly. Why would a court want the clinician to explain why this older person comprehends the information poorly?

In chapter 2, Storandt provided several possible explanations, other than cognitive disability or lack of capacity, for an older adult's poor performance on tests of ability. For example, some older adults experience test-taking fatigue more rapidly than do younger persons (Gurland, 1973).

Others may reject test-taking tasks if the items seem condescending (Lawton, 1972) or if testing itself is alien to them. Visual or hearing difficulties may reduce the quality of performance for reasons unrelated to underlying cognitive disabilities. Still others may grasp the information but may be prevented by aphasic difficulties from clearly paraphrasing what they understand.

If poor performance on functional tasks is related to factors of this type, then the data are less likely to be a basis for legal incompetence. The results seem specific to the test-taking situation, perhaps not generalizing to everyday behavior. Moreover, some of these conditions could be altered in such a way that performance on the requisite tasks could be improved. Under these circumstances, courts should be reluctant to restrict older persons' autonomy by automatically declaring them incompetent on the basis of their poor functional performance. For this reason, it is important for the examiner to determine whether the older person's poor performance during functional assessment might have been artifacts of test-taking conditions.

Clinical Explanations for Functional Deficits

Beyond this, however, when poor performance does appear to be due to an underlying clinical condition, it is still important to determine the relation between the functional deficit and the clinical condition itself. The following example demonstrates why this is important.

Imagine that the clinician has assessed an older person's memory and understanding for information in an informed consent disclosure related to a proposed surgical procedure and has found no remarkable deficits. The clinician has then asked what the older person has decided and has also asked for an explanation of the person's logic and reasoning for the decision. The clinician has found that the logic was vague or seemed not to take into account some of the most basic consequences that would be important to consider when making this decision. Judgment or problem solving, therefore, seemed to be impaired.

The clinician can find such a problem in relation to any of several different clinical conditions. For example, it could be found in a person with neuropsychological signs of frontal system dysfunction (Stuss & Benson, 1986). Such dysfunctions may leave memory and basic capacities for understanding intact, yet be manifested in failure to consider the consequences of intended actions when processing information.

However, it would not be uncommon to find this result in persons who are very depressed. They are sometimes able to grasp basic information and demonstrate their understanding; yet when asked to make a choice and describe their reasoning, their depression may impair their ability to consider the range of treatment options in their reasoning. Alternatively, because of depression, the person might have unreasonable expectancies or presumptions that might interfere with his or her judgment: for example, "I'm too sinful—nothing could help me."

Either of these explanations for poor judgment could raise the question of legal incompetence. Yet the two clinical reasons might lead to different legal responses to the person's deficits. For example, certain clinical conditions are likely to be permanent or to follow a course of progressive deterioration, whereas others—such as reactive depression—may present some prospect for improvement given time. In the latter case, perhaps the surgical treatment decision could be delayed in order to treat the depression.

Identifying clinical conditions that may be responsible for functional deficits is the type of objective for which neuropsychological evaluation methods can play an important role. They assist the clinician in determining the underlying neurological conditions or psychological problems that would explain the pattern of performance deficits in the functional evaluation.

As discussed earlier, however, the clinician's state of knowledge often does not allow for confident explanations. Many commentators have observed frequent discrepancies between performance on neuropsychological measures and actual functioning in everyday life (e.g., Dunn et al., 1990; Salthouse, 1990). The results of some recent studies, however, suggest that past failures to find empirical relations between everyday functioning and cognitive measures or clinical conditions may have been due to imperfect research designs for which current research is making corrections (e.g., Warren et al., 1989; Willis, Jay, Diehl, & Marsiske, 1992). In addition, some cognitive measures appear to relate to daily living skills in the context of some clinical conditions but not others, which produces negative results when diagnostic conditions are not sufficiently differentiated. For example, Breen, Larson, Reifler, Vitaliano, and Lawrence (1984) found that certain cognitive tests were or were not related to functional deficits in patients with Alzheimer dementia, depending on whether the patients also manifested depression.

Until such complexities are resolved empirically, clinicians may use two kinds of assistance for relating functional deficits to underlying disabilities. One kind of assistance is offered by the results of studies that have sought to validate measures of daily functioning; they often provide empirical evidence of the relations between IADL functioning and clinical conditions or cognitive test scores (e.g., Loewenstein et al., 1989; Mahurin et al., 1991). Further assistance is offered by theoretical analyses that provide guidelines for thinking through the probable relations between cognitive disabilities and functional deficits. Freedman et al. (1991), for example, discussed theoretical relations between practical decision-making abilities (in consent to treatment) and neuropsychological measures of attention, language abilities, memory, and frontal lobe functions.

Another reason for using neuropsychological measures in competency evaluations is to identify potential ways that the older person might be able to compensate for certain functional deficits. If this is feasible, then there may be no need to declare incompetence in some cases. For example, some studies have shown how difficulties in memory for informed consent information might be remediated for some older people by providing them with written descriptions or with labeled diagrams that keep critical information immediately accessible throughout the decision-making process (Tymchuk, Ouslander, Rahbar, & Fitten, 1988). In summary, there are limitations to using neuropsychological examinations to infer what an older person can or cannot do in everyday life. Functional assessments of performance on everyday tasks provide more direct evidence. Yet clinical neuropsychological measures are often essential in competence assessments in order to explain the functional impairments that the clinician has observed. In some cases, this may allow the clinician to avoid an incompetence finding by identifying cases in which poor functional performance is not a consequence of underlying disorder, or if it is, to determine whether it might be remediable or whether performance might be improved with compensatory strategies (Lawton, 1990).

THE INTERACTIVE COMPONENT OF LEGAL COMPETENCE

Merely knowing that a person has functional deficits of a particular type, which are caused by a particular clinical condition, does not complete the inquiry. Not all deficits are of equal importance in weighing questions of legal competence. Functional deficits vary in type and severity, and their importance in the older person's life cannot be evaluated by examining the person alone. A finding of legal incompetence depends, in part, on the demands of the person's environment and situation. Stated another way, legal incompetence is, in part, a conclusion about a mismatch between the individual's abilities and the specific demands of his or her circumstances.

The following discussion should clarify this person–environment interactive aspect of legal competence. Two older persons having equal types and degrees of functional deficits may be viewed differently by a court, despite their similarity in ability. This can happen if the two face very different demands in everyday life. For example, one might have a sizable and complex financial estate to manage, whereas the other may possess little of financial significance. Greater ability to manage financial matters is demanded by the first circumstance. If the two individuals have equal deficits for managing financial matters, the larger estate will create the greater incongruity between personal ability and situational demand. This is more likely to be a cause for a finding of legal incompetence, at least for the limited purposes of managing that person's personal property.

Matches or mismatches between personal ability and situational demands can vary as a function of a wide variety of circumstances, such as housing arrangements, conditions of neighborhoods, and family support systems. Therefore, courts are assisted in making legal competency decisions when they are informed of the demands that this particular older person faces and when the person's level of abilities is described in relation to those demands.

This interactive concept in the law of incompetence has been paralleled by some developments in gerontological theory and research. Kahana (1982), for example, described a "congruence model" of person–environment interaction applied to the elderly. Lawton (1982) stressed the need to conceptualize adaptations of older persons as transactions between intrapersonal abilities and environmental "press." Others have developed taxonomies of situations relevant for older persons' adaptive functioning (e.g., Scheidt & Schaie, 1978; Willis, in press).

Some instruments, such as the Older Americans Resources and Services instrument (Fillenbaum & Smyer, 1981), have been developed to assess the older person's environment and its demands. One new instrument of this type, the Assessment of Living Skills and Resources (ALSAR), is especially interesting (Williams et al., 1991). It assesses functional abilities (e.g., the person's ability to use public transportation) as well as environmental demands (e.g., the availability of various forms of transportation in that person's community). Each ability component has a parallel environmental component. The ALSAR, therefore, has special promise as an instrument that provides structure for expressing the interactive view of competency.

With or without such measures, clinicians who are performing competency evaluations should attempt to learn about specific environmental demands in the older person's life and to take them into consideration when describing the significance of the person's deficits. In some environmental circumstances, certain deficits may be relatively unimportant, which avoids the need for declaration of incompetence. In other circumstances, it may be possible to avoid a declaration of incompetence by altering the older person's environment, thereby decreasing the incongruity between ability and demand despite the person's unalterable impairment.

THE JUDGMENTAL COMPONENT OF LEGAL COMPETENCE

The judgmental component recognizes that a decision to declare incompetence hinges ultimately on a value judgment. Earlier in this chapter, I discussed the tension inherent in the notion of legal incompetence. Our society wishes to protect people from their bad decisions due to their incapacity, while it also values and protects their right to retain autonomy in decision making, insofar as this is feasible. At the heart of the concept of incompetence, therefore, there is an ultimate question: When are the person's deficits (or the incongruency between abilities and the demands of one's circumstances) sufficiently serious to warrant interference with his or her autonomy?

In cases involving severe impairment, this is often not a hard call to make. But it is more difficult in cases of moderate severity. In the latter cases, the question is not resolved by clinical logic alone. Once one knows the older person's deficits, their causes, and the particular demands of the person's environment that challenge his or her abilities, the answer to this final question depends on how much one values beneficence (or paternalism) versus a right to autonomy. Given the degree of risk involved for the older person, the question "How much risk is too much?" requires the application of ethical, moral, and legal reasoning to arrive at an answer. This is, in part, why a declaration of incompetence is determined by courts.

Nevertheless, there have been some attempts to provide guidelines or frameworks for thinking through a case. For example, Drane (1984) offered a model to assist in making this ultimate decision. In brief, the model uses what has been called a "sliding scale" threshold for competence. It requires that one consider the degree of risk associated with the older person's circumstances or choices that the person is likely to make. The greater the degree of risk associated with the consequences of a older person's choices, the greater the degree of capacity that is required to meet the standard for competence. Drane categorized such situations into three levels. His scheme does not provide an answer to the ultimate question, but it assists by structuring the problem for the clinician and courts.

CONCLUSION

Modern competence evaluations of older persons require the best neuropsychological assessments available and the best diagnostic skills that a clinician possesses. But they also require more. Incompetence is not synonymous with any particular type or degree of neurological or psychological disorder. Therefore, an assessment for legal competence is incomplete without an assessment of the older person's functional abilities for everyday tasks and decisions. This requires observing their performance on tasks that demonstrate their capacity to do those things that are required of them in adapting to the day-to-day demands of life. A few assessment tools are available for this purpose, and others appear to be in development.

The concept of legal competence also requires that the clinician examine the logical (causal) relation between the older person's functional deficits and neuropathology, as well as the relevance of those deficits in light of the actual demands of the older person's environment.

Older adults deserve careful and comprehensive assessments when the question of legal competence is raised. All clinicians are aware that a poor clinical assessment can result in inappropriate treatment. Similarly, a poor competency assessment can result in either of two types of errors. The false-positives will result in inappropriate deprivation of autonomy. The false-negatives involve a failure to recognize the older person's need for surrogate decision making, thereby placing the older person at risk of harm. The chances of either type of error can be reduced if the clinician takes the time to understand legal competence as a construct and to develop competence assessments accordingly.

REFERENCES

Allen, R., Ferster, E., & Weihofen, H. (1968). *Mental impairment and legal incompetency.* Englewood Cliffs, NJ: Prentice-Hall.

Anderer, S. (1990). *Determining competency in guardianship proceedings.* Washington, DC: American Bar Association.

Anderten, P. (1979). *The elderly, incompetency and guardianship.* Unpublished master's thesis, Saint Louis University.

Appelbaum, P., & Grisso, T. (1988). Assessing patients' capacities to consent to treatment. *New England Journal of Medicine, 319,* 1635–1638.

Appelbaum, P., & Grisso, T. (1992). *Manual for "Perceptions of Disorder."* Worcester, MA: Law and Psychiatry Program, University of Massachusetts Medical School.

Breen, A., Larson, E., Reifler, B., Vitaliano, P., & Lawrence, G. (1984). Cognitive performance and functional competence in coexisting dementia and depression. *Journal of the American Geriatrics Society, 32,* 132–137.

Caul, J. (1984). *The predictive utility of the Community Competence Scale.* Unpublished doctoral dissertation, Saint Louis University.

Christopher, F., Loeb, P., Zaretsky, H., & Jassani, A. (1988). A group psychotherapy intervention to promote the functional independence of older adults in a long term rehabilitation hospital: A preliminary study. *Physical and Occupational Therapy in Geriatrics, 6,* 51–61.

D'Andrea, J., Goldberg, M., Searight, H., Gilner, F., & Katz, B. (1991). The Community Competence Scale—short form: A competency-based measure for determining residential placement of geriatric patients. *Clinical Gerontologist, 10,* 3–10.

Drane, J. (1984). Competency to give an informed consent. *Journal of the American Medical Association, 252,* 925–927.

Dunn, E., Searight, H., Grisso, T., Margolis, R., & Gibbons, J. (1990). The relation of the Halstead–Reitan Neuropsychological Battery to functional daily living skills in geriatric patients. *Archives of Clinical Neuropsychology, 5,* 103–117.

Edelstein, H., Nygren, M., Northrop, L., Staats, N., & Pool, D. (1993, August). *Assessment of capacity to make financial and medical decisions.* Paper presented at the 101st annual meeting of the American Psychological Association, Toronto, Ontario, Canada.

Fillenbaum, G., & Smyer, M. (1981). The development, validity, and reliability of the OARS Multidimensional Functional Assessment Questionnaire. *Journal of Gerontology, 36,* 428–434.

Fitten, J., & Waite, M. (1990). Impact of medical hospitalization on treatment decision-making capacity in the elderly. *Archives of Internal Medicine, 150,* 1717–1721.

Freedman, M., Stuss, D., & Gordon, M. (1991). Assessment of competency: The role of neurobehavioral deficits. *Annals of Internal Medicine, 115,* 203–208.

Goldberg, M., Searight, H., Katz, B., Jacobi, K., Austrin, H., & D'Andrea, J. (1991). A competency-based measure to aid residential placement decisions: The Community Competence Scale—short form. *Psychosocial Rehabilitation Journal, 15,* 81–85.

Grisso, T. (1986). *Evaluating competencies: Forensic assessments and instruments.* New York: Plenum.

Grisso, T., & Appelbaum, P. (1992). *Manual for "Understanding Treatment Disclosures."* Worcester, MA: Law and Psychiatry Program, University of Massachusetts Medical School.

Grisso, T., & Appelbaum, P. (1993). *Manual for "Thinking Rationally About Treatment."* Worcester, MA: Law and Psychiatry Program, University of Massachusetts Medical School.

Gurland, B. (1973). A broad clinical assessment of psychopathology in the aged. In C. Eisdorfer & M. Lawton (Eds.), *The psychology of adult development and aging* (pp. 343–377). Washington, DC: American Psychological Association.

Heaton, R., & Pendleton, M. (1981). Use of neuropsychological tests to predict adult patients' everyday functioning. *Journal of Consulting and Clinical Psychology, 49,* 807–821.

Horstman, P. (1975). Protective services for the elderly: The limits of parens patriae. *Missouri Law Review, 40,* 215–278.

Janofsky, J., McCarthy, R., & Folstein, M. (1992). The Hopkins Competency Assessment: A brief method for evaluating patients' capacity to give informed consent. *Hospital and Community Psychiatry, 43,* 132–136.

Kahana, E. (1982). A congruence model of person–environment interaction. In M. Lawton, P. Windley, & T. Byerts (Eds.), *Aging and the environment: Theoretical approaches* (pp. 97–121). New York: Springer.

Kane, R., & Kane, R. (1981). *Assessing the elderly: A practical guide to measurement.* Lexington, MA: Lexington Books.

Kaplan, K., Strang, J., & Ahmed, I. (1988). Dementia, mental retardation, and competency to make decisions. *General Hospital Psychiatry, 10,* 385–388.

Katz, S., Ford, A., Moskowitz, R., Jackson, B., & Jaffee, M. (1963). Studies of illness in the aged: The Index of ADL, a standardized measure of biological and psychosocial function. *Journal of the American Medical Association, 185,* 94–99.

Koyano, W., Shibata, H., Nakazato, K., Haga, H., & Suyama, Y. (1991). Measurement of competence: Reliability and validity of the TMIG Index of Competence. *Archives of Gerontology and Geriatrics, 13*, 103–116.

Kuriansky, J., & Gurland, B. (1976). Performance test of activities of daily living. *International Journal of Aging and Human Development, 7*, 343–352.

Lawton, M. (1972). Assessing the competence of older people. In D. Kent, R. Kastenbaum, & S. Sherwood (Eds.), *Research, planning and action for the elderly* (pp. 122–143). New York: Behavioral Publications.

Lawton, M. (1982). Competence, environmental press, and adaptation of older people. In M. Lawton, P. Windley, & T. Byerts (Eds.), *Aging and the environment: Theoretical approaches* (pp. 33–59). New York: Springer.

Lawton, M. (1990). Aging and performance of home tasks. *Human Factors, 32*, 527–536.

Lawton, M., Moss, M., Fulcomer, M., & Kleban, M. (1982). A research and service oriented multilevel assessment instrument. *Journal of Gerontology, 37*, 91–99.

Loeb, P. (1983). *Validity of the Community Competence Scale with the elderly.* Unpublished doctoral dissertation, Saint Louis University.

Loewenstein, D., Amigo, E., Duara, R., Guterman, A., Hurwitz, D., Berkowitz, N., Wilkie, F., Weinberg, G., Black, B., Gittelman, B., & Eisdorfer, C. (1989). A new scale for the assessment of functional status in Alzheimer's disease and related disorders. *Journal of Gerontology: Psychological Sciences, 44*, 114–121.

Mahoney, F., & Barthel, D. (1965). Functional evaluation: The Barthel Index. *Maryland State Medical Journal, 14*, 61–65.

Mahurin, R., DeBettignies, B., & Pirozzolo, F. (1991). Structured Assessment of Independent Living Skills: Preliminary report of a performance measure of functional abilities in dementia. *Journal of Gerontology: Psychological Sciences, 2*, 58–66.

Maryland Estates and Trust Code Ann. 1974. 13-101(d) (1974 & suppl. 1974).

Pfeffer, R., Kurosaki, T., Harrah, C., Chance, J., & Filos, S. (1982). Measurement of functional activities in older adults in the community. *Journal of Gerontology, 37*, 323–329.

Sager, M., Dunham, N., Schwantes, A., Mecum, L., Halverson, K., & Harlowe, D. (1992). Measurement of activities of daily living in hospitalized elderly: A comparison of self-report and performance-based methods. *Journal of the American Geriatrics Society, 40*, 457–462.

Sales, B., Powell, D., & Van Duizend, R. (1982). *Disabled persons and the law.* New York: Plenum.

Salthouse, T. (1990). Cognitive competence and expertise in aging. In J. Birren & K. Schaie (Eds.), *Handbook of the psychology of aging* (pp. 310–319). San Diego, CA: Academic Press.

Scheidt, R., & Schaie, K. (1978). A taxonomy of situations for an elderly population: Generating situational criteria. *Journal of Gerontology, 33*, 848–857.

Schwartz, J., & Barone, D. (1992). Assessing civil competency in the elderly. *Journal of Forensic Sciences, 37,* 938–941.

Searight, H., Dunn, E., Grisso, T., Margolis, R., & Gibbons, J. (1989). Correlation of two competence assessment methods in a geriatric population. *Perceptual and Motor Skills, 68,* 863–872.

Searight, H., & Goldberg, M. (1991). The Community Competence Scale as a measure of functional daily living skills. *Journal of Mental Health Administration, 18,* 128–134.

Searight, H., Oliver, J., & Grisso, T. (1983). The Community Competence Scale: Preliminary reliability and validity. *American Journal of Community Psychology, 14,* 291–301.

Smyer, M. (1993). Aging and decision-making capacity. *Generations, 17,* 51–56.

Stuss, D., & Benson, D. (1986). *The frontal lobes.* New York: Raven Press.

Tobacyk, J., Dixon, J., & Dixon, J. (1983). Two brief measures for assessing mental competence in the elderly. *Journal of Personality Assessment, 47,* 648–655.

Tymchuk, A., Ouslander, J., Rahbar, B., & Fitten, J. (1988). Medical decision-making among elderly people in long term care. *Gerontologist, 28,* 59–63.

Warren, E., Grek, A., Conn, D., Herrmann, N., Icyk, E., Kohl, J., & Silberfeld, M. (1989). A correlation between cognitive performance and daily functioning in elderly people. *Journal of Geriatric Psychiatry and Neurology, 2,* 96–100.

Weinberger, M., Samsa, G., Schmader, K., Greenberg, S., Carr, D., & Wildman, D. (1992). Comparing proxy and patients' perceptions of patients' functional status: Results from an outpatient geriatric clinic. *Journal of the American Geriatrics Society, 40,* 585–588.

Williams, J., Drinka, T., Greenberg, J., Farrell-Holtan, J., Euhardy, R., & Schram, M. (1991). Development and testing of the Assessment of Living Skills and Resources (ALSAR) in elderly community-dwelling veterans. *Gerontologist, 31,* 84–91.

Willis, S. (in press). Everyday cognition: Taxonomic and methodological considerations. In J. Puckett & H. Reese (Eds.), *Lifespan developmental psychology: Mechanisms of everyday cognition.* Hillsdale, NJ: Erlbaum.

Willis, S., Jay, G., Diehl, M., & Marsiske, M. (1992). Longitudinal change and prediction of everyday task competence in the elderly. *Research on Aging, 14,* 68–91.

7

PROVIDING CLINICAL INTERPRETATIONS TO OLDER CLIENTS AND THEIR FAMILIES

BOB G. KNIGHT

In this chapter, I address the transition from assessment to treatment and, in particular, emphasize the importance of providing successful feedback in this process. In the typical scenario, the elderly client or the family (or both) initially come for evaluation with some specific questions about the older person and some decisions that the family needs to make. The assessment is then completed, the results are carefully weighed, and a diagnosis is made. Decisions about intervention strategies now need to be made. What information should be shared with the client? Should the results also be shared with the family?

Accurate clinical assessment, successful feedback, and responsible intervention depend, in my experience, on assessing the family context as well as the client's psychological functioning. The family often assumes that cognitive or emotional disorders in an older relative are due to irreversible, progressive processes (e.g., aging, Alzheimer's disease) and signal the need for the family to take care of (or take over for) the older relative.

Families are, therefore, typically highly involved at the time of assessment, regardless of whether they are physically present in the consultation room or not. Understanding the family context assists the clinician in understanding the problem, in helping the family understand the problem, and in planning interventions. For the client and the family, communicating the conclusions of the assessment begins a long process of coping with the newly understood problems that have been identified in the assessment. For these reasons, I advocate a family orientation to the feedback session, but I never lose sight of my obligation to the older adult as the principal client.

UNDERLYING PRINCIPLES FOR THE FEEDBACK SESSION

Before I describe the feedback interview, I discuss some underlying principles and values that infuse this approach to providing assessment information to the client and the family. First, older families are long-standing homeostatic systems (Neidhart & Allen, 1993; Carter & McGoldrick, 1988); their reactions to impairment of an older member are determined at least as much by system issues as by the impairment itself. The older family is a long-standing system of relationships and roles that now faces the necessity of changing in response to the problem defined by the assessment. Although understanding the diagnosis is helpful, the implications of the diagnosis for changes in the client's role in the family system are of greater relevance to the family. For example, if the client played a major role as advisor to the family, then continuing to seek advice from a moderately-to-severely demented parent is not wise. Because there is considerable inertia in family systems, absorbing the information and its implications is likely to take more than one session. However, the assessment feedback session can lay important groundwork for these changes. For both client and family, it is better (albeit uncomfortable) to know the problem and begin to address it.

Second, the older adult is presumed competent by the clinician until assessment demonstrates incompetence. Grisso (chapter 6 in this book) has provided an extensive discussion of legal competency. The same rationale and moral view applies in this nonforensic clinical context, although the application within the family context implies that decisions about intervention are likely to be more implicit and ambiguous. Many families may define the older adult who is brought for assessment as "incompetent" and may already be excluding him or her from decision making. The family may see no need for the older adult to receive the assessment results and may, in fact, be opposed to including the older adult in the feedback session. Although this exclusion from decision making within the family is sometimes based on cognitive impairment, it can be based on depression, dependency, passivity, or intrafamily power struggles. The psychologist should beware of accepting the family's viewpoint and avoid joining with the family against the older adult. In principle, the older adult is the client and owns the information. At some point in the progression of dementia, this principle may need modification. Until that modification is necessary, the older adult should decide whether the family gets the assessment results, rather than the reverse.

Third, "dementing" older adults (i.e., those in the throes of progressive dementia) may be less competent but not necessarily fully incompetent until the late stages of dementia (Grisso, chapter 6 in this book). Families are prone to "all-or-none" thinking about cognitive impairment in older family members. Concluding that the older adult has some degree of dementia does not automatically mean that he or she should be excluded from the feedback interview or from decisions about sharing the diagnosis with others. In general, dementing older adults, like the dying, have a right to know what is going on as well as the right (if competent) to participate in decision making.

Fourth, visits to physicians, hospital-based clinics, and family meetings can all be perceived as threats to the continued freedom of the dementing older adult. For these reasons, family members and physicians often underestimate the self-awareness of impairment on the part of the dementing client. Yet, in my 15 years of clinical experience in working with older adults and their families, I have found that dementing older adults are willing to discuss their impairments, their feelings about the impairments, and their methods for coping with daily life without much memory and with a declining ability to calculate, to understand complex instructions, and so on. I have also observed that when there is a real or perceived threat of institutionalization, they are much less communicative about their impairments. My experience has been almost entirely in community-based settings, and much of it has been in clients' homes. These informal settings are less threatening for the client, often being on their turf rather than my own. The dementing older adult's apparent awareness of impairment likely depends, in part, on their comfort with the environment in which the assessment takes place.

PROVIDING DIAGNOSTIC FEEDBACK

In this section, I describe ways to provide feedback to dementing clients and their families and to depressed clients and their families, while keeping in mind the principles that the older family reacts to the assessment feedback as a long-standing homeostatic system, that the older client is presumed competent, that dementing clients retain degrees of competency, and that dementing older adults often have some awareness of their cognitive impairment. I conclude the section with general comments on confidentiality, disclosing uncertainty about the assessment, and the connection between assessment and treatment.

Dementia

Giving assessment results to a family in a conjoint session can achieve several goals at once. It brings the family together, it provides the opportunity to educate everyone at once about the assessment results, and it can provide a common understanding of the interventions that are to follow. Of course, the family session should proceed only with the client's permission. The question of whether the client is capable of giving (or withholding) permission is a difficult and often ambiguous ethical and legal dilemma. In practice, I have found that dementing older adults tend to agree with most suggestions. The ones who refuse most suggestions create multiple problems for family members and professionals. It helps to have the client in the room for several reasons: It provides a chance to model open communication about the dementia; it provides opportunities to demonstrate the cognitive impairment to family members who are still in denial; it allows the client to contribute to discussions about the questions that the family faces; and finally, it allows the dementing older adult who may not be fully competent to respond to the emotional climate of the room in a candid way (i.e., "Those two are angry at each other, just like always").

Talking with dementing clients about their cognitive impairment does not seem to come naturally to most professionals. Both the resistance to discussing dementia with the client and the reasons for doing so are analogous to discussing death with the terminally ill: It is an emotionally difficult situation, but it is the client's situation, and he or she has the right to understand the illness and to participate in planning the remainder of his or her life. Clinical experience suggests that clients are virtually always aware of cognitive changes and are concerned about them.

Having a name for the cognitive changes seems to provide some sense of relief for many older clients and their families. Often these clients are relieved to know that they have Alzheimer's disease rather than psychosis, which they often fear more. Early-stage clients are often relieved to hear that the course of the illness is measured in years. Moderately demented clients are frequently rather unemotional about their cognitive impairment; however, they often have some realistic concerns about planning for future incapacity and the potential burden on other family members. Perhaps the most risky situation is feedback to intellectually focused clients with mild-to-moderate functional impairment. Among cognitively impaired clients, they are most at risk for severe depression. There is some potential for suicide in these clients as well as in clients whose personal philosophy dictates against becoming dependent on others (e.g., retired military officers). My personal experience has been that suicide is a risk in clients with multi-infarct dementia and dementia pugilistica; I have not personally encountered a truly suicidal Alzheimer's case. In these instances, the depression should be treated, and suicide precautions should be taken. However, once the depression has lifted and the treatment has been terminated, the client may still be inclined to choose death over dementia.

The family feedback session provides an opportunity to lay the groundwork for educating the family about dementia and correcting several common misconceptions. The public generally conceives of memory as a unitary ability that is either working or not working. Psychologists, in contrast, understand memory as a set of abilities that can be independent of one another. Furthermore, these abilities can each become impaired in a gradual manner. Families often struggle to understand why the client is unable to remember some things but is competent in other areas. Failing to grasp this point can support denial of the illness ("She's not demented because she can still remember how to get to the store") or can lead the family to suspect that some or all of the impairment is being deliberately faked ("Yesterday he didn't remember me, but today he recognized me right away").

Some explanation of the relationship of memory loss to behavior is also important. Family members often do not spontaneously reason from knowing that the dementing relative has Alzheimer's disease to understanding why the dementing individual gets upset when a family member is out of sight for a few minutes or that the dementing individual will forget phone messages if allowed to answer the phone. The invisibility of cognitive impairment and the general lack of understanding how brain dysfunctions relate to behavior often lead to blaming the victim for forgetting and forgetting-related behavior.

Finally, it is important to point out that in progressive dementias some symptoms disappear or improve as the disease worsens. Family members often assume that because the disease gets worse, any symptom that appears will remain and worsen for years to come. In fact, many troubling symptoms (e.g., suspiciousness, persistent wandering) vanish after several months precisely because the disease gets worse.

Depression

From the psychologist's point of view, providing feedback that the diagnosis is depression is likely to be good news. The client is likely to share this reaction to some degree: Older clients have often been worried that they had a dementing illness or that the symptoms were due to a physical illness. The assessment feedback will likely need to include information about the good prognosis for treating depression, the nature of psychotherapeutic interventions, and a rationale for trying them.

The goals of feedback to the family about depression are often to enlist the family in the therapeutic enterprise by encouraging them to understand symptoms, to reduce demands on the depressed older adult, to support optimism about therapy, to monitor potential suicidal impulses, to remove weapons, and to monitor dangerous medications if necessary. Clinical experience suggests that family members are often more negative about the possibility of change than is the depressed older adult. There can also be resentment upon discovering that increased dependency, irritability, pains, and/or signs of memory loss were due "only" to depression. Finally, depression can be rooted in conflictual family relationships, in which case the feedback session may include a recommendation for family therapy.

General Observations About Feedback on Assessment

Older clients and their families often start the assessment process with a set of unrelated signs and symptoms and a host of worries about what these problems may indicate about them. Any diagnosis rules out some of these worries, provides the relief of being able to name the problem, and starts the process of coping with the problem. In this sense, assessment feedback is generally helpful, even when the news itself is not good.

In 20 years of working with the elderly, I have been frequently surprised and appalled at the common practice of violating the confidentiality of older clients. In some cases, I have observed professionals discussing whether the older adult should be given information that had already been disclosed to a family member. Clearly, clinicians have an ethical duty to their clients to preserve confidentiality and to seek consent to share information with others. Working with dementing older adults constantly raises the question of when the ability to give and withhold consent becomes impaired (see Grisso, chapter 6 in this book). Often the professional will have to make a judgment about this ability and a judgment about who in the family has the client's best interests at heart. These are ethical and legal dilemmas that need much thoughtful exploration.

Another ethical issue is the clinician's need for candor in disclosing the degree of certainty about the assessment. More often than not, the final assessment of older adults is more accurately expressed in probabilities than in certainties. Especially when these probabilities are not very close to certainty, the client is entitled to know what the remaining options are and why the clinician chose one as the most likely. The response to treatments or the passage of time will often shed more light on the underlying problem. From a practical standpoint, it is easier to change the diagnosis later if the client (and the family as appropriate) knew from the start that the original diagnosis was a working hypothesis.

Assessments should lead somewhere, and generally, assessments are the beginning of interventions for the client, the family, or both (see Gatz, chapter 8 in this book). The feedback session itself can be used as an opportunity to educate the client and the family about the disorder and to prepare them for various helpful interventions. Without this step, assessments are of questionable value: Over the years, countless families have tearfully described being told that a relative had dementia, that nothing could be done about it, and then being ushered out of the office.

EDUCATING CLIENT AND FAMILY DURING FEEDBACK SESSIONS

The most basic level of education during the feedback session should provide information about the disorder that was diagnosed. How do the client's symptoms fit the picture of the disorder? What is the usual course and outcome? How long ago did the disorder probably start? Are there past problems that can now be understood as being caused by this psychological problem? Are there effective interventions? What are the pros and cons of various options? How long will it be until improvement is seen? or How long will it be before there is noticeable further decline?

In providing these educational spiels to dementing patients and their families, experience has made me more cautious about how much information to provide at any one time. When giving the information myself, I start by asking how much they want to know and ask to be told when enough is enough. It is also wise to watch closely for nonverbal cues. When I recommend books, I routinely suggest that they read as much as they are comfortable with and then put the book down until they want to know more. The most common dementing illnesses have typical courses measured in years. Learning about mid- and end-stage problems while dealing with an early-stage relative and coping with the news of the diagnosis can be overwhelmingly depressing. For the same reason, support groups and day care centers that expose families to the full range of stages of dementia can be depressing for families who are not ready to confront the later stages of the illness.

The next level of education should provide information on the availability of treatments or supportive resources. In many communities, there is a wide variety of supportive services for the dementing client and his or her family. For depressed older adults, there are an array of mental health services available. The ability to realistically discuss these options and to help the client choose intelligently among them is an essential skill in helping older adults connect effectively with a complex set of social, health, and psychological services (Knight, 1991).

With cases that involve an irreversible, progressive dementia, some discussion of legal and financial planning issues is also an important part of educating the family (Friss, 1990). Because of the progressive nature of the cognitive impairment, there will eventually be a need for someone to take over the impaired person's finances and become a substitute decision maker for health care and other decisions. In many states, these arrangements can be made relatively easily if the person is still competent to make the arrangements voluntarily. Unfortunately, the normal human tendency is to put off discussing these issues as long as possible. All too often, this means that more extensive legal procedures will be necessary because the affected relative will be unable to give legal consent. Waiting too long also deprives the individual of the right to have input into these decisions and shifts the burden of making the decisions to the family. Pointing these issues out at the time of assessment can greatly simplify problems that will arise years later.

There are other problems that can be anticipated and perhaps prevented by appropriate education at the time of assessment. A common problem that arises in caring for a dementing relative is that much of the care falls on one person. Encouraging the primary caregiver to "pace herself" in order to be able to last as long as possible is an important message to convey early on (Zarit, Orr, & Zarit, 1985). It can also help to prevent considerable guilt and other emotional suffering later if families can be encouraged not to promise to avoid institutional care at all costs. The point here is not a value judgment or a prediction about whether institutional care will become necessary, but rather to point out that no one can anticipate early in dementia what the late stages will be like in terms of demands for care. It is also not possible to predict what the health of available caregivers will be in 10–20 years. A promise that looks reasonable to keep in the early stages when the caregiver is healthy can become an overwhelming demand in end-stage care when the caregiver has developed chronic illnesses as well.

With depressed older adults, the main problem that can be prevented by family education is suicide. Instructing the family to "suicide proof" the depressed older adult's home by removing guns, knives, and dangerous medications is an important preventive measure. Although these steps would seem obvious to most mental health professionals, families do not always make the connection and may need encouragement to take active steps. Education can assist families in dealing appropriately with repeated suicide threats or attempts by helping them to not become frustrated or indifferent with time and repetition, which would ultimately encourage or collude with the suicide. With older adults, passive suicide by not adhering to treatment for life-threatening illness is also a possibility in depression. Educating the family to understand the role of depression in feelings of hopelessness and helplessness can enable them to remind the older adult that despair about medical treatment may be due to depression.

ASSESSMENT AS A FAMILY NETWORK EVENT

As is probably clear by now, a central theme of this chapter is that the older client does not exist in a vacuum. The older person lives in a social environment, usually one that includes one or more family members. The clinical assessment of the older client can be understood as an event that happens to the family system. The family context provides a perspective that should influence the manner in which the clinician handles the feedback session; the anticipation of a family feedback session can shape the assessment itself.

Regardless of whether families are physically present in the consulting room or not, most assessments of older persons impinge on the families, and the effects of the assessment must be considered within a family-systems approach. In principle, the disorder is the event to which the family reacts. However, for many family members, the assessment will become a symbolic event that defines the beginning of the problem, if not the beginning of the illness. The pervasiveness of this identification of the disorder and the assessment can be seen in the habit among professionals and scientists of dating the onset of dementia from the diagnosis, even though it is clear that the disorder had to exist and progress for some time before it could be diagnosed.

Illnesses in general, and especially disorders of cognition and emotion, are likely to become taboo topics in the family-systems sense (Neidhart & Allen, 1993). A taboo topic is, of course, a problem of which everyone is aware but which is not openly discussed. Often considerable energy is spent "concealing" the problem from the one person it affects the most—the person who has the disorder and who is most keenly aware of it.

Dementia and depression are both likely to be treated as taboo topics. In both cases, everyone in the family is likely to be aware that something is wrong with the affected older relative, but no one speaks of it, and in particular no one wants to speak of it with the relative. In the instance of dementia, family members seem to assume that the older adult will not be aware of any changes and should not be told. This unfortunately has the effect of creating a family social environment that is filled with secretive whispering and conversations that stop when the dementing relative enters the room. Because the cognitively impaired person is already having trouble comprehending complex social interactions, may not always know who some of the family members are, and is often anxious when overwhelmed, these secrets may naturally lead to even greater anxiety as well as suspiciousness. For depressed older adults, the result of the "family secret" is likely to be an enhanced sense of isolation and the realization that the family does not understand the problem.

In somewhat more extreme circumstances, the affected older person may be essentially cut off from the family network. An especially withdrawn depressed older adult or a cognitively impaired relative may become defined as a nonperson and treated as if he or she is not there. Although they may well "not be the person they once were," treating them as a person and keeping them connected in the family network are important strategies for helping the system deal effectively with the disorder. These principles do not imply denying the reality of the problem or the (temporary or permanent) changes in the affected relative. The family is encouraged to deal with the changes that have taken place rather than exaggerate those changes into defining the person as socially dead (cf. Sweeting & Gilhooly, 1991–1992).

Because the disorder is a network event, families respond to it as they have learned to respond to other crises in the family. These responses will typically have both emotional and instrumental components. On the emotional side, there are often various combinations and degrees of guilt and blaming. There are a remarkable number of rationales for blaming oneself or someone else in the family for both depression and dementing illness in an older relative. The rationales often involve occurrences that are years or even decades old: rebellion in adolescence or young adulthood, marrying the wrong person, years of real or imagined mistreatment by the spouse, failed careers, and so on. For depression, the depressed older adult may even be reinforcing these perceptions. For dementia, the attributions are more clearly irrational. Sibling rivalries and unresolved rivalries between a child and one parent for the other parent's affection are family issues that are interrupted rather than solved by adulthood and separate living quarters. Especially when the parent must move in with a child or when decisions must be made about finances and health care, these issues reemerge whenever the family comes back together (even when the children are over 60 years old).

The actual changes in the older adult's capabilities (whether permanent or temporary) may necessitate some changes in decades-old roles in the family system. If Mom has always "held the family together" and hosted ritual family dinners at holidays, or if Dad has resolved disputes or helped with taxes, then someone will need to take over these duties and the family will have to adjust to the new configuration. In general, the least adaptive outcomes occur when families try to maintain the status quo: Financial problems may ensue if Dad is expected to continue handling the household bills while he is in the middle stage of dementing illness, and family social life may suffer if the children wait for invitations from Mom, who is now depressed. The period of adjustment is likely to be uncomfortable, and there may be competition for taking over (or avoiding) the new roles and responsibilities, but a consciously negotiated new homeostasis is likely to be preferable to the alternatives.

Disabilities generally present families with difficult choices concerning issues of dependency and power in the family network (Brown, 1988). For both dementia and depression, as with other disabling problems, the family must strike a fine balance between doing too much, which may create excess disability by reinforcing unnecessary dependencies, and doing too little, which may overwhelm the affected relative by denying the realities of the limitations imposed by the disorder. Not encouraging the older adult to do as much as his or her ability allows creates excess disability and can deepen or create depression by inducing a sense of helplessness. On the other hand, compelling him or her to attempt activities that are not presently possible can lead to frustration and deepened depression or (in the case of dementia) to catastrophic reactions. Clearly, functional assessments can provide the family with guidance as to where the line for this balancing act may lie. The adjustments for the depressed older adult are even more difficult because they should be temporary. This balance can be even more difficult for children than for the spouse because children may see caring for the parent as a way of becoming the parent's parent and therefore (finally) becoming an empowered adult.

Because it is important to assess the family system as well as the client, I describe some of the broad features of the family that should be included in that assessment. Ascertaining the client's historical role in the family system can help the clinician to understand the disturbance in the family system that is caused by the client's disorder and thus the family's current reactions to that disturbance in the system. If the client has been impaired for several years, then it may require some careful history taking to retrieve the memory of the client as fully functioning individual and to determine the importance of the individual for this particular family.

If the clinician can interview several family members, then he or she may be able to envision the historical alliances and conflicts within the family network. As with families of any age (and with any presenting problem), histories of abuse, violence, and incest should be carefully reviewed.

The clinician should also consider the possibility that the older client is not the only impaired person in the family system. Families often seek help because several people are having problems at once. For example, Helen in *Older Adults in Psychotherapy* (Knight, 1992) was caring for a demented mother and a physically ill and depressed father, and she herself had a history of cyclothymia. On the other hand, the decision to care for an older relative may help to disguise problems that originated elsewhere in the system. That is, a couple may take in an older relative to distract themselves from their own marital difficulties. The feedback session may well conclude with a recommendation that several family members seek individual therapy or that the members seek family therapy.

ISSUES FOR THE PROFESSIONAL

A consistent thread throughout my discussions on psychotherapy with older adults has been that therapy with the elderly involves the same skills as does therapy with younger adults (Knight, 1986, 1992). On the other hand, it seems that working with older clients "feels" more difficult to many therapists. Although psychological assessment of the elderly is more complex than assessment of younger adults, providing the feedback "simply" calls for the integration of assessment skills with family-systems skills. There are, however, several reasons why the psychologist may find these sessions difficult and so avoid taking full responsibility for providing comprehensive feedback in a professional manner.

When the assessment does indicate an irreversible dementia, and especially a progressive one, the clinician may feel the very human reluctance to be the bearer of bad news. Although he or she may know that it helps the client and the family to know what the problem is, which will allow them to begin dealing with it in an informed way, it is hard to feel helpful while telling someone that the memory failures are irreversible and will get worse over the next several years. In many ways, the assessment of dementia presents the clinical geropsychologist with a dilemma that is analogous to the diagnosis of cancer by a physician. The professional's personal reaction to bringing bad news may interfere with providing accurate and complete information and guidance in a caring manner. To avoid bringing the bad news, the clinician may fall into the trap of avoiding the client.

Not all of the problems that professionals face in dealing with older adults are due to emotionally based personal motivations. In general, the literature and most course work and clinical training is much more complete regarding how to perform and interpret the assessment than on providing feedback and linking the assessment to future interventions. In short, as an emerging professional specialty, geropsychology needs to ensure that its students and interns are prepared to perform this service.

Providing feedback to older adults and their families may also expose the geropsychologist to more discussion and dispute than is typical with younger adult clients. With regard to the client and family, knowledge about psychological disorders is relatively lacking in the present cohort of older adults. Therefore, the clinician may have to explain what depression is and how depression relates to feelings of fatigue, vague pains, loss of appetite, not wanting to go out, and so on. Clients may be inclined to hold biological, moral, or spiritual explanations of these experiences and may argue for a while before accepting (or rejecting) the psychologist's explanation. Moreover, older adults almost always have one or more physicians who are involved in their treatment, and therefore, accurate assessment requires more coordination with medical findings. The physicians may not readily accept the psychologist's assessment. Finally, error rates in discriminating among possible causes of older clients' symptoms are fairly high. In short, working with older adults exposes the psychologist in a more public and interactive debate over the "real answer" to explaining the client's symptoms. Although this debate is intellectually and professionally challenging, it may provide a disquieting contrast to the security of private one-on-one practice with younger adults.

Finally, the issues of later life are issues that lie in every clinician's future. As such, when the situations of clients and their families remind the clinician of his or her own, it may be more difficult to recognize and respond to the countertransference that such reactions may arouse (Knight, 1989, 1992). Unresolved issues about the dementing illness in grandparents or parents, decisions to institutionalize a grandparent or parent, and observations of conflict between the clinician's parents and grandparents are all possible issues from the psychologist's family of origin that can cloud professional judgment in working with older families. Clinical training and supervision can prepare psychologists for dealing with countertransference issues, and given the probability that the geropsychologist will have to face some of these issues at sometime in the future, access to ongoing supervision and support is an important safeguard to assure professional treatment of one's clients.

SUMMARY

The feedback session can be regarded as the bridge between assessment and intervention. In this chapter, I have argued that the older client usually retains control of assessment feedback and decision making. The feedback session can educate the client as well as the family about the diagnosed disorder and provide information that anticipates and prevents common problems. Because the older adult usually is part of a family network, attention to family issues is an important part of accurate assessment and the handling of both education and treatment recommendations. The family orientation includes attending to the possibility that others in the family system may have problems that call for psychological intervention. Finally, the perceived difficulty of providing feedback to older adults and their families is likely to be a blend of the psychologist's discomfort in bearing bad news, his or her lack of training in providing feedback, the more public nature of working with older clients, and personal emotional reactions to the client's situation.

REFERENCES

Brown, F. H. (1988). The impact of death and serious illness on the family life cycle. In B. Carter & M. McGoldrick (Eds.), *The changing family life cycle* (pp. 457–482). New York: Gardner Press.

Carter, B., & McGoldrick, M. (Eds.). (1988). *The changing family life cycle*. New York: Gardner Press.

Friss, L. (1990). A model state–level approach to family survival for caregivers of brain injured adults. *Gerontologist, 30,* 121–125.

Knight, B. G. (1986). *Psychotherapy with the older adult.* Newbury Park, CA: Sage.

Knight, B. G. (1989). *Outreach with the elderly: Community education, assessment, and therapy.* New York: New York University Press.

Knight, B. (1991). Outreach to older adults: Matching programs to specific needs. In N. Cohen (Ed.), *Psychiatric outreach to the mentally ill* (pp. 93–111; New Directions for Mental Health Services monograph series). San Francisco: Jossey-Bass.

Knight, B. (1992). *Older adults in psychotherapy: Case histories.* Newbury Park, CA: Sage.

Neidhart, E. R., & Allen, J. A. (1993). *Family therapy with the elderly.* Newbury Park, CA: Sage.

Sweeting, H. N., & Gilhooly, M. L. (1991–1992). Doctor, am I dead? A review of social death for modern societies. *Omega, 24,* 251–270.

Zarit, S. H., Orr, N., & Zarit, J. (1985). *Hidden victims of Alzheimer's disease: Families under stress.* New York: New York University Press.

8

APPLICATION OF ASSESSMENT TO THERAPY AND INTERVENTION WITH OLDER ADULTS

MARGARET GATZ

My purpose in this chapter is to place assessment in the context of clinical practice. A framework for doing so is presented in Figure 1, which embodies phases in the assessment process, as described by Maloney and Ward (1976). The beginning point of the assessment is the stated problem. The assessor must know what the referral question is and who is the source of the question. Here are four hypothetical cases:

> "Ben seems despondent and won't do anything. What's wrong with him?" asks Ben's wife.

> "Sadie keeps annoying other residents of the rest home. What can we do about it?" asks a nurses' aide.

> "I walk from one room to the next and forget why I went there. Do I have Alzheimer's disease?" asks Hugh, an 83-year-old widower.

> "Should I make Dad stop driving?" asks Caryn, a 63-year-old daughter.

Appreciation is expressed to Michael Smyer and Martha Storandt for their critical comments on the text and to Chris Hilgeman and Donna Polisar for their technical assistance.

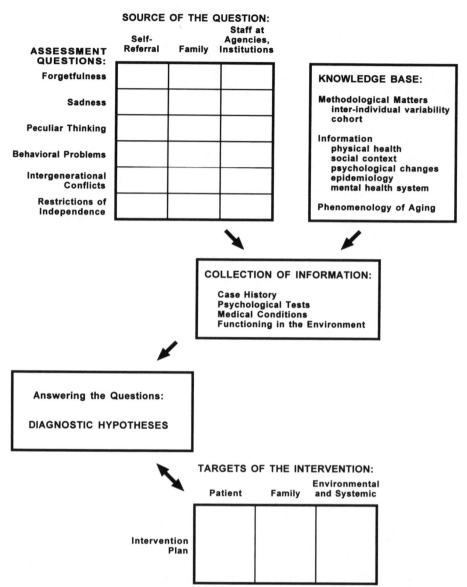

Figure 1. Schematic depiction of the assessment process, based on the perspective of Maloney and Ward (1976).

Maloney and Ward stressed that there is a second issue that must also be considered from the beginning; that is, the assessor must know the content or substance behind the problem. For example, if the question is one of memory, then the assessor must know something about memory changes in normal aging, memory complaints in older adults, and the various disorders in which memory disturbances may be observed. The middle point of assessment is collecting the data, including case history and psychological tests. The third phase of assessment involves answering the question. Maloney and Ward described the steps involved as follows:

> Based on his [or her] knowledge of the problem area, the referral question, and the specific client, he [or she] generates hypotheses and tests out whether these hypotheses are substantiated by the data he [or she] collects. In actuality, multiple hypotheses or contingency hypotheses are used. (p. 8)

The information is eventually used to generate treatment or placement recommendations. Further information that is obtained after treatment begins may be used to modify the diagnostic hypotheses.

THE ASSESSMENT QUESTION

What problems lead to referral for assessment? Extracting from the clinical experience at my own and other centers (Cohn, Smyer, Garfein, Droogas, & MaloneBeach, 1987; Gatz, 1989; Herr & Weakland, 1979; Knight, 1992), I propose six categories: forgetfulness, sadness, peculiar thinking, behavioral problems, intergenerational conflicts, and restrictions of independence. Thus, Ben's despondency is an example of sadness. Sadie's annoying other residents is an example of behavioral problems. Hugh, who is concerned about his memory, provides an example of forgetfulness. Caryn's question about whether to stop her father from driving fits under restrictions of independence.

Who is the source of the referral? In these examples, two of the sources of the request for assessment are family members, one is a staff member from a geriatric facility, and the other example is a self-referral. The combining of referral questions with sources of referral can lead to a grid. Although in no way inclusive of everything that will present itself at the practitioner's clinic or private practice, the grid will at least provide a rough guide to the scope of assessment.

Note that the first step, in which the assessment question is posed, is not straightforward at all, both because (a) the problems may be multiple and (b) the question may not be asked directly. In relation to the first of these complications, several assessment questions may be embedded in the same request. The 63-year-old daughter, to whom Dad's driving has become a behavioral problem, may also have intergenerational conflicts that are related to managing the problem. The 83-year-old widower may have both mild cognitive impairment and depression. Furthermore, as Cohen (1992) pointed out, interaction between physical and mental health is particularly common among older adults. For example, delirium may occur after anesthesia, and depression can be a side effect of certain medications for hypertension. At the same time, mental distress can cause or exacerbate physical symptoms, such as the negative effects of anxiety on gastrointestinal symptoms. Psychosocial factors can result in an inability to manage a physical health problem; for example, a diabetic with an infected foot will have greater difficulties in medical management if he or she lives alone, and his or her motivation to overcome the difficulties may be lowered by depression.

Thus, although the notion of needing to deal with a person's physical and mental health in the context of their social and physical environment is hardly unique to the aged, these issues are more obviously interrelated and have greater interactive consequences with advancing age. In addition, it means that just because the clinician has found one problem does not mean that the assessment is complete.

The second matter that makes defining the assessment problem less than straightforward is that clients tend not to ask questions in a manner in which the practitioner has learned to answer them. Clients rarely say, "Please perform a differential diagnosis between depression and dementia." Instead, they present a long complex history in which memory complaints are one feature. The assessor must then figure out the question. Indeed, figuring out the question is sometimes part of the intervention. Furthermore, clients may exaggerate their concerns or may use various cover-up strategies. Families may unintentionally mislead, for example, presenting one person as having the problem when it is really the other, or labeling the assessment request with a question that is different from the one that the clinician ultimately chooses.

Of course, before the practitioner can even begin the assessment, he or she needs someone to ask a question. Among those now old, there is a tendency to consult physicians rather than mental health professionals about their psychological symptoms. For example, Shapiro et al. (1984) determined for one site from the Epidemiological Catchment Area survey that 4.3% of older adults with psychiatric diagnoses consulted mental health practitioners, whereas 11.6% of these older adults consulted general medical practitioners. Shapiro et al. also reported that among younger adults a somewhat higher proportion sought a professional and that proportionally more of these professionals were mental health practitioners. At least in part, these cross-sectional differences may reflect a cohort phenomenon. As these younger adults become older, they may continue the same pattern, and therefore, there may be more extensive use of mental health service providers by older adults in the future. At the same time, because of co-morbidity, it is probable that substantial numbers of older adults with mental health problems will continue to see their physicians first.

A similar issue has been documented in institutional settings. Using the national Nursing Home Survey data, Burns et al. (1993) determined that, over a 1-month period, 4.5% of nursing home residents received mental health service and that half of these residents (2.3%) were served by a mental health specialist. The implication is that part of the role of the clinical geropsychologist is to (a) cultivate referral sources (e.g., physicians and staff in long-term care settings) and (b) teach them to recognize psychological problems and to call on the psychologist (Smyer, 1989).

BACKGROUND KNOWLEDGE

The topic of background knowledge was well covered by Storandt in chapter 2 of this book. I want to emphasize, however, three areas that need to be included. First, there are several methodological matters that are basic to gerontology, such as interindividual variability and cohort. The message of interindividual variability is that older adults are diverse. With respect to age alone, there are "young old," "old old," and "oldest old." With respect to nearly all psychological and demographic attributes, there is sufficient variability among older adults to produce large overlaps between distributions for old and young, even if there is a significant age difference in mean scores. The second methodological concern is cohort. Age tends to be used to separate individuals at different points of the life span; however, age is inseparable from cohort. Cohort refers to the generation into which one was born as well as all of the broad social and cultural influences that accompany growing up and growing older in a particular time in history. Thus, the extent to which age differences also reflect generational differences is not known. In trying to be sensitive to this point myself, I have adopted the phrase *individuals now old*.

Second, there is an informational base that includes physical health, social context, and psychological changes. The nature of gerontological knowledge is that there are competing bits of wisdom, each of which tells only part of the story. For example, the pervasive image is that old age is a time of multiple stressful life events. With the exception of widowhood, which seems convincingly to be among the most consequential losses of later life (Pearlin & Mullan, 1992), evidence is beginning to accumulate that major life events may not be the greatest source of stress. Rather, persistent role strains—such as struggling to make ends meet, caring for a spouse or parent who is in frail health, or balancing multiple roles—may account for more psychological burden (e.g., Franks & Stephens, 1992). Furthermore, those who study how older adults cope have two competing views. On the one hand, stress may increase geometrically as roles and stressors are accumulated. On the other hand, there may be inoculation or learning, such that with age some people may actually increase in ability to cope (Norris & Murrell, 1988). As well, there are substantial individual differences in responding to life transitions (Lieberman, 1992).

The practitioner should have a clear appreciation of the epidemiology of mental disorders in older adults as well as the mental health service system in relation to older adults. For example, Epidemiological Catchment

Area survey data (Regier et al., 1988) suggest that anxiety disorders are more common than affective disorders among those 65 years old and older. Thus, although depression is certainly a serious problem for those who are affected, anxiety is relatively overlooked despite its prevalence.

Third, a clinician requires some understanding of the phenomenology of aging. The individual is not simply the passive recipient of events and changes. The individual is an actor in his or her own life, coping and managing the various changes, creating other changes, and creating meaning. This point is especially critical because the clinician has often not yet personally experienced what it means to be an elderly person.

COLLECTING DATA

Other chapters in this book address the issue of selecting instruments to assess various conditions. The collection of information should encompass case history—which might include information from informants—and psychological tests (cognitive, personality, symptomatology). Cohen (1993) argued for the pivotal role of the case history in geriatric mental health assessment. He urged that assessment should not limit itself to present strengths and weaknesses; he also declared that "biography can be as important as biology" (p. 50). The interaction of physical health, mental health, and psychosocial factors implies that the assessment should encompass health history, current medications, history of alcohol use, social network, and current living situation, including finances. In addition, the assessment should include functional abilities within the present environment if that will be an issue in planning intervention (Lawton, 1986). The environmental context of functioning can be gathered through behavioral observations or reports of behavioral competencies, possibly including a home visit. In turn, the intervention plan needs to encompass the environmental context. Representing the perspective of an older person, Kuhn (1987) exhorted, "Without the knowledge of societal–environmental hazards to physical and mental health and well-being, I dare to observe that the diagnosis and the treatment are inadequate" (p. 381).

Note that collecting data is not something that is performed only once. Multiple re-evaluations may be necessary in order to assess change. They may also be necessary if the client is initially reluctant to engage in the testing.

ANSWERING THE QUESTION

If assessment is a matter of generating and testing hypotheses, then how are hypotheses generated and set aside or pursued? As Gatz, Smyer,

Garfein, and Seward (1991) proposed, there tend to be a series of implicit hypotheses in virtually any geriatric assessment. The starting point, of course, is the problem that was presented. A series of questions are then evaluated:

1. Does the pattern of functioning indicate normal aging, some abnormal processes, or some mixture of the two?
2. Does the complaint suggest a functional disorder (such as depression), an organic disorder (such as delirium or dementia), or a mixture of functional and organic?
3. Is the problem reversible, irreversible, or some mixture of the two? and
4. How severe or disruptive is it? [that is, is it an emergency?] (p. 295)

The first question is whether the problem suggests normal aging or some abnormal processes. An especially powerful example is the distinction between memory problems that signal nothing more interesting than normal aging and memory problems that are indeed indicative of pathology. For the client involved, it is often very helpful to have a sense of where their symptoms fit on the continuum of normal to abnormal, even when the answer is not definitive, as is often the case.

In making these judgments, the practitioner must be vitally aware of diagnostic bias. In any special population, there are twin dangers from normalizing pathology and from overpathologizing. In chapter 5 of this book, Kaszniak discussed false negatives and false postives as sources of differential diagnostic errors with Alzheimer's disease. Taking depression as another example, there is evidence that general medical practitioners minimize depression, in the sense that they fail to recognize as depressed patients who are in fact depressed (e.g., Rapp, Parisi, Walsh, & Wallace, 1988; Waxman & Carner, 1984). Older adults may also minimize or normalize feelings of depression, for example, by interpreting the symptoms as physical tiredness or by flatly denying that they are sad (see Rodin & Voshart, 1986). The danger of normalizing is that elderly people who could benefit from intervention never get to a professional.

The twin error is overdiagnosis, in which normal sadness or grief is pathologized. In essence, the professional is saying, "If I had all of those problems, I would certainly be depressed."[1] Such logic could lead to overdiagnosing depression. When there are situational factors to which it

---

[1]This point has been made by Lissy Jarvik, who asked, "Given these biological changes, the rising frequency of somatic illness, physiological decline, physical disabilities, malnutrition, overmedication (iatrogenic or self-induced), sensory deficits, reduction in mental agility, economic deprivations, social losses, and the increasing proximity of death, all of which are associated with advancing chronological age, why is not every old person in a profound state of depression?" (Jarvik, 1976, p. 326).

would be appropriate to respond with sadness or some negative affect, and when the older adult reports that he or she is not depressed, it seems important to respect the elder's phenomenological view. Overpathologizing such situations risks blaming the victim (Ryan, 1971).

In a discussion similar to that for the normalizing-versus-overpathologizing distinction, Kimmel and Moody (1990) recommended avoiding age biases in terms of "positive or negative ageist assumptions." For example, they warned against "a priori assumptions like because of their age, respondents would be more (or less) sensitive to questions about topics such as sexuality, death, bereavement, menopause, body image, or love"; they also warned against causal assumptions such as "senility is caused by living a long time, or that long-term marriages reflect marital satisfaction" (p. 494).

Either error—normalizing or overdiagnosing—could further reflect incorrect assumptions about base rates of various disorders in old age. The clinician's knowledge base should provide information about the frequency, as well as the presenting symptom profile, of various disorders, and this information should be used in formulating diagnostic hypotheses.

The practitioner must next distinguish disorders in terms of whether they are primarily functional or primarily organic. It is further necessary to distinguish reversible disorders from irreversible disorders, because this distinction does not completely overlap the functional-versus-organic differentiation.

Finally, severity must be taken into account. Suicidality and any hint that an older person is being neglected or even actively abused must be followed up immediately, as should any organic changes that might suggest the need for medical intervention (e.g., delirium or any behavioral pattern that suggests focal brain pathology, such as a tumor). Many of these actions are mandated by state laws or by the ethical guidelines of the profession. For example, states are beginning to develop laws for the reporting of elder abuse, and professions are developing diagnostic and treatment guidelines (American Medical Association, Council on Scientific Affairs, 1987). In California, as described by Eth and Leong (1992), physicians are mandated to report dementing illnesses in order to protect both operators of motor vehicles and pedestrians from drivers who may be impaired. In evaluating different diagnostic hypotheses, costs and benefits of different errors can be weighed. The cost of missing a potentially treatable organic condition or dangerous living situation, which could have increasingly serious consequences without intervention, is the greatest cost. Therefore, these hypotheses must be pursued.

Note that assessment often does not end when treatment begins. In fact, the clinician makes a best guess and develops both a treatment plan and plan for continuing assessment to refine the diagnosis.

PLANNING INTERVENTION

Various target groups for intervention can be defined that roughly parallel the sources of referrals. The first target group is individuals now old. The second target is families of frail elders. The third type of target is found at the environmental and systemic level, from physical environment to agency climate to public information to social policy considerations. Note that the source of the referral, the entity to whom assessment results are given, and the target for intervention may be the same or may differ. For example, the 63-year-old daughter who asked about her father's ability to continue to drive would want to receive the assessment results herself along with a consultation about how she should intervene. Ben's wife would want assessment results shared with Ben, and she would want Ben to be the target of an intervention to reduce his despondency.

A variety of ethical concerns are elicited when considering these different targets. Although these considerations are not unique to older adults, they are especially frequent, pertinent, and sometimes poignant. Issues of informed consent, confidentiality, and communication of information to patients at the completion of the assessment are particularly salient when working with an older adult, particularly one who has been brought to the clinic by a family member or when a family member is required as an informant (Eth & Leong, 1992; Kimmel & Moody, 1990; Knight, chapter 7 in this book). Many interventions assume involvement of the family, which means that assessment results inevitably will be shared with the family. In moving from assessment to intervention, involving the patient in setting the goals and identifying acceptable means of achieving those goals is highly desirable.

Treatment of Depression in the Aged

Depression in older adults is treatable and preventable, affording professionals a way to improve the quality of life in older adults. Indeed, there is no evidence that treatments for depression in old age are any less effective than treatments for depression at other ages (NIH Consensus Development Panel on Depression in Late Life, 1992). Moreover, the dangers of untreated depression may include increased disability stemming from medical illness and increased mortality stemming from acute illness and, to a minor extent, suicide (Baldwin, 1991; Burvill, Hall, Stampfer, & Emmerson, 1991). Interventions include antidepressant medications, electroconvulsive therapy (ECT), and psychotherapy. Antidepressant medications are the most widely used treatment, and there is some neglect of older adults as targets of psychotherapy for depression. I discuss each of the three interventions in turn.

Reviews of controlled research on the effectiveness of antidepressant medications support the conclusion that there is therapeutic benefit from a range of drugs. Tricyclics (e.g., imipramine) have received the most research attention, although trazadone and fluoxetine are gaining in usage. Monoamine oxidase inhibitors have not been used or studied as often. However, these drugs sometimes present various undesirable side effects. These include orthostatic hypotension (which increases the risk of falling), anticholinergic effects (which can cause confusion and lead to increased memory complaints), and cardiovascular side effects—to the extent that some medications are contraindicated for elderly patients, especially those with cardiac disease (Gerson, Plotkin, & Jarvik, 1988; NIH Consensus Development Panel on Depression in Late Life, 1992). In addition, relatively little is known about the efficacy of antidepressants in older adults with comorbid medical conditions (Katz, Simpson, Curlik, Parmelee, & Muhly, 1990; NIH Consensus Development Panel on Depression in Late Life, 1992). The appeal of trazadone and fluoxetine (marketed as Prozac) is that they do not have the same anticholinergic side effects. For the psychologist, familiarity with these medications permits taking into account possible side effects in the formulation and evaluation of diagnostic hypotheses and working cooperatively with the prescribing physician concerning compliance. Serial assessments with a depression scale (see Scogin, chapter 4 in this book) can be used to monitor the effectiveness of the treatment.

ECT, which is administered under general anesthesia and with a muscle relaxant, has experienced a revival in the past decade or so, after nearly having been replaced by the introduction of psychotropic medications. The literature on ECT reflects a combination of data and biases (from both advocates and detractors). What is certain is that older adults constitute a disproportionate number of those now being treated with ECT. The medical justification incorporates the following points: ECT is therapeutically effective; it avoids some of the side effects of antidepressants (and may be less dangerous than tricyclics for cardiac patients); and it acts more quickly, which is of importance if the depression is particularly profound or the patient is actively suicidal (Greenberg & Fink, 1992; NIH Consensus Development Panel on Depression in Late Life, 1992).

On the other hand, the risk of ECT is increased confusion in an already vulnerable population. Of the oldest-old patients, who are the most likely to present major coexisting medical illnesses or concurrent medications, 60–75% have been reported to experience complications (Burke, Rubin, Zorumski, & Wetzel, 1987; Cattan et al., 1990). Complications include severe confusion, falls, cardiovascular events, and respiratory problems. Occasional deaths due to myocardial infarction shortly after receiving ECT have been reported for patients with cardiovascular complications (summarized by Cattan et al., 1990), although there continues to be debate about the relative lethality of untreated depression compared with the risk associated with ECT (e.g., Kramer, 1987). For the most part, the effects of ECT on a variety of cognitive functions are short-term only (Calev et al., 1991). However, there may be different considerations for different subgroups. In one chart study of consecutive ECT patients, half of the geriatric depression patients with concurrent organic mental disorder either terminated treatment early because of confusion or were stopped because a physician judged organic symptoms to be worse (Kramer, 1987). In another study, Stoudemire et al. (1991) reported improved cognitive functioning after ECT in a subgroup that was deemed to have "pseudodementia." Clearly, hazards and benefits must be carefully weighed, and informed consent is especially important with ECT (Greenberg & Fink, 1992).

The role of the psychologist can encompass (a) prevention, crisis intervention, and early referral to assure that older adults have their depression treated before it becomes so profound that ECT seems like the only option; (b) assessment of the depression, including estimation of the source of any cognitive impairment; (c) facilitation of the consent process so that the older adult's voice is heard and the family is involved; (d) provision of therapy after ECT to prevent relapse; and (e) use of assessment instruments to monitor mood, and possibly cognition, after the ECT treatments.

Evaluations of psychotherapy have shown that behavioral therapy and cognitive behavioral therapy are effective in treating major depressive disorder in elderly outpatients (see especially Thompson, Gallagher, & Breckenridge, 1987). Most important, responsivity to psychotherapy in older adults is not different from that in younger adults. Thompson, Gallagher, and Czirr (1988) examined individuals who did not benefit from brief psychotherapy and observed that a disproportionate number presented symptoms of personality disorder. Thus, psychologists might do well to pay special attention to the presence of personality disorder during their evaluations. However, Hanley-Peterson et al. (1990) did not find any difference in therapeutic outcomes for patients on the basis of classifying their depression as endogenous or nonendogenous.

Some studies have included both psychotherapy and medications. Beutler et al. (1987) compared medication-only, medication-and-therapy, placebo-and-therapy, and placebo-only groups, all of whom received supportive counseling when they visited the medication clinic. Cognitive psychotherapy was administered in small groups. The medication was alprazolam, an anxiolytic with established antidepressant effects and fewer side effects (Gerson et al., 1988). On self-rated symptoms of depression and sleep impairment, the two cognitive therapy groups were superior, independent of medication status. In another study, Reynolds et al. (1992) combined interpersonal therapy with a tricyclic medication during the acute depressive episode. Interpersonal psychotherapy focuses on improving problematic interpersonal interactions and navigating role transitions. Reynolds et al. suggested that the combined treatment afforded a somewhat lower dropout rate and a somewhat higher success rate than was typical in the literature for medication alone or psychotherapy alone.

Relapse is a major problem in geriatric depression (Baldwin, 1991). Therefore, some practitioners strongly suggest some form of aftercare, which should be combined with continued monitoring with an assessment scale. For example, in one study, slightly over one quarter of patients who were treated with either tricyclics or ECT were rehospitalized for depression within 1 year of their first admission (Stoudemire et al., 1991). In another study of hospitalized depressives, at the 1-year follow-up, just over one quarter reported new episodes of depression (Blazer, Hughes, & George, 1992). Similarly, Gallagher-Thompson, Hanley-Peterson, and Thompson (1990) reported that just over one quarter of outpatients who were treated with psychotherapy met the criteria for major depression 1 year later. Most of these patients had not responded to the original therapeutic intervention and had remained in treatment during the year.

To prevent relapse, maintenance pharmacotherapy is sometimes recommended (NIH Consensus Development Panel on Depression in Late Life, 1992). Thus, Reynolds et al. (1992) randomly assigned patients to medication-only, medication-and-therapy, placebo-and-therapy, and placebo-only maintenance therapy. The groups that received the placebo had a relapse rate of nearly 25%, a rate similar to those of the previously mentioned studies. However, the groups that continued to receive maintenance medications had a relapse rate of 0% during the first 6 weeks.

Perhaps equally or more important is for the practitioner to try to alter the predisposing psychological and social factors. Evidence bolstering such a recommendation comes from studies of the role of psychosocial factors in depression. For instance, George, Blazer, Hughes, and Fowler (1989) found that perception of impaired social support at the time of hospital intake was associated with poorer recovery from depression at follow-up after treatment, although this relationship is not as strong for older patients as it is for younger patients (Blazer et al., 1992). Illustrating the application of this approach, the 8-month follow-up data from Frank (1991) support the efficacy of interpersonal psychotherapy as a maintenance treatment, with or without placebo, compared with the placebo-only condition. Frank emphasized preventing new depressive episodes by recognizing early warning signs. Again, psychological assessment can play a key role in this respect.

Treatment of Dementia

Treatments for dementia include psychopharmacological trials that are directed toward slowing or reversing the cognitive symptoms of dementia, treatment of behavioral problems that are secondary to the dementia, and counseling the family members who are caring for older persons with dementing illnesses. The first concern of the professional must be a careful diagnosis to distinguish reversible conditions that can be treated, even when they are coexisting with a primary degenerative dementia.

Therapeutic effects of drugs for treating Alzheimer's disease remain modest, despite progress in understanding the mechanisms of the disorder (see Hooper, 1992). Treatment strategies have reflected various theories of the pathogenesis of dementia that were in vogue at the time. Early on, there were trials of drugs to improve brain oxygenation (e.g., hydergine), vasodilators (e.g., vincamine), and drugs to enhance central nervous system cellular metabolism (e.g., noötropics). The results of these trials have provided only marginal support for the efficacy of these drugs (Salzman & Nevis-Olesen, 1992), although evaluations of newer noötropics are continuing. Building on the role of acetylcholine in memory and the established defects of this system in Alzheimer's disease, another psychopharmacological approach has involved various cholinergic-enhancing strategies, which have included the oral intake of acetylcholine precursors (e.g., dietary lecithin), the administration of cholinergic agonists by infusion, and the use of cholinesterase inhibiting drugs (e.g., physostigmine and tetrahydroaminocrine [THA]). These strategies have had some small success, although there are issues of dosage, bioavailability, problematic side effects, duration of positive change, and inconsistent replications (summarized by Raskind & Peskind, 1992; Salzman & Nevis-Olesen, 1992). The drug THA has recently received approval for use as a treatment. Reflecting continued research to isolate the mechanisms of Alzheimer's disease, there is also interest in calcium antagonists (e.g., nimodipine) as well as neurotrophic factors (Raskind & Peskind, 1992; Salzman & Nevis-Olesen, 1992). Psychologists can contribute to this ongoing research by developing neuropsychological batteries that sensitively test the efficacy of these various treatments and also by being prepared to provide accurate information to patients and families about the status of these pharmacological interventions.

Multi-infarct dementia has been treated with some limited effectiveness using strategies that follow the logic of treating cerebrovascular disorder, such as medication for hypertension (Raskind & Peskind, 1992). However, the extent of coexistence of Alzheimer's disease and vascular pathology may be greater than previously thought (Drachman, 1993), and the pathophysiology may not be entirely distinctive. Drugs such as noötropic substances (i.e., piracetam, nicergoline) are being evaluated with both Alzheimer's disease and vascular dementia patients. Nonetheless, the fact that different treatments may be appropriate for different forms of dementia illustrates the importance of initial psychological assessment.

Memory-training techniques have generally not been shown to be as effective in patients who are diagnosed as having dementia as in nondemented older adults who have concerns about their memories. After a period of early enthusiasm for memory-training groups, researchers determined that the effectiveness was greatest for depressed older adults with memory complaints, whose depression as well as perceived memory abilities were improved by the interventions (Zarit, 1980). Baddeley (1990) emphasized tailoring treatments to theories of memory and precise understanding of the specific memory problem. In this respect, the psychologist's assessment can help to target specific memory weaknesses and strengths. For example, procedural memory can be used to compensate for losses in episodic memory, and external memory aids such as calendars and alarm clocks can serve a useful prompting purpose. Bäckman (1992) recently applied what is known about the nature of the memory deficit in Alzheimer's disease to designing memory training for patients with dementia. Specifically, motor performance can be trained more successfully than can cognitive tasks, the duration of training must be lengthy, external memory aids (e.g., signs) facilitate learning, and supportive conditions are created at both encoding and retrieval. In short, convergence—possibly not yet recognized—between memory training and behavioral interventions (which are, of course, based on learning theory) is just beginning. Finally, the clinician should bear in mind that memory training should be presented carefully, so as not to reinforce the erroneous notion that the demented person would be better if only he or she would try harder to remember.

Secondary behavioral problems in dementia are treatable. These include sleep disturbance, suspiciousness, wandering, and depression. Antipsychotic drugs are sometimes used for treating these behaviors, although there is some risk of paradoxical effects (Raskind & Peskind, 1992; Small, 1988). As a consequence, geriatric psychiatrists often find themselves discontinuing the medications of older patients in order to clarify the patient's mental status.

Behavioral approaches may be the most applicable treatment techniques for secondary behavioral problems in demented patients (Teri & Wagner, 1992; Zeiss & Lewinsohn, 1986). Behavioral approaches do not unduly tax the cognitive capacities of the patient, and there are no side effects that might exacerbate the memory problems, which is a potential risk with somatic therapies. The behavioral techniques are typically taught to family members who are caring for the demented individual at home, with a family member implementing the contingencies. The use of behavioral interventions to manage a variety of problematic behaviors in nursing home residents has also been recommended (e.g., Smyer, Cohn, & Brannon, 1988).

Depression may coexist with a dementing disorder (Reifler, Larson, & Hanley, 1982; Kaszniak, chapter 5 in this book). For these patients, the professional should aggressively treat whatever may be reversible, without simultaneously instilling false hope about the possibility of affecting the underlying dementia. Antidepressants, ECT, and psychotherapy have all been used to treat coexisting depression. One controlled study compared a placebo with a tricyclic (imipramine) in depressed and nondepressed Alzheimer's disease patients (Reifler et al., 1989; Teri et al., 1991). The results showed that both imipramine and the placebo ameliorated depression but demonstrated no impact on cognition, whereas mild cognitive decline was observed in the nondepressed patients who were assigned the imipramine. Teri and colleagues have developed a curriculum for teaching behavior therapy techniques to depressed Alzheimer's patients and their caregivers, who often are also depressed. Their results indicate reduced depression in both patients and caregivers (Teri & Gallagher, 1991; Teri & Uomoto, 1991).

Families of frail elders, particularly older adults with Alzheimer's disease, have been described as the hidden clients. As a consequence, gerontologists have attempted to involve family members in intervention in order to prevent or relieve their distress. Once the patient has been properly assessed, two models are most frequently applied (Zarit, Anthony, & Boutselis, 1987). One relies on family conferences and sometimes includes the older adult. In the second, support groups are used as the vehicle for service delivery. In both models, the family member most often involved is an adult child, in fact, a daughter. Evaluations of the effectiveness of caregiver intervention typically indicate that participants feel that they benefit. In terms of effects on caregivers' self-reported subjective well-being and psychological symptoms, the enhancement of skills may be the most beneficial intervention, regardless of whether these skills are taught by support groups or by individual counselors (Lovett & Gallagher, 1988; Toseland & Smith, 1990).

Another family configuration is the older couple. The couple come to the clinic because they want to know what is wrong with one of them, which often involves some sort of memory complaints. Nearly invariably, further assessment quickly makes it apparent that there are also issues in the relationship, whether longstanding or related to the current stress. Therefore, the clinician will seek to see the couple.

CASE EXAMPLES

The following synopses of the cases encompass many of the issues brought out in the assessment, as well as how these considerations lead to a plan for intervention.

"Ben seems despondent and won't do anything. What's wrong with him?" asked Ben's wife. Ben did agree to participate in an assessment, as his wife requested. The psychologist identified some depression. The assessment included the Center for Epidemiologic Studies–Depression self-report scale (Radloff, 1977), on which Ben scored 18 (marginally clinically significant). In relation to the criteria of the revised third edition of the *Diagnostic and Statistical Manual of Mental Disorders* (American Psychiatric Association, 1987) for major depressive disorder, Ben qualified for diminished interest, psychomotor retardation, fatigue, feelings of worthlessness, but exhibited no marked sleep or appetite disturbances or thoughts of suicide. (See Scogin, chapter 4 in this book, for further considerations of instruments that are useful for assessing depression.) Ben was apparently frightened to admit to these feelings because of having seen a friend, who had sunk into a very deep depression, referred for ECT. Ben's friend had gone through a period of extreme withdrawal and refusal to eat; after treatment, Ben's friend seemed improved for a little while but had subsequently relapsed. Ben was concerned about a similar fate. Although Ben consented to his wife's describing the problem, as she saw it, to the therapist, he was initially reluctant to include his wife in receiving information from the assessment. He did agree to eight sessions of individual psychotherapy. The therapist used behavioral and cognitive behavioral approaches (Thompson et al., 1987). Ben began keeping a log of his pleasant activities, and in the sessions, the therapist addressed some of his irrational thinking. It became increasingly clear that one issue was that Ben's wife desired a more active life, whereas Ben wanted her to be around for him more. Eventually, Ben agreed to several sessions with his wife included. Assessment of the marital situation was undertaken, including a procedure in which they began to keep logs of their shared pleasant activities (Jacobson & Margolin, 1979). The therapist focused on reconciling their expectations of one another, which had changed with both of their retirements and with various physical limitations that Ben had accrued.

Hugh, an 83-year-old widower, referred himself for a dementia assessment. He dated the primary onset of his concern to an event last December, when he was subjected to an armed attack outside of his home. His garage door opener failed to function when he returned home from a restaurant one evening, and he was held up at gunpoint when he left the car to operate the garage door manually. Although he was uninjured, he remained fearful of another such episode, and he had recently installed a home security system that included a patrol service to escort him home in the evening. Hugh's outside interests had recently become curtailed, partly due to the disbanding of the local branch of a political club that he used to attend. Hugh had two married sons, whom he rarely saw, although he was quite proud of them. There had recently been a number of occasions in which Hugh forgot where he put things, such as his address book. He became concerned that he might have Alzheimer's disease, which he had learned about in the newspaper. Memory testing was within the normal range, although there was some decrement in logical memory (i.e., memory for text) and in timed tests such as a symbol–digit substitution task. (See Lezak, 1983, concerning neuropsychological test batteries, and Kaszniak, chapter 5 in this book, for discussions of differential diagnosis of dementia and depression.) Hugh tired during testing and seemed to be frustrated and anxious when he had difficulties with any item (despite the psychologist's reassurances that he should not expect to get everything correct). In further assessment of Hugh's mood, using the Brief Symptom Inventory (Derogatis & Spencer, 1982), Hugh was moderately elevated with respect to both depression and anxiety. The therapist explained that depression and anxiety can obstruct optimal cognitive functioning and proposed an intervention plan that included some counseling aimed at Hugh's depression, followed by a memory reassessment in 1 year to determine whether there was any decline.

"Should I make Dad stop driving?" asked Caryn, a 63-year-old daughter, in describing her concerns. Apparently her father had an accident about 4 months ago in which his fender was damaged when he pulled into an intersection without looking. Caryn heard about the accident from some friends who said that they would no longer ride with her father because he gets lost and will not accept help and because they did not feel safe. When Caryn asked about the accident, her father said that he had something on his mind but that there was nothing wrong with him. Caryn reported that her father had been seen by his physician and that her father told Caryn that the physician determined that he was not demented. Caryn had not spoken with the physician. She described a long history of regarding her father as controlling, but she believed that the stubbornness had recently gotten worse. Caryn subsequently persuaded her father to come for a neuropsychological assessment, which revealed quite problematic performance, especially on visuospatial tasks. (See Butters, Salmon, & Butters, chapter 3 in this book, for a review of neuropsychological instruments.) The driving situation ultimately resolved itself when the father had another minor accident. While the car was being repaired, he was hospitalized for a heart problem. During that time, he permitted Caryn's son to use the car. After being discharged from the hospital, he moved to Caryn's house to recuperate, which was a major concession on his part to not being fully independent, and he then began to investigate possible facilities where he might move. He never asked for the car back from his grandson.

Notice in this case that the primary client is the daughter. At some level, she wished to have a conversation with her father to work through how they felt about one another. In this scenario, one consequence would be improved communication, which would possibly make Caryn's father more receptive to her urging him not to drive. Through the assessment results, the therapist persuaded Caryn that the father was too impaired to achieve this sort of resolution and helped her to readjust her expectations.

CONCLUSION

In this chapter, I have provided a framework for the assessment process in which assessment and intervention are presented as interrelated elements over the course of the clinician's contact with the elderly client. Quite different treatments follow from different diagnostic hypotheses. At various times, drug, ECT, and psychotherapeutic interventions—or a combination thereof—may be recommended for depression, depending on endogenous symptoms, precipitating situation, concurrent medical conditions, suicidality, and patient preference. Dementia cases more often call upon the clinician to involve the family and to provide information. Follow-up is often essential, and cases that require differential diagnoses especially dictate periodic reassessment. Perhaps with older adults, more than with other population groups, the need to work back and forth between assessment and intervention is most compelling.

REFERENCES

American Medical Association, Council on Scientific Affairs. (1987). Elder abuse and neglect. *Journal of the American Medical Association, 257,* 966–971.

American Psychiatric Association. (1987). *Diagnostic and statistical manual of mental disorders* (3rd ed., rev.). Washington, DC: Author.

Bäckman, L. (1992). Memory training and memory improvement in Alzheimer's disease: Rules and exceptions. *Acta Neurologica Scandinavica, 139*(Suppl.), 84–89.

Baddeley, A. (1990). *Human memory: Theory and practice.* Needham Heights, MA: Allyn & Bacon.

Baldwin, B. (1991). The outcome of depression in old age. *International Journal of Geriatric Psychiatry, 6,* 395–400.

Beutler, L. E., Scogin, F., Kirkish, P., Schretlen, D., Corbishley, A., Hamblin, D., Meredith, K., Potter, R., Bamford, C. R., & Levenson, A. I. (1987). Group cognitive therapy and alprazolam in the treatment of depression in older adults. *Journal of Consulting and Clinical Psychology, 55,* 550–556.

Blazer, D., Hughes, D. C., & George, L. K. (1992). Age and impaired subjective support: Predictors of depressive symptoms at one-year follow-up. *Journal of Nervous and Mental Disease, 180,* 172–178.

Burke, W. J., Rubin, E. H., Zorumski, C. F., & Wetzel, R. D. (1987). The safety of ECT in geriatric psychiatry. *Journal of the American Geriatrics Society, 35,* 516–521.

Burns, B. J., Wagner, H. R., Taube, J. E., Magaziner, J., Permutt, T., & Landerman, L. R. (1993). Mental health service use by the elderly in nursing homes. *American Journal of Public Health, 83,* 331–337.

Burvill, P. W., Hall, W. D., Stampfer, H. G., & Emmerson, J. P. (1991). The prognosis of depression in old age. *British Journal of Psychiatry, 158,* 64–71.

Calev, A., Nigal, D., Shapira, B., Tubi, N., Chazan, S., Ben-Yehuda, Y., Kugelmass, S., & Lerer, B. (1991). Early and long-term effects of electroconvulsive therapy and depression on memory and other cognitive functions. *Journal of Nervous and Mental Disease, 179,* 526–533.

Cattan, R. A., Barry, P. P., Mead, G., Reefe, W. E., Gay, A., & Silverman, M. (1990). Electroconvulsive therapy in octagenarians. *Journal of the American Geriatrics Society, 38,* 753–758.

Cohen, G. (1993). Comprehensive assessment: Capturing strengths, not just weaknesses. *Generations, 17*(1), 47–50.

Cohen, G. D. (1992). The future of mental health and aging. In J. E. Birren, R. B. Sloane, & G. D. Cohen (Eds.), *Handbook of mental health and aging* (2nd ed., pp. 893–912). San Diego, CA: Academic Press.

Cohn, M. D., Smyer, M. A., Garfein, A. J., Droogas, A., & MaloneBeach, E. E. (1987). Perceptions of mental health training in nursing homes: Congruence among administrators and aides. *Journal of Long Term Care Administration, 15,* 20–25.

Derogatis, L. R., & Spencer, P. M. (1982). *The Brief Symptom Inventory (BSI): Administration, scoring, and procedures manual–I.* Baltimore: Johns Hopkins University School of Medicine, Clinical Psychometrics Research Unit.

Drachman, D. A. (1993). New criteria for the diagnosis of vascular dementia: Do we know enough yet? *Neurology, 43,* 243–245.

Eth, S., & Leong, G. B. (1992). Forensic and ethical issues. In J. E. Birren, R. B. Sloane, & G. D. Cohen (Eds.), *Handbook of mental health and aging* (2nd ed., pp. 853–871). San Diego, CA: Academic Press.

Frank, E. (1991). Interpersonal psychotherapy as a maintenance treatment for patients with recurrent depression. *Psychotherapy, 28,* 259–266.

Franks, M. M., & Stephens, M. A. P. (1992). Multiple roles of middle-generation caregivers: Contextual effects and psychological mechanisms. *Journal of Gerontology: Social Sciences, 47,* S123–129.

Gallagher-Thompson, D., Hanley-Peterson, P., & Thompson, L. W. (1990). Maintenance of gains versus relapse following brief psychotherapy for depression. *Journal of Consulting and Clinical Psychology, 58,* 371–374.

Gatz, M. (1989). Clinical psychology and aging. In M. Storandt & G. R. VandenBos (Eds.), *The adult years: Continuity and change* (pp. 79–114). Washington, DC: American Psychological Association.

Gatz, M., Smyer, M. A., Garfein, A., & Seward, M. (1991). Essentials of assessment in nursing homes. In M. Harper (Ed.), *Mental health assessment and long-term care* (pp. 293–309). Newbury Park, CA: Sage.

George, L. K., Blazer, D. F., Hughes, D. C., & Fowler, N. (1989). Social support and the outcome of major depression. *British Journal of Psychiatry, 154,* 478–485.

Gerson, S. C., Plotkin, D. A., & Jarvik, L. F. (1988). Antidepressant drug studies, 1964 to 1986: Empirical evidence for aging patients. *Journal of Clinical Psychopharmacology, 8,* 311–322.

Greenberg, L., & Fink, M. (1992). The use of electroconvulsive therapy in geriatric patients. *Psychiatric Disorders in Late Life, 8,* 349–354.

Hanley-Peterson, P., Futterman, A., Thompson, L., Zeiss, A. M., Gallagher, D., & Ironson, G. (1990). Endogenous depression and psychotherapy outcome in an elderly population [abstract]. *Gerontologist, 30,* 51A.

Herr, J. J., & Weakland, J. H. (1979). *Counseling elders and their families: Practical techniques for applied gerontology.* New York: Springer.

Hooper, C. (1992). Encircling a mechanism in Alzheimer's disease. *Journal of NIH Research, 4,* 48–54.

Jacobson, N. S., & Margolin, G. (1979). *Marital therapy: Strategies based on social learning and behavior exchange principles.* New York: Bruner/Mazel.

Jarvik, L. F. (1976). Aging and depression: Some unanswered questions. *Journal of Gerontology, 31,* 324–326.

Katz, R. R., Simpson, G. M., Curlik, S. M., Parmelee, P. A., & Muhly, C. (1990). Pharmacologic treatment of major depression for elderly patients in residential care settings. *Journal of Clinical Psychiatry, 51*(Suppl.), 41–47.

Kimmel, D. C., & Moody, H. R. (1990). Ethical issues in gerontological research and services. In J. E. Birren & K. W. Schaie (Eds.), *Handbook of the psychology of aging* (3rd ed., pp. 489–501). San Diego, CA: Academic Press.

Knight, B. G. (1992). *Older adults in psychotherapy: Case histories.* Newbury Park, CA: Sage.

Kramer, B. A. (1987). Electroconvulsive therapy use in geriatric depression. *Journal of Nervous and Mental Disease, 175,* 233–235.

Kuhn, M. (1987). Politics and aging: The Gray Panthers. In L. L. Carstensen & B. A. Edelstein (Eds.), *Handbook of clinical gerontology* (pp. 376–386). Elmsford, NY: Pergamon Press.

Lawton, M. P. (1986). Functional assessment. In L. Teri & P. M. Lewinsohn (Eds.), *Geropsychological assessment and treatment* (pp. 39–84). New York: Springer.

Lezak, M. D. (1983). *Neuropsychological assessment* (2nd ed.). New York: Oxford University Press.

Lieberman, M. A. (1992). Limitations of psychological stress model: Studies of widowhood. In M. L. Wykle, E. Kahana, & J. Kowal (Eds.), *Stress and health among the elderly* (pp. 133–150). New York: Springer.

Lovett, S., & Gallagher, D. (1988). Psychoeducational interventions for family caregivers: Preliminary efficacy data. *Behavior Therapy, 19,* 321–330.

Maloney, M. P., & Ward, M. P. (1976). *Psychological assessment: A conceptual approach.* New York: Oxford University Press.

NIH Consensus Development Panel on Depression in Late Life. (1992). Diagnosis and treatment of depression in late life. *Journal of the American Medical Association, 268,* 1018–1024.

Norris, F., & Murrell, S. (1988). Prior experience as a moderator of disaster impact on anxiety symptoms in older adults. *American Journal of Community Psychology, 16*, 665–683.

Pearlin, L. I., & Mullan, J. T. (1992). Loss and stress in aging. In M. L. Wykle, E. Kahana, & J. Kowal (Eds.), *Stress and health among the elderly* (pp. 117–132). New York: Springer.

Radloff, L. (1977). A self-report depression scale for research in the general population. *Applied Psychological Measurement, 1*, 385–401.

Rapp, S. R., Parisi, S. A., Walsh, D. A., & Wallace, C. E. (1988). Detecting depression in elderly medical outpatients. *Journal of Consulting and Clinical Psychology, 56*, 509–513.

Raskind, M. A., & Peskind, E. R. (1992). Alzheimer's disease and other dementing disorders. In J. E. Birren, R. B. Sloane, & G. D. Cohen (Eds.), *Handbook of mental health and aging* (2nd ed., pp. 478–515). San Diego, CA: Academic Press.

Regier, D. A., Boyd, J. H., Burke, J. D., Rae, D. S., Myers, J. K., Kramer, M., Robins, L. N., George, L. K., Karno, M., & Locke, B. Z. (1988). One-month prevalence of mental disorders in the United States. *Archives of General Psychiatry, 45*, 977–986.

Reifler, B. V., Larson, E., & Hanley, R. (1982). Coexistence of cognitive impairment and depression in geriatric outpatients. *American Journal of Psychiatry, 139*, 623–626.

Reifler, B. V., Teri, L., Raskind, M., Veith, R., Barnes, R., White, E., & McLean, P. (1989). Double-blind trial of imipramine in Alzheimer's disease patients with and without depression. *American Journal of Psychiatry, 146*, 45–48.

Reynolds, C. F., Frank, E., Perel, J. M., Imber, S. D., Cornes, C., Morycz, R. K., Mazumdar, S., Miller, M. D., Pollock, B. G., Rifai, A. H., Stack, J. A., George, C. J., Houck, P. R., & Kupfer, D. J. (1992). Combined pharmacotherapy and psychotherapy in the acute and continuation treatment of elderly patients with recurrent major depression: A preliminary report. *American Journal of Psychiatry, 149*, 1689–1692.

Rodin, G., & Voshart, K. (1986). Depression in the medically ill: An overview. *American Journal of Psychiatry, 143*, 696–705.

Ryan, W. (1971). *Blaming the victim.* New York: Vintage Books.

Salzman, C., & Nevis-Olesen, J. (1992). Psychopharmacologic treatment. In J. E. Birren, R. B. Sloane, & G. D. Cohen (Eds.), *Handbook of mental health and aging* (2nd ed., pp. 721–762). San Diego, CA: Academic Press.

Shapiro, S., Skinner, E. A., Kessler, L. G., Von Korff, M., German, P. S., Tischler, G. L., Leaf, P. J., Benham, L., Cottler, L., & Regier, D. A. (1984). Utilization of health and mental health services: Three Epidemiologic Catchment Area sites. *Archives of General Psychiatry, 41*, 971–978.

Small, G. (1988). Psychopharmacological treatment of elderly demented patients. *Journal of Clinical Psychiatry, 49*(Suppl.), 8–13.

Smyer, M. A. (1989). Nursing homes as a setting for psychological practice. *American Psychologist, 44*, 1307–1314.

Smyer, M. A., Cohn, M. D., & Brannon, D. (1988). *Mental health consultation in nursing homes.* New York: New York University Press.

Stoudemire, A., Hill, C. D., Morris, R., Martino-Saltzman, D., Markwalter, H., & Lewison, B. (1991). Cognitive outcome following tricylic and electroconvulsive treatment of major depression in the elderly. *American Journal of Psychiatry, 148,* 1336–1340.

Teri, L., & Gallagher, D. (1991). Cognitive–behavioral interventions for treatment of depression. *Gerontologist, 31,* 413–416.

Teri, L., Reifler, B. V., Raskind, M., Veith, R. C., Barnes, R., White, E., & McLean, P. (1991). Imipramine in the treatment of depressed Alzheimer's patients: Impact on cognition. *Journal of Gerontology: Psychological Sciences, 46,* P372–P377.

Teri, L., & Uomoto, J. (1991). Reducing excess disability in dementia patients: Training caregivers to manage patient depression. *Clinical Gerontologist, 10,* 49–63.

Teri, L., & Wagner, A. (1992). Alzheimer's disease and depression. *Journal of Consulting and Clinical Psychology, 60,* 379–391.

Thompson, L. W., Gallagher, D. E., & Breckenridge, J. S. (1987). Comparative effectiveness of psychotherapies for depressed elders. *Journal of Consulting and Clinical Psychology, 55,* 385–390.

Thompson, L. W., Gallagher, D., & Czirr, R. (1988). Personality disorder and outcome in the treatment of late-life depression. *Journal of Geriatric Psychiatry, 21,* 133–146.

Toseland, R. W., & Smith, G. C. (1990). Effectiveness of individual counseling by professional and peer helpers for family caregivers of the elderly. *Psychology and Aging, 5,* 256–263.

Waxman, H. M., & Carner, E. A. (1984). Physicians' recognition, diagnosis, and treatment of mental disorders in elderly medical patients. *Gerontologist, 24,* 593–597.

Zarit, S. H. (1980). *Aging and mental disorders: Psychological approaches to assessment and treatment.* New York: Free Press.

Zarit, S. H., Anthony, C. R., & Boutselis, M. (1987). Interventions with caregivers of dementia patients: Comparison of two approaches. *Psychology and Aging, 2,* 225–232.

Zeiss, A. M., & Lewinsohn, P. M. (1986, Fall). Adapting behavioral treatment for depression to meet the needs of the elderly. *Clinical Psychologist,* 98–100.

APPENDIX A

Survey of Clinicians' Practices With Older Adults

F. MARCUS BROWN III and JACK G. WIGGINS, JR.

The results of this survey are derived from forms mailed to the participants of a conference for practitioners titled "Neuropsychological Assessment of Older Adults: Dementia and Depression," which was held in St. Louis, Missouri, in May 1993. Of the 345 conference participants who were sent the form, 79 responded. These individuals had already completed the American Psychological Association (APA) Office of Continuing Education's evaluation form, which may explain the relatively low return rate of 23% for this second postconference survey. This low return may also suggest limited exposure to elders in clinical practice. Nevertheless, the survey results are given here because they provide some significant data that may be of interest to this book's readers.

SURVEY RESULTS

1. Highest degree you have completed:
   Doctoral level: 76
   Masters level: 3
   Are you licensed?
   77
   How many years have you been evaluating elders?
   The range was between 0–30 years, with a mean of 8.9 years in a somewhat biomodal distribution.
   Your gender:
   Male 50 (63%)   Female 29 (37%)
   This corresponds approximately to the male-to-female ratio in the

We thank Marianne Jahn, Department of Psychology, Connecticut Valley Hospital, for her assistance in collating quantitative data from this survey.

membership of APA. It does not correspond to the gender distribution of older adults, who are predominantly female.

Your age (in years):

26–35: 12
36–45: 34
46–55: 17
56–65: 8
66+ : 7

These data indicate that older adults are evaluated by psychologists of all ages. The distribution of ages of psychologists roughly corresponds to the age distribution of APA members.

2. How many elders do you see for evaluation in your practice each month?

The range was from 1 to 100s, with a mean of 13.9.

3. What percentage of your elderly patients are age:

65–69: 23.9%
70–74: 22.5%
75–79: 20.0%
80–84: 12.5%
85–89: 7.5%
90–94: 2.2%
95 and over: .9%

Although most of the patients that are represented are under 80 years, these data indicate a strong need to extend age norms of psychological tests to at least age 80.

4. In the last month, how many elderly patients did you see? (Please describe) Expressed in means:

a. Hospital 9.7%
b. Nursing home 12.2%
c. Private office 3.2%
d. Patient's residence 0.3%
e. Other 0.4%

Thirty comments to this question indicated locus of contact in which there are a high number of older adult patients in either residence or other specialized services. Early evaluation of the elderly in private offices is not the prevailing pattern. The total mean number of contacts (26) is nearly twice as great as the number of older adults evaluated, which suggests the need for ongoing contact with this population beyond evaluation.

5. What percentage of your elderly patients have alcohol or substance abuse problems?

16.7%

This estimate is over 12 times the National Institute on Alcohol Abuse and Alcoholism estimate (1.37%) for diagnosable abuse or dependency over age 65 using criteria of the revised third edition of the Diagnostic and Statistical Manual of Mental Disorders *(American Psychiatric Association, 1987). This suggests psychologists are either dealing with a special subset of older adults (e.g., individuals who also are on psychotropic medications that potentiate the effects of alcohol and other drugs or medications) or are overestimating the frequency of occurrence. In either event, further study is indicated.*

6. In the last month, how many of your elderly patients were referred for:

a.	Preadmission Screening and Annual Resident Review	0.8%
b.	Mental retardation	0.5%
c.	Depression	12.9%
d.	Dementia	13.7%
e.	Function/behavioral assessments	7.2%
f.	Competency to stand trial	0.4%
g.	Eating disorder	1.1%
h.	Need for conservatorship	2.2%
i.	Reversible dementia	3.4%
j.	Other	8.0%

Eight respondents reported referrals were prompted by some behavioral change creating psychological symptomatology (e.g., anxiety-, depression-, or stress-related symptoms).

7. What percentage of your elderly patients have collaterals or collateral sources of information involved in the evaluation? 65%

This reflects the importance of obtaining confirming information especially when dealing with older adults.

8. Which of the following are part of your basic assessment package for elders?

a.	Intelligence battery	0.9%
b.	Memory scales	0.9%
c.	Standardized history	0.7%
d.	Projective methods	0.1%
e.	Functional assessment scales	0.3%
f.	Depression rating scales	0.8%
g.	Standardized interview	0.7%
h.	Objective personality measures	0.6%
i.	Others	

Twenty-five individuals reported a wide assortment of psychological test instruments, including those dealing with language functions, sensory abilities, visuomotor abilities, and so on. This suggests that the practitioner who is evaluating older adults needs to be knowledgeable with a wide assortment of testing approaches. Special training in methods of assessing a range of functional and psychological abilities in elders is required in addition to the traditional formal tests of mental and psychological functions.

9. What percentage of your elderly patients cannot complete formal testing because of:
   a. Hearing impairment   4.6%
   b. Visual impairment   6.1%
   c. Motor impairment   5.5%
   d. Cognitive impairment   12.8%
   e. Language impairment   4.7%
   f. Fatigue   7.1%
   g. Other   0.5%

   The 14 responses to Other reported that the patient's medical or psychological status interfered so that some psychological functions could not be assessed without adapting test instruments for the specific patient.

10. Is any special equipment (e.g., audio amplifier, large-print written materials) part of your geriatric assessment package? Which specialized norms or tests have you found most useful? Which books have you found useful for assessment of elders? Of the 24 respondents to this question, lists of special equipment include by frequency:

Large print material:	12
Amplifiers	4
Magnifying devices	2

   Special norms found useful by frequency:

Halstead–Reitan Battery revised norms (Heaton)	6
Mayo Older Adult Normative Study (MOANS) norms (Wechsler Adult Intelligence Scale–Revised)	6
MOANS norms (Wechsler Memory Scale–Revised)	5

   Twenty-three tests found helpful, including by frequency:

California Verbal Linguistic Test	4
Dementia Rating Scale (Mattis)	4
Geriatric Depression Scale	4
Wechsler Memory Scale–Revised	4

   Of the 13 books listed the following were enumerated by frequency:

Aging and Neuropsychological Assessment (LaRue, 1992)	4
Clinical Memory Assessment of Older Adults (Poon, 1986)	2
Geriatric Neuropsychology (Albert & Moss, 1988)	4

11. Any special resources you have found helpful in the evaluation of elders? Please describe.

This item elicited only two replies.

12. Please rank-order needs for additional training (1 indicates the most important, 5 the least):

1. Substance abuse in elders	1.5
2. Tie: Differential diagnosis in elders, forensic issues, *and* disorders that cause psychological and behavioral problems	1.8
5. Tie: Assessing behavior problems *and* eating disorders in the elderly	1.9
7. Clinical evaluation of elders	2.0
8. Funding/payment issues	2.2
9. Tie: Neuropsychology of elders *and* models of normal aging	
11. Other: Sixteen individuals suggested other topics (e.g., head injury, psychopharmacology, functional-based assessment, issues involved with death and dying).	

In addition to problems common to adults, elders experience unique circumstances that require the attention of psychologists. In this survey, the respondents identified many of the special issues in the evaluation of older adults. Additional training needs were identified for future continuing education efforts.

REFERENCES

Albert, M. S., & Moss, M. B. (1988). *Geriatric neuropsychology*. New York: Guilford Press.

American Psychiatric Association. (1987). *Diagnostic and statistical manual of mental disorders* (3rd ed., rev.). Washington, DC: Author.

LaRue, A. (1992). *Aging and neuropsychological assessment*. New York: Plenum.

Poon, L. W. (1986). *Clinical memory assessment of older adults*. Washington, DC: American Psychological Association.

APPENDIX B

A Listing of References to Cognitive Test Norms for Older Adults

RICHARD C. ERICKSON, PERRY EIMON, and NANCY HEBBEN

This appendix represents updated material and references that were reported in *The Clinical Neuropsychologist* (1992, Volume 6, pp. 98–102). The data include the names of the tests, references, the age range and number of subjects involved in the geriatric samples, and the settings where the subjects lived.

Since the publication of that article, Spreen and Strauss (1991) have published a compendium that provides instructions for administration, norms, and commentary for a number of commonly used neuropsychological tests. The norms are drawn from the existing literature (marked with an asterisk) or are based on data they gathered, often otherwise unpublished. Included in their volume are norms for a number of tests of basic speech and language, as well as tests of perceptual and motor skills not referenced here.

TABLE 1
Mental Status Exams

Name/reference	Age	N	Population
Clifton Assessment Schedule			
Pattie & Gillard (1975)	$M = 70$	67	Psychiatric inpatients
Cognitive Battery for Dementia			
Christensen et al. (1991)	$M = 66$	131	Healthy older adults
Isaacs and Walkey			
Isaacs & Walkey (1963)	$M = 75$	446	Inpatients
KEW Test			
Towle et al. (1987)	58–91	53	Patients
Mattis Dementia Rating Scale			
Spreen & Strauss (1991)	65–89	85	Normals
Mental Status Questionnaire			
Haglund & Schuckit (1976)	65+	279	Male medical/surgery admissions
Kahn et al. (1960)	65+	1,077	Institutionalized
Markson & Levitz (1973)	65+	254	Psychiatric patients
Pfeffer et al. (1981)	$M = 75$	97	Retirement community
Orientation–Memory–Concentration			
Katzman et al. (1983)	65–105	322	Nursing home
Short Portable Mental Status Questionnaire			
Haglund & Schuckit (1976)	65+	279	Male medical/surgery admissions
Pfeiffer (1975)	65+	997	Community dwelling
Temporal Orientation Test			
Benton et al. (1983)	NA	434	Mixed
Levin & Benton (1975)	NA	180	Mixed
Natelson et al. (1979)	NA	254	Mixed
Cambridge Cognitive Examination			
Roth et al. (1986)	65+	17	Normals
Cognitive Capacity Screening Examination			
Haddad & Coffman (1987)	$M = 75$	46	Psychiatric inpatients
Jacobs et al. (1977)	NA	147	Patients & staff
McCartney & Palmateer (1985)	"Elderly"	182	Medical/surgery admissions
Geriatric Interpersonal Evaluation Scale			
Plutchik et al. (1971)	$M = 75$	78	State hospital inpatients
Mental Status Checklist			
Lifshitz (1960)	55–75	78	State hospital inpatients
Mini-Mental State			
Anthony et al. (1982)	60–80+	41	Medical admissions
Folstein et al. (1985)	65+	923	Community dwelling
Pfeffer et al. (1981)	$M = 75$	97	Retirement community
Extended Scale for Dementia (Mattis Demential Scale)			
Hersch (1979)	46–96	39	Normals
Neurobehavioral Cognitive Status Exam			
Kiernan et al. (1987)	70–92	59	Normals

Note. NA = not given.

TABLE 2
Neuropsychological Batteries

Name/reference	Age	N	Population
Benton Neuropsychological Assessment			
Benton et al. (1981)	65–84	162	Community dwelling
Benton et al. (1983)	Varies	Varies	Non-brain damaged
Eslinger & Benton (1983)	65–94	178	Community dwelling
Boston Diagnostic Aphasia Examination			
Borod et al. (1980)	60–85	56	Normals
Van Gorp et al. (1986)	59–80+	78	Community dwelling
Van Gorp et al. (1990)	58–85	156	Retirement community
Halstead–Reitan Neuropsychological Battery			
Borstein (1985)	60–69	107	Community dwelling
Ernst (1988)	65–75	85	Community dwelling
Harley et al. (1980)	65–79	92	VA inpatients
Heaton et al. (1986)	60+	100	Normals
Luria–Nebraska Neuropsychological Battery			
MacInnes et al. (1983)	$M = 72$	78	Community dwelling
MacInnes et al. (1984)	$M = 72$	59	Community dwelling

Note. VA = Veterans Affairs hospital.

TABLE 3
Intellectual Abilities

Name/reference	Age	N	Population
AMNART			
Grober & Sliwinski (1991)	$M = 75$	230	Community dwelling
Primary Mental Abilities Test			
Schaie et al. (1953)	65–78	28	Community dwelling
Schaie (1959)	61–70	100	Community dwelling
Quick Test			
Gendreau et al. (1973)	$M = 80$	47	Home for aged
Levine (1971)	60–100	50	Community dwelling
Shipley Institute of Living Scale			
Schear (1984)	60–69	69	VA patients
Shelton et al. (1982)	$M = 71$	24	Community dwelling
Wechsler Adult Intelligence Scale			
Doppelt & Wallace (1955)	60+	475	Community dwelling
Schear (1984)	60–69	69	VA patients
Wechsler (1955)	65+	251	Community dwelling
Wechsler Adult Intelligence Scale–Revised			
Ivnik et al. (1992a)	56–97	512	Normal elderly
Wechsler (1981)	65–74	320	Community dwelling

Note. VA = Veterans Affairs hospital.

TABLE 4
Attentional Processes and Memory Functioning

Name/reference	Age	N	Population
I. Memory batteries			
Barbizet and Cany			
Barbizet & Cany (1968)	65+	51	Normals
Denman Neuropsychological Memory Scale			
Denman (1984)	60–89	120	Normals (1986 norms)
Guild Memory Test			
Crook et al. (1980b)	60–80	228	Community dwelling
Gilbert & Levee (1971)	60–75	103	Community dwelling
New York University Memory Test			
Randt et al. (1980)	60–79	105	Mixed
Wechsler Memory Scale			
Abikoff et al. (1987)	60–80+	103	Community dwelling
Albert et al. (1987)	60–70+	40	Community dwelling
Cauthen (1977)	60–94	64	Institutional settings
desRosiers & Ivison (1986)	60–69	100	Medical/surgery inpatients
Farmer et al. (1987)	55–89	2,123	Community dwelling
Gilleard (1980)	M = 74	50	Psychiatric inpatients
Hulicka (1966)	60–89	141	Mixed
Ivison (1986)	60–69	100	Medical/surgery patients
Ivnik et al. (1991)	65–97	99	Normals
Klonoff & Kennedy (1965)	80–92	172	Community dwelling
Klonoff & Kennedy (1966)	80–92	115	Community dwelling
McCarty et al. (1982)	63–87	172	Community dwelling
Margolis & Scialfa (1984)	70–92	161	Normals
Osborne & Davis (1978)	65–75+	121	Patients
Piersma (1986)	66–88	36	Psychiatric inpatients
Van Gorp et al. (1990)	58–85	156	Retirement community
Wechsler Memory Scale–Russell Revision			
Haaland et al. (1983)	65–80+	175	Community dwelling
McCarty et al. (1980)	71–93	25	Retirement home
Russell (1988)	60–90	?	VA inpatients
Schear (1984)	60–69	69	VA patients
Wechsler Memory Scale–Revised			
Ivnik et al. (1992b)	56–94	441	Normal elderly
Wechsler (1987)	65–74	105	Community dwelling
II. Attention and concentration			
Block Span			
Corkin (1982)	55–81	15	Healthy elderly
Concentration Endurance Test (d 2 Test)			
Spreen & Strauss (1991)	50–85	61	Healthy volunteers
Digit Recall			
Benton et al. (1981)	65–84	40	Community dwelling
Crook et al. (1980a)	60–88	44	Community dwelling
Farmer et al. (1987)	55–89	2,123	Community dwelling
Paced Auditory Serial Addition Task			
Roman et al. (1991)	60–75	41	Normals
Stuss et al. (1987)	60–69	10	Community dwelling
Stuss et al. (1988)	50–69	30	Normals

TABLE 4
(*continued*)

Name/reference	Age	N	Population
Reverse Spelling			
Bender (1979)	60–90	266	Normals
Serial Sevens			
Smith (1967)	56–63	9	Normals

III. Learning and memory

Name/reference	Age	N	Population
Aronson Shopping List			
Tsang et al. (1991)	61–87	81	Community dwelling
Benton Visual Retention Test			
Arenberg (1978)	60+	288	Community dwelling
Benton et al. (1981)	65–84	162	Community dwelling
Spreen & Strauss (1991)*	60–89	173	Community dwelling
Klonoff & Kennedy (1965)	80–92	172	Community dwelling
Klonoff & Kennedy (1966)	80–92	115	Community dwelling
Block Design Learning Test			
Savage & Hall (1973)	61–93	40	Community dwelling
California Verbal Learning Test			
Delis et al. (1987)	65–80	From 273 non-brain damaged $M = 60$	
Continuous Recognition Memory Test			
Trahan et al. (1986)	66–77	54	Community dwelling
Continuous Visual Memory Test			
Trahan & Larrabee (1988)	70+	30	Nonhospitalized
Expanded Paired Associate Test			
Trahan et al. (1989)	70+	25	Healthy elderly
Fowler Non-Language Paired Associates			
Fowler (1969)	60+	20	Community dwelling
Fuld Object Memory			
Fuld (1980)	70–89	32	Community dwelling
Graham–Kendall Memory for Designs			
Haglund & Schuckit (1976)	65+	279	Medical/surgery admissions
Shelton et al. (1982)	$M = 71$	24	Community dwelling
Inglis Paired Associates			
Caird et al. (1962)	64–84	30	Psychiatric inpatients
Kendrick & Post (1967)	$M = 71$	30	Depressed & normal
LaRue et al. (1986)	$M = 73$	10	Health elderly
Whitehead (1973)	$M = 70$	26	Depressed patients
Learning and Memory Battery			
Schmidt et al. (1992)	60–79	140	Community dwelling
Tombaugh & Schmidt (1992)	60–79	200	Community dwelling
Misplaced Objects			
Crook et al. (1979)	60–88	44	Community dwelling
Modified Word Learning Test			
Bolton et al. (1967)	60+	29	Community dwelling
Rey Auditory Verbal Learning Test			
Bleecker et al. (1988)	60–89	123	Nursing home
Ivnik et al. (1992c)	56–97	530	Normal elderly
Query & Megran (1983)	65+	49	Medical inpatients
Van Gorp et al. (1990)	58–85	156	Retirement community
Rey Complex Figure Test			
Berry et al. (1991)	$M = 65$	107	Community dwelling
Berry & Carpenter (1992)	$M = 68$	60	Healthy older persons
Boone et al. (1993)	60–83	53	Healthy older adults

TABLE 4
(continued)

Name/reference	Age	N	Population
Denman (1984)	60–89	120	Normals (1986 norms)
Rosselli & Ardila (1991)	56–76+	346	Normal elderly
Van Gorp et al. (1990)	58–85	156	Retirement community
Rey Visual Design Learning Test			
Spreen & Strauss (1991)	60–84	24	Healthy older adults
Serial Digit Learning			
Benton et al. (1981)	65–84	162	Community dwelling
Benton et al. (1983)	65–74	53	Medical inpatients
Selective Reminding			
Masur et al. (1989)	$M = 80$	134	Healthy elderly
Ruff et al. (1988)	55–70	96	Community dwelling
Spreen & Strauss (1991)*	60–91	?	Unspecified
Visual Spatial Learning Test			
Malec et al. (1992)	56–97	455	Community dwelling

TABLE 5
Perceptual–Motor Speed and Coordination

Name/reference	Age	N	Population
Bender–Gestalt			
Canter & Straumanis (1969)	65–84	17	Normals
Klonoff & Kennedy (1965)	80–92	172	Community dwelling
Klonoff & Kennedy (1966)	80–92	115	Community dwelling
Lacks & Storandt (1982)	60–87	334	Senior citizen apartments
Clock Test			
Sunderland et al. (1989)	$M = 74$	83	Normal controls
Wolf-Klein et al. (1989)	$M = 77$	130	Normal
Complex Figure Test			
Berry et al. (1991)	$M = 65$	107	Community dwelling
Denman (1984)	60–89	120	Normals (1986 norms)
Rosselli & Ardila (1991)	56–76+	346	Normal elderly
Tombaugh et al. (1992)	60–79	136	Community dwelling
Van Gorp et al. (1990)	58–85	156	Retirement community
Pegboard			
Bornstein (1985)	60–69	107	Community dwelling
Schear (1984)	60–69	69	VA patients
Spreen & Strauss (1991)	60–70+	44	Healthy volunteers
Symbol–Digit Modalities Test			
Lezak (1983; p. 555)	65–74	61	Community dwelling
Pfeffer et al. (1981)	$M = 75$	97	Retirement community
Smith (1976)	65–74	61	Community dwelling
Symbol–Digit Substitution Task			
Gilmore et al. (1983)	60–80+	90	Community dwelling
Trails A and B			
Davies (1968)	60–79	180	Community dwelling
Lindsey & Coppinger (1969)	40–80	100	VA institutionalized
Schear (1984)	60–69	69	VA patients
Spreen & Strauss (1991)*	60–79	210	Unspecified
Van Gorp et al. (1990)	58–85	156	Retirement community

Note. VA = Veterans Affairs hospital.

TABLE 6
Problem Solving and Executive Functions

Name/reference	Age	N	Population
Auditory and Visual Continuous Performance Tests			
Albert et al. (1987)	60–70+	40	Community dwelling
Category Test			
Heaton et al. (1986)	60+	100	Normals
Mack & Carlson (1978)	60–80	41	Normals
Hooper Visual Organization Test			
Tamkin & Jacobsen (1984)	60–79	51	Psychiatric inpatients
Porteus Mazes			
Loranger & Misiak (1960)	74–80	50	Home for aged
Proverbs			
Albert et al. (1987)	60–70+	40	Community dwelling
Raven's Progressive Matrices			
Loranger & Misiak (1960)	74–80	50	Home for aged
Panek & Stoner (1980)	65–86	50	Community dwelling
Pfeffer et al. (1981)	$M = 75$	97	Retirement community
Raven et al. (1977)	60–80	180	Normals
Self-Regulation			
Albert et al. (1987)	60–70+	40	Community dwelling
Set Test			
Isaacs & Kennie (1973)	65+	189	Home and hospital
Similarities			
Farmer et al. (1987)	55–89	2,123	Community dwelling
Stroop			
Cohn et al. (1984)	61–90	40	Healthy males
Comalli et al. (1962)	65–80	15	Community dwelling
Spreen & Strauss (1991)	60–94	67	Healthy older adults
Verbal Fluency			
Albert et al. (1987)	60–70+	40	Community dwelling
Axelrod & Henry (1992)	60–80+	60	Healthy elderly
Benton et al. (1981)	65–84	162	Community dwelling
Farmer et al. (1987)	55–89	2,123	Community dwelling
Fuld (1980)	70–89	32	Community dwelling
Rosen (1980)	$M = 84$	10	Nursing home
Spreen & Strauss (1991)*	60–75+	532	Healthy elderly persons
Visual–Verbal Test			
Albert et al. (1987)	60–70+	40	Community dwelling
Wisconsin Card Sort			
Axelrod & Henry (1992)	60–80+	60	Healthy elderly
Boone et al. (1993)	60–83	53	Healthy older adults
Haaland et al. (1987)	64–87	75	Healthy elderly
Hart et al. (1988)	$M = 71$	18	Normals
Loranger & Misiak (1960)	74–80	50	Home for aged
Spreen & Strauss (1991)	60–94	60	Healthy older adults

REFERENCES

Abikoff, H., Alvir, J., Hong, G., Sukoff, R., Orazio, J., Solomon, S., & Saravay, S. (1987). Logical Memory subtest of the Wechsler Memory Scale: Age and education norms and alternate-form reliability of two scoring systems. *Journal of Clinical and Experimental Neuropsychology, 9*, 435–448.

Albert, M., Duffy, F. H., & Naeser, N. (1987). Nonlinear changes in cognition with age and their neuropsychological correlates. *Canadian Journal of Psychology, 41*, 141–157.

Anthony, J. C., LeResche, L., Niaz, U., Von Korff, M. R., & Folstein, M. F. (1982). Limits of the "Mini-Mental State" as a screening test for dementia and delirium among hospital patients. *Psychological Medicine, 12*, 397–408.

Arenberg, D. (1978). Differences and changes with age in the Benton Visual Retention Test. *Journal of Gerontology, 33*, 534–540.

Axelrod, B. N., & Henry, R. R. (1992). Age-related performance on the Wisconsin Card Sorting, Similarities, and Controlled Oral Word Association Tests. *Clinical Neuropsychologist, 6*, 16–26.

Barbizet, J., & Cany, E. (1968). Clinical and psychometric study of a patient with memory disturbances. *International Journal of Neurology, 7*, 44–54.

Bender, M. B. (1979). Defects in reversal of serial order of symbols. *Neuropsychologia, 17*, 125–138.

Benton, A. L., Eslinger, P. J., & Damasio, A. R. (1981). Normative observations on neuropsychological test performances in old age. *Journal of Clinical Neuropsychology, 3*, 33–42.

Benton, A. L., Hamsher, K. deS., Varney, N. R., & Spreen, O. (1983). *Contributions to neuropsychological assessment.* New York: Oxford University Press.

Berry, D. T. R., Allen, R. S., & Schmitt, F. A. (1991). Rey–Osterrieth Complex Figure: Psychometric characteristics in a geriatric sample. *Clinical Neuropsychologist, 5*, 143–153.

Berry, D. T. R., & Carpenter, G. S. (1992). Effect of four different delay periods on recall of the Rey–Osterrieth Complex Figure by older persons. *Clinical Neuropsychologist, 6*, 80–84.

Bleecker, M. L., Bolla-Wilson, K., Agnew, J., & Meyers, D. A. (1988). Age related sex differences in verbal memory. *Journal of Clinical Psychology, 44*, 403–411.

Bolton, N., Savage, R. D., & Roth, N. (1967). The Modified Word Learning Test and the aged psychiatric patient. *British Journal of Psychiatry, 113*, 1139–1140.

Boone, K. B., Ghaffarian, S., Lesser, I. M., Hill-Gutierrez, E., & Berman, N. G. (1993). Wisconsin Card Sorting Test performance in healthy, older adults: Relationship to age, education, sex, and IQ. *Clinical Psychology, 49*, 54–60.

Boone, K. B., Lesser, I. M., Hill-Gutierrez, E., Berman, N. G., & D'Elia, L. F. (1993). Rey–Osterrieth Complex Figure performance in healthy, older adults: Relationship to age, education, sex, and IQ. *Clinical Neuropsychologist, 7*, 22–28.

Bornstein, R. A. (1985). Normative data on selected neuropsychological measures from a nonclinical sample. *Journal of Clinical Psychology, 41,* 651–659.

Borod, J. C., Goodglass, H., & Kaplan, E. (1980). Normative data on the Boston Diagnostic Aphasia Examination, Parietal Lobe Battery, and the Boston Naming Test. *Journal of Clinical Neuropsychology, 2,* 209–215.

Caird, W. K., Sanderson, R. E., & Inglis, J. (1962). Cross validation of a learning test for use with elderly psychiatric patients. *Journal of Mental Sciences, 108,* 386–370.

Canter, A., & Straumanis, J. J. (1969). Performance of senile and healthy aged persons on the BIP Bender test. *Perceptual and Motor Skills, 28,* 695–698.

Cauthen, N. R. (1977). Extension of the Wechsler Memory Scale norms to older age groups. *Journal of Clinical Psychology, 33,* 208–211.

Christensen, K. J., Multhaup, K. S., Nordstrom, S., & Voss, K. (1991). A cognitive battery for dementia: Development and measurement characteristics. *Psychological Assessment: A Journal of Counseling and Clinical Psychology, 3,* 168–174.

Cohn, N. D., Dustman, R. E., & Bradford, D. C. (1984). Age-related decrements in Stroop Color Test performance. *Journal of Clinical Psychology, 40,* 1244–1250.

Comalli, P. E., Jr., Wapner, S., & Werner, H. (1962). Interference effects of Stroop Color–Word Test in childhood, adulthood, and aging. *Journal of Genetic Psychology, 100,* 47–53.

Corkin, S. (1982). Some relationships between global amnesias and memory impairments in Alzheimer's disease. In S. Corkin, D. L. Davis, J. H. Growdon, E. Usdin, & R. J. Wurtman (Eds.), *Alzheimer's disease: A report of progress in research* (pp. 149–164). New York: Raven.

Crook, T., Ferris, S., & McCarthy, M. (1979). The Misplaced Objects Task: A brief test for memory dysfunction in the aged. *Journal of the American Geriatric Society, 27,* 284–287.

Crook, T., Ferris, S., McCarthy, M., & Rae, D. (1980a). Utility of digit recall tasks for assessing memory in the aged. *Journal of Consulting and Clinical Psychology, 48,* 228–233.

Crook, T., Gilbert, J. G., & Ferris, S. (1980b). Operationalizing memory impairment for elderly persons: The Guild Memory Test. *Psychological Reports, 47,* 1315–1318.

Davies, A. D. H. (1968). The influence of age on Trail Making Test performance. *Journal of Clinical Psychology, 24,* 96–98.

Delis, D. C., Kramer, J. H., Kaplan, E., & Ober, B. A. (1987). *California Verbal Learning Test.* New York: Psychological Corporation.

Denman, S. E. (1984). *Denman Neuropsychology Memory Scale.* Charleston, SC: Author.

desRosiers, G., & Ivison, D. (1986). Paired associate learning: Normative data for differences between high and low associate pairs. *Journal of Clinical and Experimental Neuropsychology, 8,* 637–642.

Doppelt, J. E., & Wallace, W. L. (1955). Standardization of the Wechsler Adult Intelligence Scale for older persons. *Journal of Abnormal and Social Psychology, 51*, 312–330.

Ernst, J. (1988). Language, grip strength, sensory–perceptual, and receptive skills in a normal elderly sample. *Clinical Neuropsychologist, 2*, 30–40.

Eslinger, P. J., & Benton, A. L. (1983). Visuoperceptual performances in aging and dementia: Clinical and theoretical implications. *Journal of Clinical Neuropsychology, 5*, 213–220.

Farmer, M. E., White, L. R., Kittner, S. J., Kaplan, E., Moss, E., McNamara, P., Woltz, M. M., Wolf, P. A., & Feinleib, M. (1987). Neuropsychological test performance in Framingham: A descriptive study. *Psychological Reports, 60*, 1023–1040.

Folstein, N., Anthony, J. C., Parhad, I., Duffy, B., & Greenberg, E. M. (1985). The meaning of cognitive impairment in the elderly. *Journal of the American Geriatric Society, 33*, 228–235.

Fowler, R. S. (1969). A simple non-language test of new learning. *Perceptual and Motor Skills, 29*, 895–901.

Fuld, P. A. (1980). Guaranteed stimulus-processing in the evaluation of memory and learning. *Cortex, 16*, 255–271.

Gendreau, L., Roach, T., & Gendreau, P. (1973). Assessing the intelligence of aged persons: Report on the Quick Test. *Psychological Reports, 32*, 475–480.

Gilbert, J. G., & Levee, R. F. (1971). Patterns of declining memory. *Journal of Gerontology, 26*, 70–75.

Gilleard, C. J. (1980). Wechsler Memory Scale performance of elderly psychiatric patients. *Journal of Clinical Psychology, 36*, 958–960.

Gilmore, C. C., Royer, F. L., & Gruhn, J. J. (1983). Age differences in symbol digit substitution task performance. *Journal of Clinical Psychology, 39*, 114–121.

Grober, E., & Sliwinski, M. (1991). Development and validation of a model for estimating premorbid verbal intelligence in the elderly. *Journal of Clinical and Experimental Neuropsychology, 13*, 933–949.

Haaland, K. Y., Linn, R. T., Hunt, W. C., & Goodwin, J. S. (1983). A normative study of Russell's variant of the Wechsler Memory Scale in a healthy elderly population. *Journal of Consulting and Clinical Psychology, 51*, 878–881.

Haaland, K. Y., Vranes, L. F., Goodwin, J. S., & Garry, P. J. (1987). Wisconsin Card Sort Test performance in a healthy elderly population. *Journal of Gerontology, 42*, 345–346.

Haddad, L. B., & Coffman, T. L. (1987). A brief neuropsychological screening exam for psycho-geriatric patients. *Clinical Gerontologist, 6*, 3–10.

Haglund, R. M. J., & Schuckit, M. A. (1976). A clinical comparison of tests of organicity in elderly patients. *Journal of Gerontology, 31*, 654–659.

Harley, J. P., Leuthold, C. A., Matthews, C. G., & Bergs, L. E. (1980). *Wisconsin Neuropsychological Test Battery T-score norms for older Veterans Administration*

Medical Center patients. Madison: University of Wisconsin. (Distributed by C. G. Matthews)

Hart, R. P., Kwentus, J. A., Wade, J. B., & Taylor, J. R. (1988). Modified Wisconsin Sorting Test in elderly normal, depressed and demented patients. *Clinical Neuropsychologist, 2*, 49–56.

Heaton, R. K., Grant, I., & Matthews, C. G. (1986). Differences in neuropsychological test performance associated with age, education and sex. In I. Grant & K. M. Adams (Eds.), *Neuropsychological assessment of neuropsychiatric disorders* (pp. 100–120). New York: Oxford University Press.

Hersch, E. L. (1979). Development and application of the extended scale for dementia. *Journal of the American Geriatric Society, 27*, 348–354.

Hulicka, I. M. (1966). Age differences in Wechsler Memory Scale scores. *Journal of Genetic Psychology, 109*, 135–145.

Isaacs, B., & Kennie, A. T. (1973). The Set Test as an aid to the detection of dementia in old people. *British Journal of Psychiatry, 123*, 467–470.

Isaacs, B., & Walkey, F.. (1963). The assessment of the mental state of elderly hospital patients using a simple questionnaire. *American Journal of Psychiatry, 120*, 173–174.

Ivison, D. (1986). Anna Thompson and the American liner New York: Some normative data. *Journal of Clinical and Experimental Neuropsychology, 8*, 317–320.

Ivnik, R. J., Malec, J. F., Smith, G. E., Tangalos, G. E., Petersen, R. C., Kokmen, E., & Kurland, L. T. (1992a). Mayo's older Americans normative studies: WAIS-R norms for ages 56 to 97. *Clinical Neuropsychologist, 6*, 1–30.

Ivnik, R. J., Malec, J. F., Smith, G. E., Tangalos, G. E., Petersen, R. C., Kokmen, E., & Kurland, L. T. (1992b). Mayo's older Americans normative studies: WMS-R norms for ages 56 to 94. *Clinical Neuropsychologist, 6*, 49–82.

Ivnik, R. J., Malec, J. F., Smith, G. E., Tangalos, G. E., Petersen, R. C., Kokmen, E., & Kurland, L. T. (1992c). Mayo's older Americans normative studies: Updated AVLT norms for ages 56 to 97. *Clinical Neuropsychologist, 6*, 83–104.

Ivnik, R. J., Smith, G. E., Tangalos, E. G., Petersen, R. C., Kokmen, E., & Kurland, L. T. (1991). Wechsler Memory Scale: IQ-dependent norms for persons ages 65 to 97 years. *Psychological Assessment: A Journal of Counseling and Clinical Psychology, 3*, 156–161.

Jacobs, J. W., Bernhard, M. R., Delgado, A., & Strain, J. (1977). Screening for organic mental syndromes in the medically ill. *Annals of Internal Medicine, 86*, 40–46.

Kahn, R. L., Goldfarb, A. I., Pollack, M., & Peck, A. (1960). Brief objective measures for the determination of mental status in the aged. *American Journal of Psychiatry, 117*, 326–328.

Katzman, R., Brown, T., Fuld, P., Peck, A., Schechter, R., & Schimmel, H. (1983). Validation of a short Orientation–Memory–Concentration Test of cognitive impairment. *American Journal of Psychiatry, 140*, 734–739.

Kendrick, D. C., & Post, F. (1967). Differences in cognitive status between healthy, psychiatrically ill, and diffusely brain-damaged elderly subjects. *British Journal of Psychiatry, 113*, 75–81.

Kiernan, R. J., Mueller, J., Langston, J. W., & Van Dyke, C. (1987). The Neurobehavioral Cognitive Status Examination: A brief but differentiated approach to cognitive assessment. *Annals of Internal Medicine, 107*, 481–485.

Klonoff, H., & Kennedy, M. (1965). Memory and perceptual functioning in octogenarians and nonagenarians in the community. *Journal of Gerontology, 20*, 328–333.

Klonoff, H., & Kennedy, M. (1966). A comparative study of cognitive functioning in old age. *Journal of Gerontology, 21*, 239–243.

Lacks, P., & Storandt, H. (1982). Bender–Gestalt performance of normal older adults. *Journal of Clinical Psychology, 38*, 624–627.

LaRue, A., D'Elia, L. F., Clark, E. O., Spar, J. E., & Jarvik, L. F. (1986). Clinical tests of memory in dementia, depression, and healthy aging. *Journal of Psychology and Aging, 1*, 69–77.

Levin, H. S., & Benton, A. L. (1975). Temporal orientation in patients with brain disease. *Applied Neurophysiology, 38*, 56–60.

Levine, N. R. (1971). Validation of the Quick Test for intelligence screening of the elderly. *Psychological Reports, 29*, 167–172.

Lezak, M. D. (1983). *Neuropsychological assessment* (2nd ed.). New York: Oxford University Press.

Lifshitz, K. (1960). Problems in the quantitative evaluation of patients with psychoses of the senium. *Journal of Psychology, 49*, 295–303.

Lindsey, B. A., & Coppinger, N. W. (1969). Age-related deficits in simple capabilities and their consequences for Trail Making performance. *Journal of Clinical Psychology, 25*, 156–159.

Loranger, A. W., & Misiak, H. (1960). The performance of aged females on five non-language tests of intellectual functions. *Journal of Clinical Psychology, 16*, 189–191.

MacInnes, W. D., Gillen, R. W., Golden, C. J., Graber, B., Cole, J. K., Uhl, H. S. M., & Greenhouse, A. H. (1983). Aging and performance on the Luria–Nebraska Neuropsychological Battery. *International Journal of Neuroscience, 19*, 179–190.

MacInnes, W. D., Golden, C. J., Gillen, R. W., Sawicki, R. F., Quaife, M., Uhl, H. S. M., & Greenhouse, A. H. (1984). Aging, regional cerebral blood flow, and neuropsychological functioning. *Journal of the American Geriatric Society, 32*, 712–718.

Mack, J. L., & Carlson, N. J. (1978). Conceptual deficits and aging: The Category Test. *Perceptual and Motor Skills, 46*, 123–128.

Malec, J. F., Ivnik, R. J., Smith, G. E., Tangelos, E. G., Petersen, R. C., Kokmenn, E., & Kurland, L. T. (1992). Visual Spatial Learning Test: Normative data and further validation. *Psychological Assessment, 4*, 433–441.

Margolis, R. B., & Scialfa, C. T. (1984). Age differences in Wechsler Memory Scale performance. *Journal of Clinical Psychology, 40,* 1442–1449.

Markson, E. W., & Levitz, G. (1973). A Guttman scale to assess memory loss among the elderly. *Gerontologist, 13,* 337–340.

Masur, D. M., Fuld, P. A., Blau, A. D., Thal, L. J., Levin, H. S., & Aronson, M. K. (1989). Distinguishing normal and demented elderly with the Selective Reminding Test. *Journal of Clinical and Experimental Neuropsychology, 11,* 615–630.

McCartney, J. R., & Palmateer, L. M. (1985). Assessment of cognitive deficit in geriatric patients. *Journal of the American Geriatric Society, 33,* 467–471.

McCarty, S. M., Logue, P. E., Power, D. G., Zeisat, H. A., & Rosensteil, A. K. (1980). Alternate form reliability and age-related scores for Russell's revised Wechsler Memory Scale, *Journal of Consulting and Clinical Psychology, 48,* 296–293.

McCarty, S. M., Siegler, I. C., & Logue, P. E. (1982). Cross sectional and longitudinal patterns of three Wechsler Memory Scale subtests. *Journal of Gerontology, 37,* 169–175.

Natelson, B. H., Haupt, E. J., Fleischer, E. J., & Grey, L. (1979). Temporal orientation and education. *Archives of Neurology, 3,* 444–446.

Osborne, D., & Davis, L. J., Jr. (1978). Standard scores for Wechsler Memory Scale subtests. *Journal of Clinical Psychology, 34,* 115–116.

Panek, P. E., & Stoner, S. B. (1980). Age differences on Raven's Colored Progressive Matrices. *Perceptual and Motor Skills, 50,* 977–978.

Pattie, A. H., & Gilleard, C. J. (1975). A brief psychogeriatric assessment schedule: Validation against diagnosis and discharge from hospital. *British Journal of Psychiatry, 127,* 489–493.

Pfeffer, R. I., Kurosaki, T. T., Harrah, C. H., Jr., Chance, J. M., Bates, D., Detels, R., Filos, S., & Butzke, C. (1981). A survey diagnostic tool for senile dementia. *American Journal of Epidemiology, 114,* 515–527.

Pfeiffer, E. (1975). A short portable Mental Status Questionnaire for the assessment of organic brain deficit in elderly patients. *Journal of the American Geriatric Society, 23,* 433–441.

Piersma, H. L. (1986). Wechsler Memory Scale performance in psychogeriatric patients. *Journal of Clinical Psychology, 42,* 323–327.

Plutchik, R., Conte, H., & Lieberman, M. (1971). Development of a scale (GIES) for assessment of cognitive and perceptual functioning in geriatric patients. *Journal of the American Geriatric Society, 19,* 614–623.

Query, W. T., & Megran, J. (1983). Age-related norms for ALVT in a male patient population. *Journal of Clinical Psychology, 39,* 136–138.

Randt, C. T., Brown, E. R., & Osborne, D. P., Jr. (1980). A memory test for longitudinal measurement of mild to moderate deficits. *Clinical Neuropsychology, 2,* 184–194.

Raven, J. C., Court, J. H., & Raven, J. (1977). *Manual for Raven's Progressive Matrices and Vocabulary Scales: Standard Progressive Matrices*. New York: Psychological Corporation.

Roman, D. D., Edwall, G. E., Buchanan, R. J., & Patton, J. H. (1991). Extended norms for the Paced Auditory Serial Addition Task. *Clinical Neuropsychologist, 5*, 33–40.

Rosen, W. G. (1980). Verbal fluency in aging and dementia. *Journal of Clinical Neuropsychology, 2*, 135–146.

Rosselli, M., & Ardila, A. (1991). Effects of age, education, and gender on the Rey–Osterrieth Complex Figure. *Clinical Neuropsychologist, 5*, 370–376.

Roth, M., Tym, E., Mountjoy, C. Q., Huppert, F. A., Hendrie, H., Verma, S., & Goddard, R. (1986). CAMDEX: A standardized instrument for the diagnosis of mental disorder in the elderly with special reference to the early detection of dementia. *British Journal of Psychiatry, 149*, 698–709.

Ruff, R. M., Quayhagen, M., & Light, R. H. (1988). Selective reminding tests: A normative study of verbal learning in adults. *Journal of Clinical and Experimental Neuropsychology, 11*, 539–550

Russell, E. W. (1988). Renorming Russell's version of the Wechsler Memory Scale. *Journal of Clinical and Experimental Neuropsychology, 10*, 235–249.

Savage, R. D., & Hall, E. H. (1973). A performance measure for the aged. *British Journal of Psychiatry, 122*, 721–723.

Schaie, K. W. (1959). Cross-sectional methods in the study of psychological aspects of aging. *Journal of Gerontology, 14*, 203–215.

Schaie, K. W., Rosenthal, F., & Perlman, R. M. (1953). Differential mental deterioration of factorially "pure" functions in later maturity. *Journal of Gerontology, 8*, 191–196.

Schear, J. M., (1984). Neuropsychological assessment of the elderly in clinical practice. In P. E. Logue & J. M. Schear (Eds.), *Clinical Neuropsychology* (pp. 227–230). Springfield, IL: Charles C Thomas.

Schmidt, J. P., Tombaugh, T. N., & Faulkner, P. (1992). Free-recall, cued-recall and recognition procedures with three verbal memory tests: Normative data from age 20 to 79. *Clinical Neuropsychologist, 6*, 185–200.

Shelton, M. D., Parsons, O. A., & Leber, W. R. (1982). Verbal and visuospatial performance and aging: A neuropsychological approach. *Journal of Gerontology, 37*, 336–341.

Smith, A. (1967). The serial sevens subtraction test. *Archives of Neurology, 17*, 78–80.

Smith, A. (1976). *Symbol Digit Modalities Test: Adult Norms Supplement*. Los Angeles: Western Psychological Services.

Spreen, D., & Strauss, E. (1991). *A compendium of neuropsychological tests*. New York: Oxford University Press.

Stuss, D. T., Stethem, L. L., & Poirier, C. A. (1987). Comparison of three tests of attention and rapid information processing across six age groups. *Clinical Neuropsychologist, 1*, 139–152.

Stuss, D. T., Stethem, L. L., & Pelchat, G. (1988). Three tests of attention and information processing: An extension. *Clinical Neuropsychologist, 2,* 246–250.

Sunderland, T., Hill, J. L., Mellow, A. M., Lawlor, B. A., Gundersheimer, J., Newhouse, P. A., & Grafman, J. H. (1989). Clock drawing in Alzheimer's Disease: A novel measure of dementia severity. *Journal of the American Geriatric Society, 37,* 725–729.

Tamkin, A. S., & Jacobsen, R. (1984). Age-related norms for the Hooper Visual Organization Test. *Journal of Clinical Psychology, 40,* 1459–1463.

Tombaugh, T. N., & Schmidt, J. P. (1992). The Learning and Memory Battery (LAMB): Development and standardization. *Psychological Assessment, 4,* 193–206.

Tombaugh, T. N., Schmidt, J. P., & Faulkner, P. (1992). A new procedure for administering the Taylor Complex Figure: Normative data over a 60–year span. *Clinical Neuropsychologist, 6,* 63–79.

Towle, D., Wilcock, G. K., & Surmon, D. J. (1987). The KEW Test: A study of reliability and validity. *Journal Clinical and Experimental Gerontology, 9,* 245–256.

Trahan, D. E., & Larrabee, G. J. (1988). *Continuous Visual Memory Test: Professional manual.* Odessa, FL: Psychological Assessment Resources.

Trahan, D. E., Larrabee, G. J., & Levin, H. S. (1986). Age-related differences in recognition memory of pictures. *Experimental Aging Research, 12,* 147–150.

Trahan, D. E., Larrabee, G. J., Quintana, J. W., Goethe, K. E., & Willingham, A. C. (1989). Development and clinical validation of an expanded paired associate test with delayed recall. *Clinical Neuropsychologist, 3,* 169–183.

Tsang, M. H., Aronson, H., & Hayslip, B., Jr. (1991). Standardization for a learning and retention task with community residing older adults. *Clinical Neuropsychologist, 5,* 66–77.

Van Gorp, W. G., Satz, P., Kiersch, M. E., & Henry, R. (1986). Normative data on the Boston Naming Test for a group of normal older adults. *Journal of Clinical and Experimental Neuropsychology, 8,* 702–705.

Van Gorp, W. G., Satz, P., & Mitrushina, M. (1990). Neuropsychological processes associated with normal aging and the early detection of "at risk" elders. *Developmental Neuropsychology, 6,* 279–290.

Wechsler, D. (1955). *Manual for the Wechsler Adult Intelligence Scale.* New York: Psychological Corporation.

Wechsler, D. (1981). *Wechsler Adult Intelligence Scale: Revised.* New York: Psychological Corporation.

Wechsler, D. (1987). *Wechsler Memory Scale–Revised.* New York: Psychological Corporation.

Whitehead, A. (1973). Verbal learning and memory in elderly depressives. *British Journal of Psychiatry, 123,* 203–208.

Wolf-Klein, G. P., Silverstone, F. A., Levy, A. P., & Brod, M. S. (1989). Screening for Alzheimer's disease by clock drawing. *Journal of the American Geriatric Society, 37,* 730–734.

AUTHOR INDEX

Page numbers in italic refer to listings in reference sections.

206   AUTHOR INDEX

SUBJECT INDEX

Family feedback, 141–53
    and dementia, 144–45
    educational aspects, 147–48
    ethical issues, 146–47
    systems issues, 142, 149–51
Family informants, 74–75, 97
Family intervention, 169
Family network 149–51
"Family secret," 149
Fatigue
    as depression criterion, 62
    and test performance, 21
Feedback to client/family, 141–53
    and dementia, 144–45
    and depression, 145–46
    educational aspects, 147–48
    ethical issues, 146–47
    professional issues, 151–53
    underlying principles, 142–43
Fluency deficits, 36, 46–50
Fluoxetine, 164
Forgetting rate
    Alzheimer's dementia, 41–43, 102–3
    clinical utility, 43, 102
    depression versus Alzheimer's disease, 102–3
    Huntington's dementia, 42–43
    limitation as diagnostic tool, 102–3
    normal elderly, 41–42
    savings scores as sensitive measure, 42
Fowler Non-Language Paired Associates, 187
Frailty, and test performance, 18–19
Fuld Object Memory task, 187

Generational differences, 8–9, 159
Geriatric Depression Rating Scale, 74
Geriatric Depression Scale, 69–71
    advantages and disadvantages, 71
    dual diagnosis advantages, 96–97
    psychometrics, 69–70
    short form, 70–71
Geriatric Interpersonal Evaluation Scale, 184
Graham–Kendall Memory for Designs, 187
Grammatical abilities, 36
Guardianship, 120–23
Guild Memory Test, 186
Guilt, in families, 150

Halstead–Reitan test, 11, 185
Hamilton Rating Scale for Depression
    Alzheimer's disease inappropriateness, 96
    limitations, 73
    severity rating, 72–74
    and somatic symptoms, 93
Health problems
    depression assessment artifact, 93
    depression relationship, 63–64
    prevalence, 9–10
    and test performance, 9–22
Hearing
    age-related changes, 16–18
    sex differences, 16–17
    and test performance, 18
Hooper Visual Organization Test, 189
Hopemont Capacity Assessment Interview, 129–30
Hopkins Competency Assessment Test, 129
Huntington's disease
    intrusion errors, 45
    recognition memory, 40–41
    remote memory deficit, 46
    semantic memory, 47–49
    as subcortical dementia, 34–35
Hydergine, 167
Hypertension, and test performance, 10–11

Illumination, and testing, 13–15
Imaging studies, 100
Imipramine
    coexisting depression and Alzheimer's disease, 84, 169
    depression treatment, 164
In-home assessment, 18–19
Independent Living Scale, 128
Individual differences, 8–9, 159
Informants. See Collaterals
Information–Memory–Concentration test, 37
Informed consent
    and competence, 120
    and decision-making capacity, 129, 131–33
    inferential approach, 125–26
Inglis Paired Associates, 187
Insomnia, 62

Neuropsychological tests (*continued*)
    in legal competence assessment, 125–26, 132–33
    norms, 185
    predictive use, 100
Neuroticism, age-related stability, 23–24
New York University Memory Test, 186
Nicergoline, 167
NIMH Dementia Mood Assessment Scale, 75
Nimodipine, 167
Nootropic drugs, 167
Normal elderly
    forgetting rate, 41–42
    memory complaints, 94–95

Object Memory Evaluation, 103
Object naming. *See* Confrontation naming
Older Americans Resources and Services Instrument, 134
Oldest old, 159
Old-old, 8, 159
Onset age, depression, 92
Orientation–Memory–Concentration exam, 184

Paced Auditory Serial Addition Task, 186
Parkinson's disease
    motor impairment effects, 22
    remote memory deficit, 46
Passivity, and dementia, 25
Patient history, 98
Pegboard test, 188
Perceptual–motor speed/coordination, 188
Peripheral vision, 15–16
Personality
    influence on assessment, 23
    stability with age, 23–26
Personality disorders, 165
Pharmacotherapy
    coexisting depression and Alzheimer's disease, 84
    in depression, 164–66
        psychotherapy combination, 165–66
    maintenance use, 166
Physical health problems. *See* Health problems
Physicians, as consultation source, 158
Physostigmine, 167

Piracetam, 167
Polypharmacy, 93
Porteus Mazes, 189
Preadmission Screening and Annual Resident Review, 3
Prescription medications, 11–13
Primary Mental Abilities Test, 185
Problem-solving deficits
    assessment instruments, norms, 189
    dementia feature, 36
Projective techniques, 76
Proverbs test, 189
Prozac, 164
Pseudodementia
    and depression, 82–83
    electroconvulsive therapy, 165
Psychologists, feedback skills, 151–53
Psychomotor performance, 98–99
Psychopathology, and aging, 23–26
Psychotherapy, in depression, 165–66
Public event memory, 46

Quick Test, 185

Rapid forgetting. *See* Forgetting rate
Raven's Progressive Matrices, 189
Reaction time, 19–20
Reading speed, 19, 21
Recall tasks
    depression versus dementia, 101–3
    as effortful processing, 101
Recency effect, and recall, 40
Recognition memory
    Alzheimer's versus Huntington's patients, 40–41
    depression versus Alzheimer's disease, 101–3
Referral source, 157
Remote memory, 45–46
Reporting laws, 162
Response bias, memory tasks, 101–3
Response times, slowing of, 19–21
Retrieval deficits
    depression versus Alzheimer's disease, 103
    Huntington's disease, 47–49
    and remote memory, 46
Retrograde amnesia, 45–46
Reverse Spelling task, 187
Rey Auditory Verbal Learning Test, 187
Rey Complex Figure Test, 187–88

Visual Form Retention Test, Revised, 22
Visual Reproduction (Wechsler) subtest, 42–44
Visual Spatial Learning Test, 188
Visual–Verbal Test, 189
Visuospatial impairment, 37, 50–51

Wechsler Adult Intelligence Scale, 185
Wechsler Memory Scale, 186
Wechsler Memory Scale, Revised
    Alzheimer's patients, 42–44

intrusion errors, 44
norms, 186
Wechsler Memory Scale, Russell Revision, 186
Wisconsin Card Sort, 189

Yes–no recognition memory, 102
Young-old, 8, 159

Zung Self-Rating Depression Scale, 66, 93

ABOUT THE EDITORS

Martha Storandt is Director of the Aging and Development Program in the Department of Psychology and Associate Director for Clinical Research for the Alzheimer's Disease Research Center at Washington University. Her research interests focus on the clinical psychology of aging, including both depression and dementia, with a substantial emphasis on assessment of older adults. In addition to editing and writing several books on aging, Dr. Storandt has authored numerous scientific articles on the normal aging process as well as on Alzheimer's disease. She also leads the specialization in aging in the clinical psychology training program at Washington University.

Gary R. VandenBos is Executive Director of Communications of the American Psychological Association (APA). Among his professional interests is facilitating the application and dissemination of psychological research knowledge into clinical practice and policy formulation. He has participated in various national and international committees and task forces on adult development and aging, and he has directed four APA grant projects focusing on aging issues and the mental health needs of the elderly. He has coedited two previous aging-related volumes: *Psychology and the Older Adult: Challenges for Training in the 1980s* (with J. F. Santos) and *The Adults Years: Continuity and Change* (with M. Storandt).